More Praise for *Do I Stay Christian?*

Publishers Weekly, Best P... ...t..., Religion

"Solidifies McLaren's place as one of t... ... ...s of modern Christianity."   *y*)

"If you're a former Christian . . . you are precisely the reader Brian McLaren hopes to reach."   *—Spirituality & Practice*

"What I appreciated most about *Do I Stay Christian?* was McLaren's honesty about his own ongoing struggle with that question."   *—Texas Observer*

"[For] those who can't quite accept a Christianity that they have outgrown."   *—Church Times*

"Any change, however, will rest on the foundation that proceeds from an honest assessment of what is. And that assessment is the most valuable contribution by McLaren."   *—National Catholic Reporter*

"Woven with beautiful personal stories, this book will give you many things to consider as well as some clarity."
                            —Jo Luehmann, host of *The Living Room Podcast*

"If you're wondering whether it's time to shake off your sandals and walk away from Christianity, I beg you to read this book before making up your mind."
                    —Jonathan Merritt, author of *Learning to Speak God from Scratch*

"Answers from one of our most eloquent Christian teachers for those asking: Why bother?"   —Jon M. Sweeney, author of *The Pope Who Quit*

"This book gives me a map for finding what lies beyond—a Christianity that's bigger, wiser, and more powerful than I dared to dream."
                                      —Jana Riess, author of *Flunking Sainthood*

"I recommend this book for . . . those seeking honest conversation about the very complex realities of Christianity."
                            —The Rev. Wil Gafney, PhD, Brite Divinity School

Do I Stay Christian?

A Guide for the Doubters,
the Disappointed,
and the Disillusioned

Brian D. McLaren

ST. MARTIN'S
ESSENTIALS
NEW YORK

Published in the United States by St. Martin's Essentials, an imprint of St. Martin's Publishing Group.

www.stmartins.com

Design by Meryl Sussman Levavi

The Library of Congress has cataloged the hardcover edition as follows:

Names: McLaren, Brian D., 1956– author.
Title: Do I stay Christian? : a guide for the doubters, the disappointed, and the disillusioned / Brian D. McLaren.
Description: First edition. | New York : St. Martin's Essentials, 2022. | Includes bibliographical references. | Identifiers: LCCN 2022000928 | ISBN 9781250262790 (hardcover) | ISBN 9781250262806 (ebook)
Subjects: LCSH: Christianity—Essence, genius, nature. | Apologetics. | Christianity—Controversial literature. | Faith.
Classification: LCC BT60 .M35 2022 | DDC 270.8/3—dc23/eng/20220322
LC record available at https://lccn.loc.gov/2022000928

ISBN 978-1-250-89005-4 (trade paperback)

Our books may be purchased in bulk for promotional, educational, or business use. Please contact your local bookseller or the Macmillan Corporate and Premium Sales Department at 1-800-221-7945, extension 5442, or by email at MacmillanSpecialMarkets@macmillan.com.

First St. Martin's Essentials Trade Paperback Edition: 2024

10 9 8 7 6 5 4 3 2 1

This book is dedicated to two dear friends whose presence and absence I will always associate with the writing of this book.

Bill Duncan died of COVID-19 in March 2021. Bill was my friend across five decades of life, and he was my partner in planting a new church in the early 1980s (Cedar Ridge Community Church, http://crcc.org/). It is one of the greatest blessings of my life to have had such a wise, deeply rooted, forgiving, supportive, and delightful friend. Bill was kind enough to read my books and offer me encouragement about each one. I am quite certain this book would have been his favorite, and he would have said something like, "I think you finally were able to say what you've been striving to say for your whole adult life."

Fran McKendree was a gifted singer, songwriter, guitarist, and worship leader whose music and friendship brightened my life, especially over the last decade. While he was undergoing treatment for aggressive cancer in 2020 and 2021, he produced some songs that I had written or co-written with him. (You can find some of them here: http://brianmclaren.net/celebrating-a-life-of-wonder-goodness-and -creativity/). He passed away in June 2021. These lines from his song "Haul Away" could serve as an epigram for this book (from *Times Like These*, McKendree Spring, 2013, available here: https://vimeo .com/119998423/):

Break these chains and, flying, let me go.

Dance me out and let me see

How this storm can paint a rainbow

And how beginnings come to be.

CONTENTS

❧

✼

A Religion Is Many Things

It was about ten-thirty at night. I had just fallen asleep in a hotel room in San Francisco. My hotel phone jangled at full volume and I fumbled in the darkness to find it. "Brian, my name is Carl. I'm terribly sorry to bother you so late, and I apologize for hunting you down at your hotel," the caller said with a deep southern accent. "I work for a Christian campus ministry here in the Bay Area. My whole staff team and I were at your lecture this evening, and we're fans of your books, and we wondered if it would be possible for us to meet with you before you leave town. I hope that's not too presumptuous to ask."

"I'm sorry," I said, trying not to sound too groggy. "I have to catch a plane at 9:00 a.m. That means I need to be at the airport at eight, which would mean leaving here before seven so I could return my rental car."

"You don't understand," Carl said. "We're desperate. Is there any way?"

It turned out that Carl lived near the airport, and I agreed to meet Carl's team at his apartment at 5:30 a.m. The small living room was already crowded with about a dozen people when I arrived. Delia, Carl's wife, had prepared a last-minute breakfast buffet that didn't look last minute at all: scrambled eggs, sausage, fresh biscuits, toast, fruit, orange juice, and coffee. We sat around the room elbow to elbow, our breakfasts on our laps, and Delia began in a Louisiana drawl even more pronounced than her husband's: "Brian, bless your heart for getting up so early to meet with a ragamuffin bunch of perfect strangers like us. I might as well get the ball rolling. We came from Louisiana to reach secular college students for Christ here in liberal, heathen San Francisco. But the truth is, they've reached us more than we've reached them. Now, the Christianity we came here with just doesn't make much sense anymore. If I had my way, I would leave campus ministry today, and then I think I'd leave Christianity tomorrow."

Carl went next, and then, one by one around the room, each person shared a similar story. "I'm hanging on to Christian faith by a fingernail," one said. "I don't even know if there's a God anymore," said another. "I had to stop reading the Bible," another said, "because I'm about one chapter away from complete atheism."

When we came full circle back to Delia, she said, "When we heard you speak last night, we felt that you might understand our predicament and be able to help us. We just don't know what to do."

By this time, it was 6:20, and I realized I only had forty minutes before I needed to leave for the airport. What could I say in forty minutes to help these sincere and conflicted people?

Fast-forward twenty years, and I found myself in a similar conversation, this time in a Chinese restaurant just outside Chicago. I looked around the table and saw a sampling of Mainline Protestant clergy: an Episcopal priest and a Presbyterian pastor to my left, two Methodists and a Lutheran across from me, and two post-Evangelicals now in the United Church of Christ to my right. They were the organizers of a daylong event for clergy at which I had just spoken.

One of the Methodist pastors across from me had just told our little group that she had seriously considered leaving ministry earlier in the year. Then she caught my eye: "Brian, do you ever feel tempted to just throw out the whole thing and do something else with your life?"

"Sometimes I do," I said. "Lately, more often than you'd think."

Everyone froze for a second. My companions clearly didn't expect my admission.

One of the post-Evangelicals to my right leaned toward me and made eye contact over his reading glasses. "I think Jesus would be pretty embarrassed about what we've made of the movement he started," he said. "Sometimes I think he wouldn't want to be a part of it either."

Over their kung pao chicken, egg drop soup, and vegetarian fried rice, one by one my companions shared their ambivalence not just about staying in ministry, but about staying Christian.

I can't count how many similar conversations have unfolded since that early morning breakfast with Evangelicals in San Francisco and that dinner with Mainline Protestants near Chicago. Surprising numbers of Roman

Catholics have told me, almost as if reading from the same script, "I have no hope for the church reforming or renewing. My only hope is that it collapses and dies soon, before it does too much more harm, so something new can be resurrected." Others had hope for renewal but talked in terms of centuries, not years or even decades. Latter-Day Saints, Adventists, Unitarians, and many others have reached out to me about their similar spiritual frustrations in their unique contexts.

As I recall these conversations, I hear echoes of literally thousands of others in hallways, over meals, via email, or in chance encounters in airports. "I wouldn't be a Christian anymore if I hadn't found your books," a young youth pastor told me in a book-signing line. "I was a Mennonite pastor for twenty years," a middle-aged man explained at an event, "but this is the first time I've set foot in a church of any kind since I left the pastorate seven years ago. These days I call myself post-Christian." "You saved my life (spiritually speaking) through your books while I was deployed in Iraq," a military chaplain wrote me. "I came out as an atheist and left Christianity," a former Methodist minister wrote. "Maybe my journey would have been different if I'd met people like you in time."

Over time, I've come to realize that when people speak of leaving Christianity, part of their struggle is that *Christianity* doesn't refer to one simple thing. Like any religion, Christianity is a complex mixture of many different things, a diamond of many facets, or a meal of many ingredients.

1. Christianity can be understood **historically** or **culturally**, as a legacy you are born into or enter by choice. To be a Christian is to inhabit a cultural or historical tradition.
2. Christianity can be defined **institutionally**, as a power structure or hierarchy in which you participate. To be a Christian is to affiliate with an institution and accept its authority structure.
3. Christianity can be defined **doctrinally**, as something you believe. To be a Christian is to affirm a system of beliefs or teachings.
4. Christianity can be defined **liturgically** or **pragmatically**, as a set of rituals you practice. To be a Christian is to engage in some version of Christianity's rituals or practices.
5. Christianity can be defined **spiritually** or **experientially**, as something you feel or a conversion experience you've had. To be a Christian is to have, foster, and share a set of experiences.

6. Christianity can be defined **moralistically**, as a shared set of moral values or precepts. To be a Christian is to live your life by a moral or ethical framework.

7. Christianity can be defined **missionally**, as a program, plan, or movement for intentional action in the world. To be a Christian is to take on that mission as your own.

8. Christianity can be defined **demographically**, as a sociological or anthropological identity. To be a Christian is to identify yourself as a member of a recognized group.

9. Christianity can be defined **politically**, as a way of organizing people for political action (or inaction). To be a Christian is to act as part of a coalition with shared theo-political aims.

10. Christianity can be defined **socially**, as a community of people in whose presence you feel safe, welcome, needed, accepted, or supported. To be a Christian is to enjoy an experience of social belonging with others who identify as Christian.

11. Christianity can be defined **linguistically**, as a shared set of words and ways of communicating.

In my case, as a person of Scottish, English, Irish, Dutch, and other European descent, it was almost inevitable that I would inherit some form of Christianity as part of my family heritage (#8). As a child, I was inducted into the doctrines, practices, and morals of one stream of conservative Protestantism (#3, 4, and 6). I learned respect for the living and dead authority figures in our tradition from my parents and later mentors (#2).

At youth groups and summer camps, I felt drawn into the welcoming fellowship of my peers (#10), and I had some life-changing spiritual experiences in my teens and early twenties that marked me deeply (#5). I never thought much about the history of my faith until I was in my twenties, but then I was introduced to a telling of Christian history that made me feel proud to be part of an exceptional tradition (#1). We were deeply committed to something we called "world missions," so I wholeheartedly threw myself into that endeavor (#7). For many years, I avoided taking overtly political stances so I could focus on "spiritual matters" as my tradition taught me to do, not realizing how political inaction ends up strengthening the powers that be and is therefore a type of tacit political action (#9). Through wide reading and broad relationships, I became reasonably fluent in the terminology of many other denominations as well as my own (#11).

By the time I was finished with college, I had affiliated with Christianity on eleven out of eleven markers. I was *really, truly, seriously* Christian! But in the years that followed, every single marker became problematized for me. I discovered I had been given a whitewashed version of Christian history. I got a behind-the-curtain look at Christian institutions and their structural design flaws and dysfunctions. I saw serious problems with the doctrines, liturgies, and language of Christianity. I saw how essential Christian experiences— from being *saved* or *born again* to being *filled with the Spirit* and *called to ministry*—were often carefully stage-managed and manipulated. I began to see serious unintended negative consequences of conventional Christian morality and missions. I witnessed both in history and in my own lifetime how Christianity as a demographic or social reality can be manipulated for ugly political purposes.

I felt like a boy who was born into a loving family. His parents, uncles, aunts, and cousins were close-knit and fiercely protective of one another, and the whole extended family was successful and prosperous. The boy's childhood was filled with delicious food, spacious homes, new cars, great vacations, exciting entertainment, everything that anyone could wish for. "Family is everything," his dad said at every holiday, "and there is no family like our family." The little boy felt in his bones that his father's words were true. In his teenage years, however, the boy began discovering that his family had secrets. One discovery led to another, until the boy realized his happy, close-knit family was part of something called the Mafia. When he confronted his father about this, he was told that if he wasn't willing to become part of the family business, to keep its secrets and maintain its loyalties, he would be disowned forever . . . or something even worse might happen to him. He was either all in or completely out.

That's the kind of identity crisis I have struggled with through my years as a Christian.

Many challenges to my Christian identity have come from my fellow Christians who advocated versions of Christianity that horrified me and made me want to run for my life in the opposite direction. One such moment— equal parts mortifying and clarifying—particularly stands out. It was the evening of August 5, 2007. I was sitting on my couch watching a televised debate among Republican presidential candidates.[1]

The moderator asked one candidate, Tom Tancredo, what had been the "defining mistake" of his life. Tancredo answered that his defining mistake was waiting too long before accepting that "Jesus Christ is my personal savior." A little later, the moderator came back to Mr. Tancredo with a question about terrorism: "Last week you said that, in order to deter an attack by Islamic terrorists using nuclear weapons, you would threaten to bomb Mecca and Medina. The State Department called that 'reprehensible' and 'absolutely crazy.'" Tancredo doubled down. He saw his willingness to nuke the holiest sites of Islam as proof of his fitness to be president. He saw no conflict between killing over two million innocents and having "accepted Christ as his personal savior."

I knew that there was a name for punishing innocent civilians for deeds done by others: "collective punishment." I knew that collective punishment had been condemned by the Geneva Conventions of 1949 as a war crime. Tragically, collective punishment has had a long history, including within Christianity.

So here was an outspoken Christian unapologetically threatening to commit a war crime as a plank in his campaign platform, notwithstanding the likelihood that such an atrocity would likely lead to a global nuclear war that would kill untold millions more.

"If this fellow wins the presidency, and if he follows through on his threat, the jig will be up for me," I thought. "I will be done. I will have to stop identifying myself as a Christian as an act of protest against such idiocy and evil."

That thought hadn't even fully settled before another thought rushed in: "Who am I kidding? Similarly horrific idiocies and atrocities have already been done by Christians and in Christ's name, and not just once, but again and again and again across history. Maybe it's time to be done with the whole thing now. Maybe every day I stay Christian, I add legitimacy to the next group of Christians who are about to commit the next atrocity."

Fast-forward nine years, and a majority of white Christians lined up to support someone more crude and shortsighted than Mr. Tancredo. No matter how many lies their candidate told, no matter how small-minded and vengeful he showed himself to be, when he advocated violence against protesters engaging in free speech, when he normalized white supremacists and neo-Nazis, when he bragged of adultery and sexual assault, when he boasted he could shoot someone on Fifth Avenue with no repercussions, and even when he dared to disagree with one of Jesus' central teachings—while at the National Prayer Breakfast, no less—even then, white Christians, especially Evangelicals, stood by him. Along with too many of their white Catholic and Mainline Protestant brothers and sisters, white Evangelical Christians remained the most loyal segment of his loyal base, even when he botched the response to COVID-19, even when his toll of lies topped thirty thousand, even when he incited a mob to storm the Capitol just before his turbulent presidency ended.[2] It became increasingly clear that they loved him not in spite of his faults but because of them. He might be tough, crude, dishonest, vicious, and self-serving, but he was *their* tough, crude, dishonest, vicious, and self-serving champion.

In that light, you can see why, as recently as ten minutes ago, I felt sick to death of the armed platoon of harm that hides in the Trojan horse of many forms of Christianity. All too often, the Christian industrial project reminds me less of a religion and more of the tobacco, fossil fuel, and weapons industries: willing to harm millions to keep their business going.[3]

I hope you can see that "Do I stay Christian?" is not a theoretical question for me. It is a matter of the heart, a matter of identity, a matter of ultimate concern. It confronts me each morning when I look in the mirror.

In telling you all this from the start, I hope you will understand my purpose for this book. I am not writing this book to convince you (or myself) to stay Christian. Nor am I writing this book to convince you (or myself) to leave Christian identity behind forever. Instead, I want to think through the question of retaining or shedding Christian identity with you looking over my shoulder. And I want us to consider *how we are going to live*, whether or not we identify as Christian.

So in Part I of the book, I present the best reasons I am aware of for answering "Do I stay Christian?" with a decisive *no*. If Christianity has been nothing but a blessing to you personally, this section may be painful and disruptive for you to read. But I plead with you to grapple with it humbly, honestly, with eyes and heart wide open.

In Part II, I offer the best reasons I know for answering with a sincere *yes*, without in any way minimizing the problems we address in Part I. Then, in Part III, I turn to a related question: whatever we decide about staying Christian, how can we do so in a good, honest, and loving way? In other words, this *how* question will apply whether you stay or go, whether you say *yes* or *no* (or *I don't know*) to the question raised by the title.

I am aware that every word I write is filtered through my own experience as a white male Christian, born in 1956 near the peak of the baby boom, who has lived a middle-class life on the East Coast of the United States ever since. I am also aware that people from different vantage points will have different insights, some, no doubt, at odds with my own. I know that my experience is not universal nor should my vantage point exclude anyone else's. For that reason, I encourage you to be as honest about your experience as I've tried to be about mine. Rather than pitting our experiences against one another, I hope we can learn from one another, approach one another with curiosity and empathy, and look for ways to seek the common good together.

Now you may have picked up this book leaning in one direction or another. For example, you may be thinking, "I already have one foot out the door of Christianity. If you have any good reasons to stay, I need to see them fast." If that's you, you may want to skim the "No" section of the book and focus on "Yes" and "How." If you are happily and firmly Christian and simply want to understand the reasons why friends or family members are leaving the faith, the "No" section is probably the part you need most, even though it may upset you. Ultimately, I hope you will engage with all three sections.

Wherever you're coming from, I make this promise: I won't try to push any foregone conclusion upon you. This is a serious subject, and a personal one. As a thoughtful and morally responsible person, you are the only one who can decide whether you will stay Christian or not. And only you can decide how you will live your wild and precious life after you choose to stay or leave.

Before we jump in, I want you to know three things.

First, in most of my previous books, I included questions for reflection and discussion at the end of each chapter. For this book, I would like to offer a slightly different way for you to engage more deeply, whether as an individual or as a group. You'll find that resource in Appendix I. It might be best to read that appendix before Chapter 1.

Second, in these pages I tell lots of stories of people I've met. Unless they're public figures or grant me permission, I protect their privacy by changing names and identifying details. Sometimes, I combine elements of two or more stories into one. I do so for the sake of clarity and brevity, and never to mislead.

Third, I want to tell you a brief story. When I was in college, I went through a period of deep doubt (one of many) about the existence of God. For a while, I kept my secret, but then I confided in one of my closest friends. "I think I'm on my way out of Christian faith," I said. He looked at me across the room, with great kindness on his face. "Whether you stay Christian or not," he said, "I am your friend no matter what."

If we were in the same room, that is what I would say to you.

PART I

No

When you're writing, you're trying to find out something which you don't know. The whole language of writing for me is finding out what you don't want to know, what you don't want to find out. But something forces you to anyway.

—James Baldwin

✒

BECAUSE CHRISTIANITY HAS BEEN
VICIOUS TO ITS MOTHER
(ANTI-SEMITISM)

Nobody is born a religious jerk. It takes a religion to help someone become that way.

Unfortunately, I know this from personal experience.

I put my whole heart into parenting my four kids. They're now adults, two with kids of their own, and judging by the way our kids turned out, you would think I was an amazing dad. But last night I wrote a letter to one of our adult children to ask forgiveness for a significant flaw in my fatherhood: my approach to discipline.

In the letter I explained that my approach to parenting was strongly influenced by Christian leaders whose teachings I am now repulsed by.[1] I trusted those leaders because they were respected in the Evangelical community to which I belonged and because they used a magic word, *biblical*, to describe their teaching. Now, I've come to see that what they called *biblical* was actually *authoritarian*, and I am coming to terms with how much better a parent I could have been if I had found better teachers. This breaks my heart, I wrote, because fatherhood has been the most meaningful experience of my life and I sincerely wanted to do it right.

I explained all this not as an excuse but as part of my apology, because I now see how some aspects of my parenting were insensitive, unwise, and hurtful. I've told all my children, "I sincerely did my very best for you as a father, but you deserved so much better." If only I knew when they were born what I know now! In some ways, my Christian commitment probably helped me be a better parent than I would have been otherwise, but in others, I think it made me worse. The situation recalls a time Jesus spoke of religious people traveling over land and sea to make converts, only to make them "twice the sons of hell" they were before (Matthew 23:15).

Our religion can "hell-ify" us by inspiring in us an impenetrable sense of rightness or even superiority. That sense of rightness can inoculate us against humility, infusing in us an excessive confidence or addiction to certainty that keeps us from seeing our mistakes until after the harm has been done—to others (including our children) and to ourselves. *Our religion is right,* we believe, *which makes us right.* As a result, the more devoted we are, the more stubborn and unteachable we become. And everyone can see it but us, because we're blinded by our sincerity and zeal.

The stories we typically tell ourselves about Christianity keep us living in our comfortable delusion of innocence. For example, as a young Christian, I was taught that heroic Christians like William Wilberforce ended slavery. (I wasn't taught that other Christians gained unimaginable wealth through slavery, or that the vast majority of white Christians in the South defended slavery either actively or tacitly, or that America's largest denomination formed to perpetuate slavery on biblical grounds.[2])

I was taught that devout Christians like Sir Isaac Newton were responsible for many of humanity's great scientific breakthroughs. (I wasn't taught how their fellow Christians mocked, persecuted, and opposed many brilliant thinkers, from Copernicus and Galileo to Charles Darwin and Rachel Carson.[3])

I was taught that Christians like George Mueller and Mother Teresa had been champions of orphans and widows, the downtrodden and poor, the sick and destitute. (I wasn't taught that their fellow Christians, including many of their major donors, created, profited from, and defended the systems that produced so many orphans, widows, downtrodden, sick, destitute, and poor.)

I was taught that Christians like Rev. Dr. Martin Luther King, Jr., and Archbishop Desmond Tutu courageously fought to overcome the American and South African versions of apartheid. (I was never told that their fellow Christians created those very systems and defended them with elaborate theological justifications, deceptive legal machinations, and plenty of violence.)

I was even taught that Christianity was the incubator of humanity's greatest art and literature, from da Vinci and Rembrandt to Bach and Handel to Shakespeare and Dostoyevsky. (I was seldom if ever taught to appreciate the magnificent art of other traditions or acknowledge the proliferation of Christian schlock.)

I was taught the heroic stories of Christian missionaries, of special interest to me because my paternal grandfather was a Scottish missionary to Angola. (But I was never taught about the harmful legacy of much missionary activity or about the catastrophic effects of European colonialism, to which the modern missionary movement was often fused at the hip.[4])

I was taught that Christians saw the earth as God's handiwork and that we were its stewards. (But I had to discover for myself how Christians use doctrines of "dominion" and "the Second Coming" and "election" as excuses to exploit the earth since God gave it to "us," and besides, since God is going to destroy the earth soon anyway, we might as well use it all up while we can.)

I was taught about the heroic Christian martyrs who faced torture and death with courage and equanimity. (But I wasn't ever taught about how often Christians had made martyrs of others, torturing and killing both people of other faiths and their fellow Christians in the name of God, Jesus, the Church, the Bible, and Christianity.)

Through sermons, books, radio/TV "ministries," and other media, I was repeatedly informed about the worst atrocities across history committed by non-Christians. (But about our own Christian atrocities, I was kept shockingly ignorant.)

In short, I was taught my religion's historical upsides and few of its downsides, and I was taught about other religions' historical downsides and few of their upsides.

That's a perfect recipe for creating ignorant and arrogant religious jerks.

Through the years I have tried to rectify my ignorance about my own religion's downsides and the upsides of other religions. But honestly, even after years of research, I can't be certain how much I still don't know simply because Christian institutions have so effectively denied, minimized, and rationalized our faults, recalling the old bromide about the victors writing history.

The earliest atrocity of my religion began just decades after Jesus lived and died. He taught and modeled love and radical forgiveness, but the religion that sprang up around his name very quickly showed a hateful face, and the first victim of its hostility was its own mother: Judaism.

The irony is so stark that it's hard to process: a Jewish movement with a Jewish founder and all-Jewish original followers becomes, in the matter of a couple of decades, viciously anti-Jewish. From late in the first century onward, beginning with the author of the Fourth Gospel and later including Tertullian, Origen, Chrysostom, Jerome, Ambrose, and Augustine, many of Christianity's most revered leaders vilified Jews, setting the stage for inhumane acts of persecution against Jewish people in the coming centuries, from ghettoization and banishments to forced conversions and mass executions.[5]

During the COVID-19 pandemic in 2020, many scholars reviewed the history of plagues in Christian civilization and saw how these plagues often stirred up anti-Jewish sentiment and scapegoating. For example, historian Frank Snowden, author of *Epidemics and Society*, recounted how as the bubonic plague spread from body to body in the fourteenth century, a social plague of violence spread from mind to mind, with symptoms of "divisiveness, xenophobia, witch-hunting, blaming, finding a guilty party—the great 'other' that we can attack."[6] The Jews became the other of choice upon whom European Christians repeatedly projected their pent-up anxiety and violence.[7] Over two hundred pogroms—or organized massacres—erupted during that plague outbreak alone, with an especially horrific massacre occurring in Strasbourg, France, on Valentine's Day, 1349. Snowden writes,

> The citizens of Strasbourg rounded up the community of [2,000] Jews, brought them to the Jewish cemetery, and said that it was their religion that was leading them to poison the wells where Christians drank— and that was the source of the bubonic plague. They had either to renounce their religion or be killed on the spot. Half of the Jews held to their religion, and they were burned alive.

A priest/historian from later in that century, Jakob Twinger von Königshofen (1346–1420), recounted that the motives for the massacre included money as well as plague-inspired panic. After the slaughter,

> Everything that was owed to the Jews was cancelled. . . . The council . . . took the cash that the Jews possessed and divided it among the working-men proportionately. The money was indeed the thing that killed the Jews.

If they had been poor and if the feudal lords had not been in debt to them, they would not have been burnt.[8]

Later that year, Charles IV, emperor of the Holy Roman Empire, officially pardoned the city for its crimes of mass murder and theft. Some might call that pardon an act of mercy, but it has the scent of coverup and complicity.

Less than a hundred years later, the Protestant Reformation was born. It too perpetuated anti-Semitism with venomous fervor, as exemplified in the bone-chilling words of Martin Luther:

Their private houses must be destroyed and devastated, they could be lodged in stables. Let the magistrates burn their synagogues and let whatever escapes be covered with sand and mud. Let them be forced to work, and if this avails nothing, we will be compelled to expel them like dogs in order not to expose ourselves to incurring divine wrath and eternal damnation from the Jews and their lies . . . we are at fault in not slaying them.[9]

It's not hard to see how this kind of vicious Protestant rhetoric, together with its Catholic counterpart, smoldered deep in the German Christian psyche and caught fire in the Nazi death camps, gas chambers, and mass graves four centuries later.[10]

I was born a decade after the Holocaust, at a time when fundamentalist Christians like Jerry Falwell, Sr., seemed to embrace Judaism as Christianity's equal partner in creating the West in general and the United States in particular. Falwell constantly spoke of the "Judeo-Christian tradition." (A rabbi friend of mine noted, with appropriate skepticism, "Judeo-Christian usually just means Christian.") Falwell's son carried on the pairing.[11] Along with TV preacher John Hagee and many others, the Falwells became fervent supporters of the nation of Israel, offering further evidence, to some at least, of their anti-anti-Semitism. It's clear, however, that their brand of Christian Zionism bears only superficial resemblance to Jewish Zionism. In the end, Christian Zionism reduces Jews to the status of pawns in the fulfillment of end-times prophecies that many Christian preachers love to speak and write about.

By the time I was a young pastor, all things Jewish were downright trendy, and many Evangelicals started celebrating "messianic Passover Seders" and many joined "messianic synagogues."

Rabbi Danya Ruttenberg diagnosed our problem succinctly in a tweet: "Philosemitism is antisemitism, too. Fetishization of Jews and Judaism is also an objectification of us and a denial of our humanity, and also often comes with a side order of appropriation."[12]

Rabbi Danya's assessment makes sense to me, especially after a tour of Israel and Palestine I helped organize several years ago. Our trip wasn't a typical holy land tour. We spent half of our time in the West Bank and half in Israel, seeking to understand the Israel-Palestine situation by actually meeting Israelis and Palestinians.[13] We met settlers whose settlements were funded and defended by "philosemitic" Christians in the United States. We met Palestinians whose lands had been taken by those Christian-supported Israeli settlements. We met Israeli Jewish activists who were working to end house demolitions and assure equal human rights for their Palestinian neighbors. We visited Palestinian refugee camps and met with a leader of the Palestinian Liberation Organization—who was, by the way, a dedicated Christian. We were guests at a Shabbat service in a synagogue near Jerusalem. It was full of friendly people, few of whom had ever had a personal relationship with a Palestinian or understood what life was like for Palestinians. Over our ten-day trip, we went through several checkpoints and saw the "wall of separation" from both sides.

We came away seeing the ugly underbelly of Christian Zionism and "philosemitism." We saw with heartbreaking clarity how Christian Zionism hurts Palestinians, whether they're Christian or Muslim. We also saw how Christian Zionism has become a fundraising tool for extreme right-wing political alliances that many Jews find morally horrifying. We saw how Christian Zionism perpetuates a simple but terribly dangerous theological idea, an idea that Christian missiologist Lesslie Newbigin called "the greatest heresy in the history of monotheism," the idea that God chooses some people for exclusive privilege, leaving everyone else in a disfavored (or we might say "dis-graced") status.[14] *They are the other. They don't belong here. They are in the way. Their rights don't count.*

This elitist attitude has been central to Christian anti-Semitism through the centuries. Large swaths of Christians embraced and still embrace a doctrine called "supersessionism." Yes, the Jews were "God's chosen people" in the past, this doctrine says, but ever since they rejected Jesus, we Christians have replaced (or superseded) them. Some modified their supersessionism to say that God chose two groups of people, first Jews and then Christians. But either way, the supposed pro-Israel stance of many conservative Christians today has a chilling dimension: Jews in Israel are useful to these Christians because of their supposed role in bringing in "the last days," during or after which they will either convert or be sent to the fires of hell—as if God in the end will outdo the worst Christian hate crimes against Jews.

Not only that, but I suspect another unsavory motivation is at work. After the Holocaust, the Jews were seen as a group of innocent victims. By associating ourselves with innocent victims, we Christians could, in a sense, enhance our own sense of innocence. (We'll return to this theme of innocence in Chapter 16.) Christians could derive other benefits from Jews too, as I saw some years ago during a preaching trip to Guatemala. I noticed that every second or third car on the road had a bumper sticker of an Israeli flag or star of David. "I had no idea there were so many Jewish Guatemalans," I said to my driver. "Those aren't the cars of Jews," he explained. "They're the cars of Pentecostals. Pentecostals teach that God will bless whoever blesses the Jews. So they sell those bumper stickers at their churches. It's a way for Christians to buy a blessing from God. Life is hard here, so we want to get blessings any way we can!"

The Christian community still remains largely ignorant of or in denial about its detestable history of anti-Semitism. It remains equally oblivious to how its contemporary "philosemitism" fetishizes, objectifies, appropriates, and exploits Jews in anti-Semitic ways. Until these dangerous underlying conditions are fully and effectively addressed, they remain like loaded guns hidden in the glove compartment, even among Christians sporting pro-Israel bumper stickers on their minivans.

I have felt this danger even more acutely since the weekend of August 10–11, 2017, when I was asked to be part of a clergy witness in Charlottesville, Virginia. There I watched as hundreds of young khaki-clad white men (along with a few women) carried tiki torches and baseball bats through the city, chanting anti-Semitic Nazi slogans and waving Nazi and Confederate flags. I rallied, sang, prayed, and marched with a multi-faith group of counter-witnesses standing for Black, minority, and Jewish lives. I was among those who ran into the chaos to help care for the wounded after a white supremacist terrorist drove his car into a crowd, injuring many and killing one young woman. I saw with my own eyes that anti-Semitism continues to ferment in many American souls.

Until the Christian faith unites more passionately and decisively in acknowledging its ugly anti-Semitic history (which is ongoing and, in some places, experiencing a resurgence), I must be sympathetic to those who say they can't stay Christian for this reason alone.

I think of two people I've met, one born in a Mainline Protestant family in the United States, the other born in a Lutheran family in Germany. After learning the realities of Christian anti-Semitism, each felt that the most faithful and moral thing they could do was convert from Christianity to Judaism. One became a rabbi in the United States, the other, an activist in Israel. When their kind faces and thoughtful eyes come to mind, I feel a deep and complex irony: might it sometimes be necessary, to follow Jesus' example of deep solidarity with the oppressed, to leave the religion associated with Jesus entirely? Might the most truly Christlike choice be to disassociate from Christianity and associate with a religion that Christians have persecuted? Might the nonviolent example of Jesus require a true follower or friend of Jesus to defect from any religion with a long track record of doing violent harm in Jesus' name? No morally serious person can minimize the gravity of these questions.

The psychology of anti-Semitism is as complex and convoluted as its history. But one thing is clear: anti-Semitism is not like a freak accident that happens randomly to individuals. It's more like a conspiracy theory that an unscrupulous cable news station spreads among susceptible groups, recruiting the naive as accomplices in ignorance, lies, and bigotry. For most of its history, the Christian religion has been this tawdry cable news station, hosting a wide array of dangerous anti-Semitic conspiracy theorists, and in many places, it continues to do so.

So it is for reasons of moral integrity that I must ask myself: might it be necessary to turn off the religious network that turned so viciously on its own mother, and that continues to put her under threat? Might a religion that could make me a worse father also make me a worse neighbor or citizen? Don't I owe it to my neighbors, especially my Jewish neighbors, to seriously reconsider my involvement in a religion that has been so cruel to them for so long?

2

✌

BECAUSE OF CHRISTIANITY'S
SUPPRESSION OF DISSENT
(CHRISTIAN VS. CHRISTIAN VIOLENCE)

I've lost touch with Chad in recent years. He was a likable leader of a Christian organization who read my books and sought me out privately for guidance on a few occasions. He once invited me to speak at a large conference he organized. When I arrived, he escorted me through the crowd and whispered in my ear, "We're glad to have you speak to our conference. But we almost lost some of our major donors when they found out we invited you. That's why we couldn't have you give a lecture, but could only let you be interviewed onstage. We had to title your session 'Interview with a Heretic.' I hope you don't mind us calling you a heretic. It's the only way we can get you in front of our constituency."

I didn't know whether agreeing to speak under those conditions was an act of humility or folly on my part, but I did know that the term *heretic* was loaded. Historically, it empowers those who apply it and disempowers those to whom it is applied.

Early in Christian history, *heretic* was a neutral word, roughly equivalent to *nonconformist*. By the middle of the second century, the word changed to an epithet. Early in the fourth century, heresy became a crime with increasingly dire consequences.[1] Labeling someone *heretic* or *apostate* made almost any cruelty possible. It put the presumed heretic under great threat, and it gave the heresy hunter great power. It targeted the heretic as an enemy not only of the Christian church but also of the Christian empire.

The historical reality of Christian empire, like Christian anti-Semitism, is bathed in irony. Jesus was an oppressed brown Palestinian Jew, living in a Middle Eastern nation that was occupied by a European empire centered in Rome. Jesus challenged the empire of Rome by proclaiming an alternative empire, the empire of God. The similarity of the terms highlighted the radical contrasts between the two empires:

Rome's empire was violent. God's empire was nonviolent.

Rome's empire was characterized by domination. God's empire was characterized by service and liberation.

Rome's empire was preoccupied with money. God's empire was preoccupied with generosity and was deeply suspicious of money.

Rome's empire was fueled by the love of power. God's empire was fueled by the power of love.

Rome's empire created a domination pyramid that put a powerful and violent man on the top, with chains of command and submission that put everyone else in their place beneath the supreme leader. God's empire created a network of solidarity and mutuality that turned conventional pyramids upside down and gave "the last, the least, and the lost" the honored place at the table.

Not surprisingly, the Roman Empire saw Jesus and his nonviolent movement as a threat to their violent regime, so they had him tortured and publicly executed as a matter of standard procedure. By pinning a naked human being to wood the way a dead butterfly or grasshopper is pinned in a display case, the empire showed its own absolute dominance and its victim's absolute defeat. The message was clear: Jesus' message of truth and love meant nothing in the face of the empire's crushing power and domination.

In defiance of the empire, Jesus maintained nonviolence to the end. He cried neither "Goddamn you filthy Roman dogs for what you are doing to me!" nor "I'll be back, hunt you down, and make you all pay someday!" Instead, with his dying breath he uttered a prayer for his torturers and killers to be forgiven because they didn't know what they were doing.

Echoing its founder's nonviolence, the Christian faith initially grew as a nonviolent spiritual movement of counter-imperial values. It promoted love, not war. Its primal creed elevated solidarity, not oppression and exclusion: "For in Christ Jesus you are all children of God through faith. As many of you as were baptized into Christ have clothed yourselves with Christ. There is no longer Jew or Greek, there is no longer slave or free, there is no longer male and female; for all of you are one in Christ Jesus" (Galatians 3:26–28). The early Christians elevated the equality of friendship rather than the supremacy of hierarchy (John 15:15; 3 John 14, 15). Because of their counter-imperial posture, including their refusal to be soldiers in the Roman army or to participate in the imperial cult that proclaimed the divinity of the emperor, they were often mocked, distrusted as unpatriotic, and persecuted.

But then, in the early fourth century, Constantine became emperor. He was determined to unite the empire's many factions and fortify his regime, and like thousands of political leaders since then, he saw the Christian religion as a useful tool.

Constantine needed the religion's help because over the previous century, the Roman Empire had been weakened by political corruption and a series of invasions, mass migrations, rebellions, plagues, trade problems, economic downturns, political corruption, and insurrections. The support of a zealous and growing religion would help him unify his empire, pacify his diverse constituents, and gain moral authority for his actions. Similarly, the bishops of the church had a lot to gain from a deal with the emperor. To have the emperor's support would elevate their status, attract new converts, protect them from persecution, increase their power, and perhaps even add to their wealth.

Just before a critical battle, Constantine claimed to have had a vision. In this vision, the Christian cross became a sword and spear of warfare, and a heavenly voice promised Constantine military victory if he painted the cross on the shields of his soldiers.[2] When the visionary promise came true, the union of Christianity and the Roman Empire seemed to be a match made in heaven.

From that time forward, the primary Christian institution on earth was branded (in multiple senses of the word) as Roman, and the *Roman Catholic Church* became an imperial rather than counter-imperial community. Church and state, we might say, became both bedfellows and brothers in arms, united in heart and mind.[3]

The bishops derived great benefits from this relationship, but they paid a high price too. Before Constantine, Christians could have said, "Inspired by the cross of Christ, we heal, forgive, serve, welcome, transform, resist tyranny, and demonstrate love." But after Constantine, their mission and ethos were profoundly altered: "Inspired by the cross of the Empire, we conquer, kill, dominate, crush, rule, exploit, gain power, and impose law and order to retain our power. (And we make a handsome profit while doing so wherever possible.)"

What the empire wanted to do, the church generally blessed. Church leaders may occasionally have complained a bit, but in general, they offered the empire either compliant support or ready forgiveness. This cozy relationship with the empire continued long after the Roman Empire had fully collapsed. The church supported the empire's many reincarnations in French, German, Spanish, Portuguese, Dutch, British, Russian, German, and American imperial ventures. Each empire could count on the mainstream Christian church to bless its successes, pardon its failures, and pacify and unify its masses.

A community with a history of violence to Jews (as we saw in Chapter 1) does not sound like a safe place for non-Christians. But as a chaplain to empire, Christianity was not a particularly safe place for Christians either—at least not those who chose to differ from the authorities of church or state. *Choosing to differ*, in fact, was the root meaning of the word *heresy*.

When I look back across Christian history, I can't help but see that there is a fine line between a would-be reformer and a heretic. Successful reformers are revered as heroes and saints by their followers of later generations, but failed or rejected reformers are remembered as heretics by the victorious anti-reformers who write the history. When the heretic to some is the heroic reformer to others, and when the orthodox commit crimes against humanity in the name of orthodoxy, the terms *heresy* and *orthodoxy* seem equally problematic, and say as much about power struggles as they say about either theology or morality. Because of these complexities and others, going forward I'm going to employ the term *doctrinal nonconformist* (or simply *nonconformist*) instead of *heretic*.

Constantine set the stage for state violence against Christian nonconformists by ordering that all writings of Arias, the leading nonconformist of the day, be burned, and all who hid Arias's writings be killed. The theologian Athanasias (296–373) similarly called for violence against the followers of Arias. Even Augustine, who early in his career advocated persuasion rather than persecution of nonconformists, eventually condoned fines, imprisonment, banishment, and floggings to punish members of the nonconformist Donatist movement. His defense of violence against nonconformists stopped short of the death penalty, however.

Following Augustine, for the next six hundred years, the church typically responded to nonconformists with trials, censure, imprisonment, punishment, and banishment but stopped short of killing. But beginning in the late twelfth century, a new wave of nonconformist movements spread across Europe, and in response, popes and bishops became more aggressive than they had ever been before.

In France and Italy, the church hunted down and killed members of the Albigensians, Waldensians, and other similar reform movements. In 1252, the ill-named Pope Innocent IV issued a document that authorized torture for doctrinal nonconformists, unleashing a wave of heresy hunts (collectively known as the Medieval Inquisition) that spread across Europe, especially concentrated in Spain. Thomas Aquinas, medieval Christianity's greatest teacher, defended these actions in 1271: "With regard to heretics . . . they deserve not only to be separated from the Church by excommunication, but also to be severed from the world by death."[4]

Historians generally agree: while the records are unreliable and incomplete, at least tens of thousands of suspected nonconformists were prosecuted by church courts between 1180 and 1450; many thousands were tortured; over a thousand were executed by church authorities. If those numbers seem small, remember that the 6,500 lynchings of Black Americans between Reconstruction and World War II weren't failed attempts at genocide; they were successful acts of terrorism.[5] Their purpose was to frighten Black Americans into submission. Fewer than seven thousand terrorist lynchings led six million African Americans to leave everything—farms, homes, work, savings, as well as family—in a flight for their lives known today as the Great Migration.[6]

The numbers swell when women accused of being witches are included. Historians estimate that in a seventy-year period starting in 1560, 80,000 women were tried as witches and 40,000 were killed. Protestants had a special appetite for witch trials; over 90 percent of the trials took place in Protestant lands. In fact, some scholars suspect that Protestants used witch hunts as a means of gaining "market share" from Catholics: if you're going to be a Christian, why not join the most zealous, anti-Satan variety?[7]

A late edition (1578) of an Inquisition manual produced by the church made explicit the actual purpose of the violence: "for punishment does not take place primarily and *per se* for the correction and good of the person punished, but for the public good in order that others may become terrified and weaned away from the evils they would commit."[8] The word *terrified* strengthens my earlier use of the term *terrorist organization*. The term feels even more accurate when you consider the tools of terror the church employed: the Red X, the hair shirt, branding irons, the strappado, the Judas cradle, the Spanish boot, the brodequin, the heretic's fork, and the rack.[9] When compared with these brutal forms of torture, banishment and even death by burning at the stake might seem merciful.

Again: these ecclesial atrocities were used upon baptized Christians, all for the crime of questioning doctrines that many Christians in good standing now question, or believing things that many Christians in good standing now believe. Again: most Protestant Reformers did not reform the violence to which the Catholic Church had surrendered itself. As soon as they had the chance, they also used violence to suppress the nonconformists of the Radical Reformation, including those who were themselves nonviolent. (Some Anabaptists, as they were called, were true nonconformists in that they chose to differ from both Catholic and Protestant norms by rejecting violence in all forms, in imitation of Christ. Both branches of so-called orthodoxy persecuted them violently.[10])

Since Constantine, Christianity has repeatedly claimed a legitimate right to do violence to its members to protect its interests and conserve its supremacy. It has sought far-reaching and sometimes almost limitless control over the behavior and minds of its subjects. At times, it has behaved like a totalitarian power, suppressing dissent and claiming divine and absolute authority, capable of absolute corruption. At times, it has behaved like a terrorist organization, intimidating the many by graphic public violence to a relative few. At times (as we will see in the next chapter), it has behaved like a regime of genocide, with a death toll in the millions. Both Catholic and Protestant Christians have covered up pedophilia scandals and mass killings of children in Christian orphanages and boarding schools, protected perpetrators, and silenced victims, showing haunting similarities to a crime network. The tragic irony, once again, makes me grimace: the Christian religion began as a peasant peace movement whose leader said we should all call one another sisters and brothers, but it quickly reduced sisters and brothers to subjects to be dominated, punished, imprisoned, and worse.[11]

Before moving on, I'd like to include a final story of Christian-on-Christian violence, as told by my friend Mirabai Starr. It represents thousands of untold stories of Christian-on-Christian violence that were not part of official inquisitions by church authorities and therefore don't show up in historical records. These episodes were more intimate and spontaneous and happened in secret in churches, schools, monasteries, and families. We only know this story today because it involved someone who later became so famous that he could be neither forgotten nor suppressed. In the early 1570s, an idealistic young monk in his late twenties was a reformer in the making:

> Juan de la Cruz was twenty-nine years old and madly in love with God. The great living saint Teresa of Ávila had recognized a rare sanctity and brilliance in this humble young friar and placed him in charge of her first reform convent.
>
> Then late one night, threatened by this movement to return the order to the contemplative path embodied by the Desert Fathers and Mothers, the mainstream Carmelites whisked him away and imprisoned him in Toledo.
>
> His cell was a tiny closet that had formerly served as a latrine. There was not enough room to lie down, and the only window was far above his head. . . . Twice a day the friars took him out and flogged him.
>
> "Denounce Teresa!" they demanded. "Renounce the heresy of this so-called reform!"
>
> But he would not betray the dream. The dream of a life of voluntary simplicity, solitude, and silence. A contemplative life based on the Gospel teachings of poverty of spirit and charity of heart. A life of stripping away rather than accumulating. Of relinquishing power and seeking nothing. Of nothing but loving friendship with the divine and loving service to [God's] creation.[12]

Juan de la Cruz is better known to English speakers today as St. John of the Cross, one of the most beloved monastics and mystics in Christian history.

If you were to dismiss this chapter by arguing that such things only happened in the distant past, I would agree that imprisonment, beatings, and burning at the stake have not been used to punish Christian nonconformists for centuries, thank God. But then I would gently remind you how contemporary Christian leaders in the United States, starting in 2016, have defended or tolerated children being torn from the arms of Christian parents and kept in cages.[13] Or I would remind you of the continuing use of banishment by Christian parents whose teenaged Christian children come out as gay. Or I could refer you to contemporary religious leaders defending torture, including waterboarding, in a so-called Christian nation.[14] Or I could recount the story of Protestant and Catholic "troubles" in Ireland.[15] Or I could point you to right-wing Catholic activist Steve Bannon, who recently advocated placing the severed heads of opponents on pikes in front of the White House, or white Evangelical and Charismatic preachers who continue to call for civil war in support of Donald Trump.[16]

Today, abuse of Christians by Christians tends to be more emotional and spiritual than physical. But shunning and disowning (forms of relational banishment), public shaming and character assassination, private humiliations, church trials of nonconformists, blacklisting, and other forms of Christian-on-Christian cruelty continue, and more and more traumatized people are coming forward with their stories, often accompanied by the hashtag #churchtoo.[17]

To state the obvious: Jesus never tortured or killed or ruined the life of anyone, but the same cannot be said for the religion that claims to follow him.

Knowing what I now know, if I were not already a Christian, I would hesitate in becoming one, at least until the religion in all its major forms offers a fearless, searching, public moral accounting for its past crimes . . . first, against Jews, and also against its own nonconformist members.

%

3

BECAUSE OF CHRISTIANITY'S HIGH GLOBAL DEATH TOLL—AND LIFE TOLL (CRUSADER COLONIALISM)

"What religion you, teacher?" Sisavanh asked.

It was 1982, and I was teaching English as a second language to a class of recent refugees, adults from Vietnam, Cambodia, Laos, Afghanistan, and Iran. Sisavanh was from Laos, and I was pleased to hear him using his new language to establish personal contact with me, although it appeared he still hadn't discovered the joy of using verbs.

"I'm a Christian," I said. "What religion *are* you, Sisavanh?" I hoped he might notice the emphasis I put on the verb, but alas, he answered, "I Buddhist."

Then he added—with a bounty of actual verbs, "Teacher, I *love* Christian. Christian save my life in refugee camp. Christian give me food, give me book English, give medicine when I sick. Christian good. Good religion." He flashed a smile and two thumbs up.

I looked around the room. I was glad Christians had earned a good reputation with this Buddhist refugee. But I couldn't help but think how the Muslims in the room might have had different stories to tell. Christians and Muslims had been killing one another for centuries, and—little did we know in 1982—we would soon be killing one another again.

If Christianity's attitude toward Judaism could be compared to a violent child turning upon its mother, and if Christianity's attitude toward nonconformists could be compared to authoritarian parents browbeating or abusing their children, its relation to Islam could be compared to violent sibling rivalry. When Mohammed testified in 613 that he had received a revelation from the God of Adam, Abraham, Mary, and Jesus . . . the same God worshipped by Christians, Christians could have welcomed him as a brother, or at least entered into respectful dialogue. Some Christians did enter into neighborly relationships for a while, but as Muslim civilization grew, predictable tensions grew as well.

By 746, John of Damascus had identified Mohammed as a false prophet, and later Christian writers added the infamous "H word" (heretic) to describe him. The Christian West saw the growing Islamic empire as a threat, and in 1093, Pope Urban launched the First Crusade against Islam.[1] Five more Crusades followed, along with other wars that are sometimes included among the Crusades. What gave the Crusades a special religious character was the fact that the church launched or supported them and promised forgiveness of sins for those who went to fight.

The rivalry between the world's two largest religions continues today. September 11, 2001, re-ignited the coals of Christian Islamophobia that had been quietly smoldering during most of my lifetime, usually overshadowed by the Cold War. The reality of that abiding Christian Crusader mentality became clearer than ever to me back in 2007 when a popular Christian talk show host accused my colleagues and me of being Al-Qaeda sympathizers simply because we advocated loving our Muslim neighbors rather than killing them.[2]

Christianity's conflicted relationship with Islam set the stage for its attitude toward other religions it encountered, from Hinduism, Buddhism, and Confucianism in the East to Indigenous religions around the world.

In nearly every encounter between Western Christians and global non-Christians, Christians have continued the Crusader mentality, seeing their neighbors as dangerous opponents in a holy conflict and presenting them with the same three options: *convert* to become one of us, *get out* of our way and *leave*, or *submit* to our dominance, subjecting yourself to a second-class status.[3]

That would be bad enough, but these options have often been supplemented by a fourth: *or die.*

If you ask when the Crusades ended, some historians would say about 1300. But you could make a case that for another five hundred years, the Crusades continued by going global, and doing so under an alias: *European Christian colonialism.* Christian crusader colonialism has been a clever way of hiding the ultimatum of *convert, leave, submit, or die* in plain sight.

By the time Columbus "sailed the ocean blue" in 1492 (inspired by bizarre prophecies and end-times ambitions), the theological stage had already been set for his voyage.[4] One papal document in particular opened the door to the global conquest by European Christian nations. It was a permission slip of sorts from Pope Nicholas V (1397–1455) to the king of Portugal, allowing him to conquer and colonize parts of West Africa. King Alfonso had helped the pope raise an army to fight Muslim forces expanding into Europe from Turkey, and so the pope rewarded him handsomely through a document now popularly known as the Doctrine of Discovery:

> Justly desiring that whatsoever concerns the integrity and spread of the faith, for which Christ our God shed his blood, shall flourish in the virtuous souls of the faithful . . . we grant to you by these present documents, with our Apostolic Authority, full and free permission to invade, search out, capture and subjugate the Saracens [Muslims] and pagans and any other unbelievers and enemies of Christ wherever they may be, as well as their kingdoms, duchies, counties, principalities, and other property . . . and to reduce their persons into perpetual slavery, and to apply and appropriate and convert to the use and profit of yourself and your successors, the Kings of Portugal, in perpetuity, the above-mentioned kingdoms, duchies, counties, principalities, and other property and possessions and suchlike goods.[5]

The document was expansive in its geographic scope, chilling in its intent, mercenary in its goal, and horrific in its impact and duration.

Pope Alexander (1431–1503) followed up with a similar permission slip to Spain in 1493 (retroactively granting Columbus permission for his famous voyage). In 1494, a treaty clarified that it was only the lands of non-Christians that could be taken, and additional papal documents made it clear that the church was giving the Portuguese and Spanish carte blanche to colonize the whole world for the "spread of the faith, for which Christ our God shed his blood." Other nations, like France, asked to be admitted to the colonization frenzy, and the church offered its blessings on their ambitions. After the Protestant Reformation in 1518, nations of Northern Europe had an additional reason to break from Rome: they could conquer the world and convert other nations "to their use and profit" without needing to ask the pope's permission—or share any of their profits with him.

Among the Protestant nations, the British created the world's largest colonial empire. After thirteen of its colonial holdings in America rebelled, the revolutionaries quickly became the new colonizers, using the benign agrarian term *settlers* instead of the more accurate *colonizers* or *conquistadors*. Citizens of the newly formed United States went on—in the name of life, liberty, and happiness—to take all three from millions of Indigenous people, unleashing many of the worst atrocities of the colonial period.

To this day, with the help of the Christian religion in its many denominations, many of my fellow Christians, especially in the United States, maintain a self-image of pristine innocence and exceptional superiority. They assume, as I once did—terribly naively, I admit—that colonialism was a political and economic project with no Christian involvement. We celebrate our religious and national virtues with grandiose fireworks, as if bright lights and loud noises could distract us from our past. Meanwhile, we quietly camouflage today's incarnations of the Christian crusader colonial spirit in terms like *American exceptionalism, Western civilization, patriot*, and *law and order*.

The Doctrine of Discovery (perhaps better called *The Doctrine of White Christian Supremacy*) unleashed a wave of catastrophes that continue to shape our global situation today:

- Millions of Indigenous people around the world have suffered genocide, land theft, cultural humiliation, displacement, and apartheid.
- Millions of human beings were kidnapped in Africa, shipped in horrific conditions to the New World, and then exploited for their labor in "perpetual slavery." Women were routinely raped by the enslavers, and they had to watch their families be separated as their children and spouses were traded like livestock, all while the enslavers justified their actions using the Bible.
- Millions experienced a first set of wars to resist initial subjugation followed by a second set to achieve liberation.[6]
- In addition to the death tolls of war, colonizers inflicted new *life tolls* upon colonized peoples. The colonized suffered constant traumatic humiliation, exploitation, and abuse, intensified by the knowledge that their children would suffer under similar conditions, generation after generation.
- Even after liberation, descendants of the colonized faced a long, pain-

ful, usually violent process of recovery after independence as they tried to build new social and political infrastructure in the context of deep-seated corruption, intertribal conflict, insupportable debt, arbitrary borders, and other lasting consequences of colonialism.

Whatever the death toll of the colonization project from 1492 to 1899, one researcher estimates that 50 million were killed *in the twentieth century alone* as one colonized nation after another fought to be liberated from colonial domination, and as the "civilized Christian West" fought to retain colonial dominance as long as it could.[7] When we add the death toll to what I've called the life toll, the devastating impact of Christian crusader colonialism is incalculable.

Of course, Christian crusader colonizers have reaped obscene profits from their domination. No wonder the crusader colonial spirit lives on, reincarnated in enduring ideologies like white supremacy and white Christian nationalism. Many white Christians would be appalled to think of themselves as white supremacists, but they would be proud to think of themselves as Christian supremacists. As a result, their whiteness is concealed in their Christianity, hidden to both others and themselves. The personal suffering of millions is captured in works of nonfiction like *The Half Has Never Been Told* and works of fiction like *Things Fall Apart*, which help humanize the victims of the global Christian invasion. But still, the half has never been told of how the world fell apart as a consequence of a Christian mandate to "go into all the world and make slaves of all nations."[8]

Centuries of crusader colonization have produced deep trauma that still inhabits the global human psyche, demon-like. This trauma expresses itself in internalized presumptions of superiority and privilege among the descendants of the colonizers, along with an almost desperate obsession to remain in power, for fear, perhaps, that if they let up for an instant, the colonized will do to them in the future what their ancestors did to the colonized in the past.[9] Among the descendants of the colonized, the trauma often manifests as a mirror-image presumption of internalized inferiority and hopelessness . . . or as an unending besiegement by lament and rage, recalling the words of James Baldwin: "To be a Negro in this country and to be relatively conscious is to be in a rage almost all the time." The summer of 2020, with its unforgettable image of a white knee on a Black neck, demonstrated that the time for outrage is far from over.

Wherever Christians have gone, we have brought a legacy of schools, hospitals, and other institutions intended to improve our quality of life and the lives of others. But make no mistake: we have also brought the fourfold ultimatum of *convert, leave, submit, or die*, which is the unwritten contract of crusader colonial Christianity, past and present.

If I walk into the average Christian church this Sunday, few of my fellow Christians will know much about this tragic legacy. Instead, sincere but uninformed Christians will share a deep sense of moral innocence, if not superiority. I find our widespread self-deception so outrageous that I can only borrow these fiery words from a speech delivered on July 4, 1852, by Frederick Douglass, as he addressed the white Christian crusader colonialism of his day:

> [The] church regards religion simply as a form of worship, an empty ceremony, and not a vital principle, requiring active benevolence, justice, love and good will towards humanity. . . . A worship that can be conducted by persons who refuse to give shelter to the houseless, to give bread to the hungry, clothing to the naked, and who enjoin obedience to a law forbidding these acts of mercy, is a curse, not a blessing to humankind. . . .
>
> The church of this country is not only indifferent to the wrongs of the slave, it actually takes sides with the oppressors. . . . Many of its most eloquent Divines . . . have shamelessly given the sanction of religion and the Bible to the whole slave system. . . . For my part, I would say, welcome infidelity! welcome atheism! welcome anything! in preference to the gospel, as preached by those Divines! . . . These ministers make religion a cold and flinty-hearted thing, having neither principles of right action, nor bowels of compassion. They strip the love of God of its beauty, and leave the throng of religion a huge, horrible, repulsive form. It is a religion for oppressors, tyrants, man-stealers, and thugs. . . .
>
> [A] religion which favors the rich against the poor; which exalts the proud above the humble; which divides humankind into two classes, tyrants and slaves; which says to the person in chains, stay there; and to the oppressor, oppress on; it is a religion which may be professed and enjoyed by all the robbers and enslavers of humankind.[10]

Because of the American Christian church's complicity in the racist "system of crime and blood," as diagnosed by Douglass, the nation fell into a civil war full of yet more crime and blood. It is not impossible—it is not even difficult—to imagine this nineteenth-century history repeating itself in the twenty-first. The events at the U.S. Capitol on January 6, 2021, illustrate that grim possibility. Researcher/pollster Robert P. Jones documents the sad, statistically verifiable truth that white Christians have not yet faced our past and turned from it: "White Christian churches, both Protestant and Catholic, have served as institutional spaces for the preservation and transmission of white supremacist attitudes," so that "the more racist attitudes a person holds, the more likely he or she is to identify as a white Christian."[11]

If the human species survives the twenty-first century, I suspect that unbiased historians of the future will look back on the six hundred years beginning in 1452 as (among other things) the era of white Christian colonization and genocide. I imagine our descendants will wonder how any person of conscience during this period could have stayed Christian.

I wonder too. I wonder too.

4

¾

BECAUSE OF CHRISTIANITY'S
LOYAL COMPANY MEN
(INSTITUTIONALISM)

Over my lifetime as a Christian, whenever the underbelly of Christian history has been exposed (which isn't often), a little voice pops up inside my head with counter-arguments. I call this voice my Inner Fundamentalist. Here's a sample of how our conversations go.

> My Inner Fundamentalist: You were being so negative in the previous chapters! You're minimizing all the good we Christians have done.
>
> Me: I'm glad to acknowledge all the good we've done. But that isn't the point. The point is that we have some ugly skeletons in our closet that we don't acknowledge, and that lack of acknowledgment creates a sense of false innocence that leads to superiority that looks a lot like pride. That pride increases the chances that we'll fall into the horrors of our past again . . . or even worse horrors.
>
> My Inner Fundamentalist: OK. There may have been some failures, but these were exceptions, minor imperfections committed by men of their times, or flaws that have been exaggerated by our critics and enemies. The good far outweighs the bad. Think about all the hospitals and schools, all the . . .
>
> Me: Sorry to interrupt, but that sounds a little like the abusive spouse who says, "Don't you remember the diamond rings I bought you and the luxury vacations I took you on? You're complaining about a few black eyes and bruises? How ungrateful is that! What's wrong with you?"

So your objection proves my point: *we Christians still don't get it.* We're the richest, largest, and most well-armed religion on the planet, and if we remain unwilling to acknowledge and learn from our past, we pose a serious threat to the very existence of humanity.

My Inner Fundamentalist: OK. No need to preach. But you make it sound like Christians are worse than anyone else.

Me: Jesus said that his followers should display better fruit than they would have otherwise. He said they should be the light of the world and the salt of the earth, not that they would be no shadier or more rotten than anybody else. As an insider, I know: we work from a posture of moral superiority, and that assumption of moral superiority fuels our sense of spiritual privilege and religious exceptionalism. It's reinforced by our sermons, our liturgies, our rituals, our theologies.

My Inner Fundamentalist: But we constantly talk about our sins. We confess our sins every Sunday.

Me: That response troubles me on many levels. First, yes, we constantly talk about our sins, but have you noticed that nearly all the sins we preach and pray and sing about are *personal* sins? I spent my entire childhood and young adulthood without hearing a single serious sermon about the *social* sins of racism and white supremacy, exploitation of the poor, economic injustice, nuclear proliferation, or destruction of the earth, arguably the most serious sins happening during my lifetime on this planet!

My Inner Fundamentalist: But those are liberal matters. Christians are supposed to be conservative.

Me: Who told you this? Our conservative focus on personal and especially sexual sins strikes me now as a weapon of mass distraction. It keeps us from addressing the more "weighty matters of the law," as Jesus said. And don't even get me started about how many of us Christians use abortion and homosexuality as trump cards to neutralize any other issue that's brought up. Imagine if we Christians had expended even half the energy on combating racism that we've spent in opposing gay marriage or making abortion illegal. Not to mention the fact that criminalizing abortion is one of the least effective methods possible for reducing it. If we really wanted to reduce abortion, we would provide better health care and . . . [1]

My arguments with my Inner Fundamentalist tend to end like this . . . or not end. They just go on and on.

Some of my Catholic friends tell me they have their own version of this inner voice. They may call it their Inner Vatican or Inner Mother Superior. The details differ, but the process is the same: even though they hardly ever attend Mass anymore, they still hear that inner voice scolding them for eating steak (instead of fish) on Fridays or using birth control (or voting for a Democrat).

I've come to understand my Inner Fundamentalist not simply as a part of my own psyche but also as an outpost or colony, if you will, of a larger Christian authority structure. That structure might have a physical headquarters in a building somewhere—in Rome, for example, or Nashville, Atlanta, Kansas City, or New York. But Christianity's primary headquarters is not in a building in a city, but in our heads. Like a piece of downloaded software, Christianity occupies our neurons, silently monitoring and influencing our behavior, occasionally intruding into our conscious thoughts, often through the voice of our Inner Fundamentalist, Inner Vatican, or whatever.

Although I'm no expert in brain science, I am fascinated by the subject and read all I can about it. I've become convinced of this one obvious yet far-reaching truth: *we humans are wired by our brains to be social creatures, herd animals if you will.* We may think of ourselves as independent individuals, but our brains are hardwired for herd belonging. This wiring keeps us vigilant for any sign of social rejection or disapproval from members of our herd, especially its leaders. It also makes us crave the acceptance and approval they offer, which gives our Inner Fundamentalists or Inner Vaticans (or Inner Imams or Inner Rabbis) a lot of power.

Religions, then, are networks of brains under a shared influence. Sometimes the networks may harmonize our brains and lead us to collaborative behavior for the common good. Sometimes the networks may trigger our brains to fear, hate, attack, reject, or kill each other.

The more you think about this, the more you realize: you don't want to give just any schmo the keys and passcodes to your brain. In my experience, Christian leaders tend to fit into three broad categories:

First, there are many *vital spiritual leaders* in Christian organizations: sincere souls, deeply devoted, who are wise, authentic, humble, skillful, and generous, constantly learning and growing. When they are trusted with precious access to your brain, they will be careful to use that access only for your good and the common good, to the best of their ability.

Second, there are many *exhausted and burned out leaders*, people who used to be in the first category but who have been worn down by, among other things, their fellow leaders in the third category. It's a little dicier to entrust these leaders with your keys and passcodes.

In the third category, I've observed a large number of what I call *Christian company men*. (Given the persistence of male domination in most Christian communities, men dominate this category.[2]) Most are unquestionably sincere, utterly convinced that loyal service to their religious institutions equals service to God. That loyalty becomes their primary qualification. Because of their loyalty, their fellow company men promote them, often to the very highest places of power, even if they must overlook deficits in spirituality, insight, or virtue. Loyalty trumps all else.

At this moment, my Inner Fundamentalist is clearing his throat: "Ahem. Ahem! What's so bad about loyalty? Isn't loyalty a virtue?"

And, of course, as usual, my Inner Fundamentalist is partly right. Loyalty is indeed a virtue. But loyalty is easily abused. That's why we reserve our trust for people who actually care about the common good. When people we trust have interests that may actually harm us and our neighbors, we call it a *conflict of interest*. Conflicts of interest can lead to all kinds of corruption, injustice, and damage.

For example, imagine a Catholic bishop or cardinal who makes decisions out of loyalty to his fellow clergy at the expense of children in his church who are being sexually abused by some of those clergy. Or imagine a pastor who does not speak out on behalf of Black, Indigenous, or other people of color for fear of alienating major donors who consider any talk of racism and injustice to be "left-wing." Or imagine the board members of a Christian organization who do not properly investigate allegations of sexual misconduct for fear that bad press about their staff will result in a drop in donations. In each case of conflict of interest, some benefit and some suffer.

So we have every right to be curious, if not downright skeptical, about the divided loyalties and competing interests of those to whom we give access to delicate and powerful real estate in our brains.

Jesus had a lot to say to the loyal religious company men of his day. He told them that their love for God could never be an excuse for apathy or hate toward a neighbor.[3] He noted how institutional loyalty led them to put even their parents' well-being in jeopardy.[4] He told them that they had lost perspective, confusing "weightier matters" and trivialities.[5] He showed them that there were times when they should look at their history and tradition and dare to say, "You have heard it said . . . but I say to you."[6] He told them that saying the right words counted for nothing if they didn't put those words into right action.[7] He warned them about straining at gnats and swallowing camels.[8] In word and deed, in parable and practice, Jesus made it clear that constricted loyalties and constrained interests couldn't be reconciled with God's boundless mercy.[9]

As I mentioned, I began writing this book during the COVID-19 pandemic. Many churches around the world defied commonsense rules of social distancing and quarantine because the common good of public health conflicted with their personal and institutional ability to conduct business as usual, including the collection of in-person offerings. Misplaced, constrained, or absolutized loyalty, we now see, can be lethal. That fact is obvious in death cults like Jonestown, when the poisoned Kool-Aid is literal. It is less obvious but no less lethal when followers drink metaphorical Kool-Aid by defying public health guidelines or refusing to get vaccinations, or by denying climate science because trusted religious company men told them to do so.

The Christian company men who inhabit each of our brains, speaking out as our inner fundamentalists, can cause us great harm. They can also direct us to harm others—*in exactly the terrifying ways we described in the previous chapters.* They see themselves as loyal followers, obeying orders and fulfilling the wishes of those they trust above them in the hierarchy. They don't realize that the glue of upward loyalty that holds the organization together can also be an acid that eats away at their integrity, even their humanity.

If you are part of a religious system that derives its invisible power through one-directional loyalty to those above you, you had better be careful. You may wake up one day to discover that you have become a religious company man (or woman) yourself. Then, you will see how easily Christian company men can become *Christian con men* or *con artists.* The *con* is all about *confidence.*[10]

To join a religion and stay in a religion means giving its religious leaders the keys or passcodes to very deep, very sensitive regions of our brains—on a regular basis at weekly gatherings, but also in life's most pivotal and vulnerable moments . . . on sacred holidays, in rites of passage that mark new seasons of life, and in times of great crisis, moments of life and death. That access to our brains is a sacred trust. I can see why many are choosing to change their passcodes and deny further access to Christianity's company men.

Because of Christianity's Real Master (Money)

During my twenty-plus years as a pastor, I took over a thousand offerings, wrote hundreds of fundraising letters, and led one major fundraising campaign for a church facility.

Although I felt uncomfortable at first, I eventually discovered that raising money for worthy causes is meaningful, wonderful work. If we don't raise money for good purposes, it will be wasted on lesser purposes, even evil purposes. So I have great respect for the good work of philanthropic fundraising.

I have not only been on the receiving end of Christian fundraising: my wife and I have made giving a priority in our family budget for our whole married lives, following the generous example of my parents and grandparents, who lived frugally so they could give generously. To put it bluntly, I believe in giving and find great joy in it. But I also believe that every religious system, like every individual, faces the perpetual danger of being corrupted by money.

This danger has become clearer to me over the last decade, since the U.S. Supreme Court issued a landmark decision known as *Citizens United*. The ruling gave wealthy individuals and powerful corporations freedom to spend unlimited amounts of money to influence elections. Money, the court said, was a form of speech, and to limit political donations was to limit free speech.

Many saw the court's decision as a victory for free speech, but many (including me) saw it as a tragic loss for the average person. The super-rich, who already had a disproportionate amount of power and influence in our country, were given carte blanche to use their wealth to further bias the political system in their favor. They could buy expensive airtime on mass and social media, magnifying and amplifying their free speech and drowning out the voices of their neighbors, especially people of color, who lacked similar wealth. They could hire lobbyists to court politicians, winning them over to their own greedy agenda through the supposed free speech of donations.

Citizens United seemed like a perfect plan to funnel ever more power and money from the poor and middle class to the ultra-rich, in a seemingly unstoppable cycle. That's why so many of us were and are concerned about it. What's happened in U.S. politics since 2010 has confirmed that our concerns were justified: every year, a larger and larger percentage of wealth (and the power that goes along with it) is owned by a smaller and smaller percentage of wealthy families and corporations.[1]

In the aftermath of *Citizens United*, I realized that donation-dependent religious organizations and leaders are as beholden to their major donors as political parties and politicians are to their major donors. (And often, the lists of religious and political major donors have a lot of overlap.) In other words, *Citizens United* has been the standard operating practice of Christianity for centuries.

The penny (pardon the pun) dropped, and questions that had troubled me for decades suddenly had answers: Why didn't more white American preachers preach more courageously against land theft and slavery in the first four centuries of my country's history? Why haven't more white American preachers spoken out against lynching, segregation, voter suppression, and other expressions of white supremacy in the last two centuries? Why don't more Christian leaders today speak out against climate change and the fossil fuel industry, about the long-term environmental cost of short-term economic growth? Why don't they speak out against nationalism, militarism, and the NRA's campaign of gun proliferation? Why are they skittish about addressing white supremacy, police violence against minorities, and mass incarceration? Why do so many preach so frequently against abortion and gay marriage but so rarely against economic inequality and systemic injustice?

In each case, the answer is the same: we clergy (I speak as part of the problem) are caught in a tangled web of conflicts of interest, most (if not all) involving money.

Because of my years in parish ministry, I feel the pain on all sides. I understand why a large percentage of our pastors become the kinds of company men we considered in the previous chapter. They must constantly negotiate among their own moral and spiritual instincts, the interests of their institutions, their personal concerns about their own salaries and retirement accounts, and professional and social status. In short, they must master the art of ethical compromise as a matter of vocational survival.

In this process, many congregations and pastors create a kind of enmeshed identity, where the personal ego of the pastor and the institutional ego of the congregation fuse; they merge their interests and render themselves a co-dependent mutual appreciation society, based on an unwritten contract of mutual payoffs. What do you call it when a preacher needs the people for his own ego and advantage, and the people need the preacher for their own ego and advantage? The best word I've found to describe such a relationship is *narcissistic*.

My Inner Fundamentalist is on the verge of uttering a barrage of four-letter words right now. But he doesn't cuss:

> My Inner Fundamentalist: This is devilishly unfair! There are many wonderful, happy churches that aren't like this.
>
> Me: As always, my dear Inner Fundamentalist, you are partly right. But I can't help but notice something: to the degree I let your words pacify me into complacency, I'll stay Christian and keep giving. And then, more money will keep coming in to keep the system going just as it is.

There's a quote commonly attributed to Dorothy Day, founder of the Catholic Worker movement. I've seen it often on posters and internet memes through the years: "Our problems stem from our acceptance of this filthy, rotten system." The system in question is assumed to be the capitalist system. But a Catholic Worker named Brian Terrell did some detective work and found what Day actually said.

Day was interviewed in an article titled "Money and the Middle-Class Christian" in the *National Catholic Register*. She spoke about problems plaguing the institutional church, including the decline in numbers of men applying for the priesthood and the closing of church buildings. When asked what the cause of these problems might be, she didn't blame them on secularism or external persecution. She said, "I feel that over and over again in history the church has become so corrupt it just cries out to heaven for vengeance. . . . I think it's a result of the corruption in the institutional church, through money and through their acceptance of this lousy, rotten system."[2]

For Day, what was rotten and lousy was *corruption in the institutional church*, and especially systemic corruption related to money.

When I let this all sink in, I know that institutions aren't in themselves the problem; the problem is the *institutionalism*: the tendency of institutions to abandon the mission for which they were created and instead redefine their mission as absolute loyalty to their own bottom line.

I come back to Jesus' words about divided loyalties: "You can't serve two masters. Either you hate one and love the other, or you cling to one and despise the other." In other words, if you love money, you'll hate God, and if you love God, you'll hate money.

Some find such language shocking, extreme, exaggerated. Our imaginations are so imprisoned by our economic systems that we find the idea of hating money to be . . . almost blasphemous! But at this moment, I don't feel Jesus was exaggerating at all. At thirty, he saw with great clarity what I saw only dimly well into my fifties. Money is useful, even necessary, in our current culture. But it is also dangerous. Locate an evil, and you'll find the love of money at or near the root of it. That's true of the issues we've considered in the preceding chapters of this book, and it will be equally true in the chapters that follow.

Suddenly, in my mind's eye, I see Jesus flipping the tables of the money changers in the Temple. As the coins scatter across the stones, he leaves the Temple, never to return.[3]

I wonder if I should follow him out the door.

✎

6

Because of the White Christian Old Boys' Network (White Patriarchy)

About a decade ago, I met a young pastor we'll call Raymond who shared my love for fly fishing. We fished together a time or two and then lost touch. Recently, he found my book *Faith After Doubt*, which presents a four-stage model of faith development: Simplicity, Complexity, Perplexity, and Harmony. (I'll summarize the model in Chapter 21.) After reading the book, Raymond emailed me:

> I wanted to reach out and say thank you for putting *Faith After Doubt* out into the world. The last handful of years I've read very little in the realm of Christian theology/ecclesiology/whateverology. I just couldn't handle too many excursions into such waters while trying to keep faith in Jesus and pastor a church in TRUMP's America. . . .
>
> As I started reading, your narrative of moving through the stages felt almost autobiographical. I have been hovering between Perplexity and Harmony for some time now. I think the radical revealing of the white evangelical church in the 2016 election was when I first started asking the question, "Is the church in America a net gain for compassion in the universe?" . . .
>
> At the same time, my sense of connection and belonging to the church and my pastoral vocation within it has been deeply strained. This past year, the pandemic and the politicization of responses to it, anger about restrictions, the Black Lives Matter movement, the most divisive and hateful election in our history, and our denomination coming to a breaking point

around LGBT inclusion have all formed a confluence of stressors. . . . There are many days where I think, "If you gave me a viable exit strategy and handed me a ripcord, I'd pull that thing so fast it would make your head spin!"

I trust you that there is a good and beautiful field in which Harmony is reality on the far side of Perplexity. I've already been making excursions there! I just don't know if I can dwell there and remain a pastor. As you clearly know, that is a pretty sobering thought to engage when I have invested my whole life up to this point in this work.

On page 185 you say, "I hold out hope that our religious institutions can take on this mission of moral and spiritual development. But I have to admit that sometimes I feel I am hitting my head against a closed box. . . ."

Do I share your hope? My honest knee-jerk response is, "I don't know Brian, and I'm too f*ing tired and beat up to care."

Christianity in its dominant forms today is exhausting, even to its most promising young leaders, like Raymond. They're seeking new sources of inspiration, especially sources that don't come from the white male institutional centers. I understand. I feel the same way.

When Raymond went to seminary, the vast majority of books he was required to read were written by white male theologians and churchmen. The same was true for most of his fellow seminarians, even if they were of Black, Indigenous, Asian, Latinx, or other backgrounds. Most descendants of both the colonizers and the colonized still learn their theology from the colonizers and their defenders. As a result, when young clergy pass on what they've learned to their congregations, white religious company men typically occupy prime mental real estate in their brains. Since powerful white men have been writing the history and theology, it's no surprise that powerful white men have been at the center of it. But they have been less forthcoming when it comes to reporting how men like them have also been the center of humanity's problems.

For example, when it comes to lethal personal violence, male humans nearly always take center stage: about 96 percent of murderers are male in the United States, where I live.[1] When it comes to wars, men are also in the center. From our ancient legends until today's headlines, men battle it out with other men as violent rivals for status, prestige, sexual satisfaction, money, land, and power. When they're not committing murder or going to war, they're often fighting in other ways, working out their aggressions through institutional power struggles, political partisanship, professional jealousies, ideological polemics, and religious controversies. (No wonder my colleague Richard Rohr often says that Jesus had to be incarnated as a nonviolent man because men were [and are] so violent that we needed a new model of manhood as the next step in our redemption.)

Male aggressiveness has been causing problems for millennia.[2] Over time, most cultures fought fire with fire, so to speak: they sought to manage male aggressiveness by elevating one male to an alpha position of supremacy. The hope was that this concentration of power would reduce the total amount of violence and social disruption in the society. As a reward for shouldering the hazards of concentrated power and assuming the mantle of "chief violence officer," the alpha male was given a wide array of perks, including increased status and prestige, expanded sexual access, extravagant wealth, and tacit permission to engage in various forms of corruption such as nepotism, cronyism, and self-dealing.

The name for this time-honored system is *patriarchy*, defined by feminist author bell hooks as "a political-social system that insists that males are inherently dominating, superior to everything and everyone deemed weak, especially females, and endowed with the right to dominate and rule over the weak and to maintain that dominance through various forms of psychological terrorism and violence." She adds that patriarchy is "the single most life-threatening social disease assaulting the male body and spirit in our nation."[3]

Patriarchy has evolved into a million forms and can be found today in countless families, clans, businesses, industries, schools, sports organizations, tribes, nations, empires, nonprofits, and religious communities. Even all-women groups can function as quasi-patriarchies, adopting the male dominance hierarchy and adapting it to their situation.

As we saw in Chapter 3, about five centuries ago, the kings, popes, and rich elites of Europe extended their patriarchal regimes globally. As a result of colonization, patriarchy expressed itself as *white Christian male supremacy* for much of the world.

The cocktail of whiteness, Christianity, and patriarchal machismo packs such a punch that white Christian males can occasionally confer limited power on a non-white Christian man or even a woman. (It helps if she is his submissive wife or daughter and for that reason under the patriarch's control.) On rare occasions, non-Christians may even be given some limited power, as long as they show proper deference to the dominant Christian males who rent them their platform.[4]

Patriarchy has shown a remarkable tenacity in spite of its one great design flaw: patriarchal succession. First-born sons often lack their father's charisma (or sanity, or insanity), and their younger brothers often want to edge them out. For these and other reasons, patriarchal transitions have often been bloody and chaotic. In response, societies developed a kinder and gentler form of patriarchy called democracy. Democracy gave men the right to vote to elect their next patriarch.

Of course, men were still running the show. But that began to change—very slowly at first—over the last few centuries. In different societies around the world, a few nations experimented with allowing some women the right to vote in some elections. The lone state of New Jersey in the newly formed United States allowed voting for women (until 1807), as did Wyoming when it became a state in 1869. After a long period of slow and uncertain change, in the 1890s the tide began to turn. New Zealand was the world leader: it was the first self-governing colony to allow women to both vote and run for office. In the coming decades, women's suffrage steadily gained ground around the world.

The white Christian patriarchy of the United States became alarmed by the growing strength of what it called "the weaker sex," just as it had been alarmed nearly a century earlier when other nations (especially Britain in 1833) began to outlaw slavery. To allow women to vote was rebellion against the social order imposed by God, Christian preachers intoned, with a long list of Bible verses to bolster their argument. Equally threatening, equality for women was a slippery slope: might calls for full racial equality be next?[5]

Even after the Nineteenth Amendment guaranteed women in the United States the right to vote, progress toward equality has been slow. It wasn't until 1984, 2008, 2016, and 2020 that Walter Mondale (D), John McCain (R), Ted Cruz (R), and Joe Biden (D) chose women as their vice presidential running mates. Such a move kept men in the lead but acknowledged the rising power of women. In 2016, Hillary Clinton became the first woman to win a majority of votes to lead the nation (although the Electoral College trumped the popular vote). If she had won the U.S. presidency, she would have joined a small but powerful group of women heads of state around the world.[6]

Such an election would have done far more than break a glass ceiling.

It would have signaled a milestone in a global shift beyond patriarchy. The 2020 election added a new chapter to this story. Joe Biden, a kinder and gentler white patriarchal figure, positioned himself as a truly transitional leader. He was the vice president to the nation's first Black president, and then became president to the nation's first female and Black/South Asian vice president. Just as Obama's election in 2008 stirred a vitriolic whitelash (a backlash by white supremacists), a similar anti-feminist whitelash has unfolded against the Biden/Harris administration. White patriarchy doesn't let go of power without a fight.

Trump's presidency offered the world a crash course in patriarchy. Trump constantly used threats of violence, threats of lawsuits, outrageous insults, and displays of wealth to either bully his rivals into submission or drive them from the field. He employed physical posturing and braggadocio about his genitals' size to prove that he was the alpha male fittest to be trusted. One of his favorite—almost messianic—expressions, "Believe me," invited people to put aside critical thinking about the man's competence and moral character and revert to confidence in a more primal, pre-rational authoritarian patriarchy.

We might have expected crude sexual braggadocio and "kick-ass" attitudes like these to turn off sincere Christians, but actually, traditional Christian theology, being a male-dominated project, remains easily seduced by patriarchy.[7] After all, God in traditional monotheism is commonly imaged as a Zeus-like super-patriarch, ready to smite with violence all who besmirch his patriarchal honor. Trump's strongman persona felt familiar, even comforting, to believers in a patriarchal universe, making it easier for them to forgive a bit of p*ssy grabbing, punch-him-in-the-face pugilism, racial dog-whistling, and unself-conscious arrogance. After all, they told themselves, patriarchal white boys will be boys.

Patriarchy may have made sense (to men at least) in addressing the problem of male aggressiveness back in the days of swords and spears. But in a world of nuclear, biological, and chemical weapons, patriarchy is not the solution: it is the problem. When an aggressive "kick-ass" male ego is connected to the finger on a nuclear button, patriarchy poses an existential threat to us all.

As the ancient foundations and glass ceilings of patriarchy crack, we are finally taking seriously the suffering inflicted by white Christian patriarchal social systems. That cost begins when women and children are required to subordinate themselves to the heads of their families. Although a woman in a patriarchal system may think of herself as under her man's protection from the violence of other men, she has little if any protection from *his* violence.

LGBTQ people who don't fit into the sexual roles defined by patriarchy often fare even worse than straight women and children. They are classified as perverts or misfits and are subject to special cruelties and degradations. Religious and racial minorities similarly suffer, and sadly, those who have been abused or humiliated by those deemed "above them" in the power pyramid often pay the pain downward. The abuse and humiliation accumulate like a flood of sewage surging downstream.

A white Christian patriarchal universe is not a safe place for women, children, racial and religious minorities, and nonconformists, and neither is it a safe place for the earth and its nonhuman creatures. After all, in white Christian patriarchal minds, the earth and all its creatures exist for the "use and profit" of white Christians (to recall a toxic phrase from the Doctrine of Discovery).

A white Christian patriarchal universe is, in contrast, a super-hospitable place for two kinds of men: dominant, aggressive, often narcissistic alpha males characterized by what is often called "toxic masculinity," and the beta males who gain power by being the alphas' subservient, loyal yes-men. The alphas and the betas, whom we called *Christian company men* back in Chapter 4, coexist in what is often called an "old boys' network" of mutual protection and mutual benefit.

Social scientists, it turns out, have been doing wide-ranging research for decades on these beta males (and the females who align with them). This research accelerated in the aftermath of World War II, when scientists wanted to understand why millions of seemingly normal people in Germany, Italy, and Japan abandoned their normal morality and became willing to torture, kill, and die for authoritarian leaders like Adolf Hitler, Benito Mussolini, and Hideki Tojo.[8] Researchers developed the term *authoritarian followers* to describe them.

Authoritarian followers favor centralizing power in a single individual, party, religion, and ideology. They use *fear of a real or concocted enemy* so that their strongman can present himself as their protector. They *divide society based on a loyalty test* to the strongman and his regime. They *distort or distract from the truth* to build and maintain unquestioning support for the strongman. And they *suppress dissent by any means necessary*. Any personal values that authoritarian followers previously held are sacrificed, one by one, for the supreme value of all authoritarians: *winning*, by concentrating power in the hands of their group and its supreme leader. Winning becomes the singular end that justifies any means.

At this very moment, all the largest institutional forms of Christianity on earth (Roman Catholicism, Eastern Orthodoxy, and Evangelicalism, including most Charismatic and Pentecostal movements) render people vulnerable to authoritarianism because they continue to perpetuate patriarchy and proclaim a patriarchal universe. They exclude women from high-level decision-making and from leading their most sacred rituals. They marginalize LGBTQ people, condemning them as "objectively disordered" or "an abomination." They defend their power based on an inerrant Bible or infallible papacy and magisterium. They uncritically deploy verses like Romans 13:1–2 to squash dissent ("Submit to the governing authorities, for all authority is instituted by God and anyone who opposes authority is standing against what God has established"). They link the power of human authorities with God's authority, which, they say, is absolute and unquestionable. They deride critical thinking and praise simple, unquestioning faith.

Two thousand years after Jesus launched a subversive spiritual movement of equality, emancipation, and peace, two thousand years after women were among his inner circle and the first messengers of resurrection, two thousand years after Jesus defended Mary of Bethany's place in the all-male circle of disciples, the Christian religion still remains subservient to patriarchy and the authoritarian control it engenders.[9] Yes, thankfully, there are vital movements of Christian feminism and LGBTQ equality and post-colonial theology in the academy and around the margins. But in most of its institutional centers, Christianity remains an old white boys' club, a patriarchal religion with a violent past it has yet to acknowledge and address, a haven for authoritarian leaders and the followers who serve them, happy to exploit the labor and enjoy the adulation of women, people of color, and sexual minorities, but defiant against accepting them as equal partners in ministry.

Similarly, two thousand years after Jesus said God loved all the world, no exceptions; two thousand years after Pentecost, when it became clear that God "spoke all languages" and therefore loved all ethnicities; two thousand years after an Ethiopian eunuch (a racial and sexual "other") was baptized without stigma and Gentiles in general were welcomed as equals into an all-Jewish movement; two thousand years after Paul said that in Christ there was neither Jew nor Greek, slave nor free, and male nor female; two thousand years after the author of the Book of Revelation envisioned people of every tribe and nationality united in God, the Christian religion is still by and large characterized by white patriarchy.[10] True, there are vital movements of Black, Latino, Asian, Indigenous, and mestizo Christianity, and we shall return to their pivotal importance in more detail in Chapter 18. But even though they are growing globally and white Christianity is shrinking, Christians of color are still being colonized, co-opted, marginalized, dominated, or vilified by the same old wealthy inner circle of patriarchal white supremacist Christians.[11]

When you watch the vigor with which members of the white Christian old boys' network seek to control the lives and bodies of women, and the languor with which they seek to control the bodies and behavior of their own pedophile priests and abusive pastors, you have to wonder.

When you observe the passion and persistence with which they speak out against LGBTQ equality, and the nonchalance with which they seek to eradicate abuses of power by their own, you have to wonder.

When you see how resolutely they resist saying *Black lives matter* and how readily they affirm *law and order* (which has long been the slogan of racial oppression), you have to wonder.

But you don't have to wonder why so many people—including white men like Raymond . . . and like me—are ready to pull the rip cord and make our escape from the white Christian old boys' network.

❧

7

BECAUSE CHRISTIANITY IS STUCK
(TOXIC THEOLOGY)

I sometimes see Christianity as a huge ship capable of amazing voyages. It has tall masts and wide sails, a strong hull, a deep keel, and a powerful rudder. But it is going nowhere because its anchor is so heavy that its crew cannot pull it up.

By reducing its mysteries to beliefs, by codifying those beliefs in systems, and by defining itself by those belief systems, it has rendered itself a paradox: a ship that floats but doesn't sail.[1]

For most Christians I encounter today, *beliefs are simply what Christianity is*. If I point out that in its early years, Christianity was a way of life, not a set of beliefs, they will protest that it was both, and the beliefs had priority. If I point out that the earliest Christians were widely divergent in their beliefs, they are surprised and doubtful; that's not what they have been taught. If I point out that arguing about beliefs leads to arguments about words, and the New Testament repeatedly and consistently condemns that kind of obsession, they start arguing with me—and if I argue back, there we are, multiplying words, words, and more words, unintentionally proving my point. Christianity's fervent belief in beliefs has a circular quality to it.

Imagine if scientists reduced science to a list of facts. Imagine if scientists stopped being curious, stopped hypothesizing, stopped designing experiments, stopped replicating those experiments, and stopped subjecting findings to peers for review. Imagine if scientists spent their time policing fellow scientists to be sure they remained faithful to those lists. Science, you might say, would no longer be scientific.

That's because the genius of science, its heart and essence, is the scientific method, a method by which it can and in fact must amend its facts. Its method helps it sail onward toward greater and greater alignment with reality.

In that light, imagine a Christianity that deploys reflective practitioners whose quest is to follow the life and example of Jesus, teaching others by their example to live by Jesus' spiritual method of radical, nondiscriminatory love and courageous truth-telling. These disciples would be defined by their ongoing quest or mission rather than by the beliefs they hold at this moment.

Now, in contrast, imagine a Christianity that tirelessly sends out belief teachers to promote a list of beliefs about Jesus, God, life, and the afterlife, and then deploys belief police to be sure those teachers are following the list required by their guild. Two very different Christianities, indeed.

I am not against beliefs, any more than a scientist is against facts. But I think Christianity has sabotaged its capacity to sail by hardening its identity in a heavy anchor of unalterable beliefs that it treats as unquestionable facts.

I think you can be a very good human being if you believe in the factuality of the virgin birth, the physical resurrection, a literal second coming, the "one, holy, catholic and apostolic church," a literal hell, or a literal six-day creation. But both history and my own experience convince me that you can just as easily be a very terrible human being while holding these beliefs. And the reverse is also true: you can be a wonderful human being and not hold to some or all of these beliefs. As far as I can tell, as someone who has been around a while, your beliefs—your Christian beliefs—cannot be correlated with your moral quality as a human being, *even though they are supremely relevant to your status as a Christian.*

And so Christianity faces a very practical dilemma: do we Christians want to continue to enfranchise scoundrels who hold the right beliefs but perpetuate harm? And conversely, do we want to exclude good and genuine people—Christlike people, in fact—who in good conscience cannot affirm our lists of beliefs, even though they are wholeheartedly following the way of Christ?

That's a big enough problem. But there's an even bigger problem hidden underneath this one. Our problem is not just the beliefs articulated in our creeds and other doctrinal statements; it's the pre-critical assumptions—the view of the universe—that underlie many if not most of those beliefs.

Think of it like this: our beliefs are like the tips of icebergs. When we affirm them, we unwittingly also affirm a much larger mass of hidden assumptions that uphold them from beneath the surface. Those unacknowledged assumptions often support an archaic view of the universe that further renders Christianity incapable of evolving into something better.

For example, in the old model of the universe, there were two categories of stuff: temporal *worldly* things and eternal *spiritual* things. The temporal category included physical objects, bodies, and the like, things that come and go, are born and die, grow and decay, evolve and diversify. This temporal category included the entire physical universe, all of creation, all its matter and energy, and even time, all its past, present, and future.

The eternal category consisted of spirit, which is hard to define, except to say it is immaterial and therefore sacred, transcendent, and "supernatural," meaning not subject to the laws of physics. The realm of the eternal was perfect, which meant it was inherently unchangeable. After all, when something is perfect, there is only one way to go: *down*. So evolution could happen everywhere in this temporal universe, but in the realm of the eternal, *nothing could ever evolve*.

With minor variations and few exceptions, every conventional Christian belief, creed, doctrinal statement, sermon, prayer, and book I've ever encountered was situated in this dualistic universe and shared the assumption that if something was perfect and holy, it was necessarily unchangeable. Which means if Christianity is from God, it must never, ever evolve. Which means it is forever stuck either being perfect or pretending to be perfect.[2]

Like millions of people, I've moved out of this universe. I was raised in it. I remember it. But I simply don't live there anymore. To have opinions about arguments based on the rules of that universe feels like being asked to vote in an election in a country in which I was born but no longer have citizenship.

In the universe I inhabit, there aren't two eternal, fundamental, unchangeable categories: temporal versus eternal, physical versus spiritual, sacred versus secular, saved versus damned, perfect versus "fallen," and so on. No: the cosmos is far more interesting, rich, and interconnected than that.

I can try to explain by offering a simple analogy, drawing from my love of fly-fishing. I'm standing in a stream, and I cast my fly (a lure made of feathers and thread) to a seam in the water, a place where fast-flowing water meets slower or still water. What is that seam? It certainly is not a set of atoms; every second, one set of atoms is replaced by new ones. If we suddenly froze the stream to stop the atoms from moving, to capture that seam as in a photograph, the seam would no longer exist. That's because the seam, we might say, isn't a fixed and static thing. It's a pattern of things, a relation and flow of things. It is temporary, contingent, more of an event than a thing. I look upstream and see a hump of water in front of a rock: another pattern or event. I see the stream itself . . . also an event. I look at the rounded rocks beneath my feet: before the stream smoothed them, they were jagged boulders on a mountain, and before that, bedrock under the mountain, and before that, fluid magma deep beneath the earth, and before that, space dust drawn into orbit around the sun. What I see as a solid round rock is just one event in a long, long story.

Then I look down to see my reflection in the water, and behold! I realize that I too am an event, a flow, a pattern of relationships!

I used to think that things were real, and change was something that happened to them over time. Now I think that change is real, and things are events that happen over time. Change is the constant and things come and go, appear and disappear, form and fade away.

My parents and grandparents lived in the old familiar universe of concrete things in eternal categories: temporal/eternal, matter/spirit, natural/supernatural, profane/sacred, worldly/heavenly, changing/unchangeable. Just over a hundred years ago, a fellow named Einstein rudely interrupted their dualistic universe. He proposed that energy and matter were less like oil and water (two things that normally don't mix) and more like water and ice (two manifestations of the same thing). One could, in fact, be turned into the other. If you "freeze" energy, you experience it as matter. If you accelerate matter enough, you experience it as energy. Matter and energy were no longer fundamentally different things, but rather, they became different expressions and experiences of the same . . . thing.

Ah, but there my language throws me back into the old universe, because what do I mean by "thing"? Now, everything—a rock, a mountain, a government, a star, a flower, a person, a civilization—looks less and less like a thing and more and more like that seam in a trout stream. It is less a thing that exists and more an event that is happening, one part of uncountable other events and processes over time. This is the unfolding, ever-changing universe I live in. It is a universe of constant motion, becoming, evolving, decomposing, recomposing. It is a universe of events in process, of dynamic interactive evolution rather than static, inert being. It's the expanding, evolving universe of Albert Einstein (and Edwin Hubble, Charles Darwin, A. N. Whitehead, John Cobb, Catherine Keller, and others) rather than my grandparents' mechanical, dualistic universe of things.

If you live in this new universe too, you know what I'm saying. If you don't, you might at least be able to imagine it. And in case you're wondering, yes, of course we can speak of God in this universe. But we can't simply import our old understandings of and beliefs about God from the old universe. Instead, we must hypothesize, experiment, test, and retest to see how God shows up for us in this new context.

So when I ask, "Do I stay Christian?," in part I'm asking if there is any place in Christianity for a person like me who inhabits this different universe and can only speak sincerely of God in my native environment. When I ask, "Do I stay Christian?," in part I'm asking, "Is Christianity allowed to evolve? Or is its marriage to the old view of the universe perpetual . . . even if the spouse dies?"[3]

Again, it's not that I *refuse to* believe in the old universe; it's that I simply cannot honestly be somewhere I no longer am. I cannot see what I used to see from a vantage point I no longer occupy; I can remember it, but I can no longer see it.

Why can't we Christians admit that we, like everything else in the universe, are in process, and that our religion, like all religions, is actually an event, constantly, unavoidably changing, for better or worse? Why can't we allow our leaders' job descriptions to evolve from belief police to . . . actual leaders who help lead the way? Why can't we admit that we are stuck in an old model of the universe and that it's time to rethink everything? Why can't we admit that beliefs are important, but they aren't the point? Why can't we admit that focusing on getting our words and beliefs right has not succeeded in helping us be good?

Why are we more loyal to our heavy old anchor than to our call to adventure?

I imagine what grappling with these questions would do for us. It would allow us to humble ourselves and face the issues that are driving so many of us away. It would allow us to go back to ground zero and start afresh, seeing what we now see, in the way we now see it. It would allow us to utter one of the truest, most honest sentences of our lives: "Wow, we don't really know." It would then allow us to ask one of the most exciting questions of our lives: "In light of this new universe—the conceptual universe of process and evolution that more and more of our descendants will be born into—what can Christianity—and we Christians—become?" It would rekindle in us a sense of wonder, which must surely be one of the most essential theological virtues of all. It would let us cut the old anchor line and start sailing again. (And yes, we could acquire a new anchor for those times we need it.)

In short, it would allow us to get unstuck and get back on the path of maturing as a religion, and doing our part to help our species mature as well, before we, in our immaturity, blow the whole thing to smithereens.

At this moment, I hope you feel the acute, almost unbearable irony: more than ever before, the world needs religions that teach us to value and love the planet, to see its inherent value and sacredness apart from the human economy. The world needs religions that teach us to love our neighbor as ourselves, remembering that our neighbor includes the refugee, the sick, the poor, the outsider, the outcast, the other, and even the enemy. The world needs religions that teach us to transform our swords into plowshares, our bullets into trumpets, and our nuclear submarines into artificial reefs. The world needs religions that value love and interdependence, not money and competition. The world needs religions that are anti-racist, anti-authoritarian, gender-equal, and characterized by compassion and wisdom rather than greed, arrogance, and dogmatism.

And Christianity could be one of those religions. In fact, I would say that it has exactly the resources we need for this moment of existential threat. Christianity has evolved before; it could evolve again.

It could. But the odds are against it doing so. In its dominant forms, it has become conservative, nostalgic, arthritic, cramped, stuck. Its anchor is too heavy to lift. It is going nowhere.

No wonder so many adventurous souls are jumping overboard.

⁂

8

BECAUSE CHRISTIANITY IS A FAILED RELIGION (LACK OF TRANSFORMATION)

Michael Luo recounts a story from the early life of Frederick Douglass, when Douglass was enslaved by a man named Thomas Auld. Auld experienced a Christian conversion at a Methodist camp meeting in 1832:

> Douglass had harbored the hope that Auld's conversion . . . might lead him to emancipate his slaves, or at least "make him more kind and humane." Instead, Douglass writes, "If it had any effect on his character, it made him more cruel and hateful in all his ways." Auld was ostentatious about his piety—praying "morning, noon, and night," participating in revivals, and opening his home to traveling preachers—but he used his faith as license to inflict pain and suffering upon his slaves. "I have seen him tie up a lame young woman, and whip her with a heavy cowskin upon her naked shoulders, causing the warm red blood to drip; and, in justification of the bloody deed, he would quote this passage of Scripture—'He that knoweth his master's will, and doeth it not, shall be beaten with many stripes.'"[1]

When I read those chilling words, I thought back to my years as a pastor. I thought about how many people I met who became more "kind and humane" when they came to Christian faith. There were many. But other faces came to mind too, the faces of people who, like Thomas Auld, absorbed Christianity as a new fuel in their unchanging trajectory of bitterness and spite, or ambition and pride. In almost every case, when I tried to help them see what was happening, they simply left for another church where the pastor would appreciate their zeal and conviction.

I remember one woman whose departure particularly saddened me. When Rose first came to our congregation, she was not a Christian. I remember long conversations with her where she complained about what narrow-minded and judgmental hypocrites Christians were. But over time, she saw in our church something different, and she came to Christian faith. For several years, Rose became a model of Christian growth, a truly "kind and humane" person. I admired her and, frankly, took some pride in her as one of the success stories of our ministry.

But over time, Rose started listening to a particular type of radio preacher and reading a particular set of authors. Under their influence, she became increasingly critical of our church and of me as its pastor. (There was, of course, always plenty to criticize.) I wasn't surprised when she made an appointment to tell me she was leaving. We were too "liberal" and "unbiblical," she explained, and I understood what she meant. As she left my office, Rose turned back to me and said, "It's kind of ironic, Brian. I've become exactly the kind of Christian I used to hate before I came to this church."

For a moment, I thought she was expressing remorse and having a change of heart. But then she added, "I can't believe how blind I was back then." That was the last time I saw Rose.

Christianity has become the world's largest, wealthiest, most powerful religion. By all obvious measures, it is the most successful religion that has ever existed on the planet. But its apparent success hides its egregious failure.[2] The religion has failed to transform surprisingly high numbers of its adherents into Christlike people. Some Christians become vicious, cruel, monstrous, and, like Thomas Auld, all the more dangerous because of their sanctimoniousness. Some become more judgmental and narrow-minded, as Rose did. To twist the lyrics of a beloved hymn, they were blind, then they saw, and then they became blind again in a whole new way.[3]

Meanwhile, many, perhaps most, just stay more or less the same.

It's one of the things that disturbs pastors on sleepless nights: *why do so many Christians change so little?* No wonder they see Christians who are growing and changing as trophies of sorts, proof that their labors have not been in vain. That's how I had felt with Rose.

One thing pastors and parishioners have in common: when they notice the lack of transformation, they tend to blame themselves. "Maybe if I were a better preacher, or prayed and fasted more, or could hire a better worship leader, maybe then my flock would change," the pastor thinks. Meanwhile, the parishioners think, "Maybe if I studied the Bible and prayed more, or went on more retreats, or gave more money, maybe then I would change." When the self-blame becomes too much, they generally start blaming each other. "Maybe if I found a different congregation . . ." a thousand pastors wonder, while a thousand parishioners simultaneously wonder, "Maybe if we had a younger, more dynamic and Spirit-filled preacher . . ."

These attempted diagnoses keep a lot of pastors and parishioners feeling more or less depressed or desperate, like people with a mysterious illness—call it "lack of transformation syndrome," or LTS. They hear about a new program, a new movement, a new book, a new church that is *really dynamic and growing*, and they think, "Finally, I'll be cured of LTS." They spend years having their hopes raised and disappointed. They spend a lot of money too.

That's when they realize they are suffering from something even worse: ATES—attempted transformation exhaustion syndrome.

After exhausting themselves for years with blame and shame, after hiring and firing a string of worship pastors, after changing churches repeatedly, after reading lots of books and going to lots of conferences and retreats, a few may dare to whisper, "Actually, maybe the problem is not us. Maybe the problem is Christianity. Maybe the product doesn't perform according to its advertising. Maybe there's something wrong with the religion itself, at least in its current form. Maybe it really doesn't transform people after all. Maybe those who get better over time, or stay the same, or get worse would have done so anyway. Maybe Christianity, in terms of actual personal transformation, is a placebo, a sugar pill, snake oil."

It's a pretty sure bet: in the coming days and weeks, another famous pastor will flame out in some way, whether through sexual scandal, financial malfeasance, fraud, or just plain old bullying and meanness. Meanwhile, another headline will announce that another bishop has covered up rampant sexual abuse among his priests, or that another mass grave has been found behind an old church-sponsored boarding school or orphanage, or that another famous Christian has made another insulting and ignorant comment about science, LGBTQ people, Muslims, Jews, people of color, or poor people. And once again, people with ATES will have all the more reason to say, "Stay Christian? No thank you. I tried it. It doesn't work."

If Christianity were failing only individuals, that would be serious enough. But we have to imagine a space alien visiting the earth and asking, "What effect is the largest, most successful religion on this planet having on global well-being?" They would look at earth's most serious problems—climate change, economic inequality, racism, and other forms of hostility and war, for example. And they would see how much time and energy the world's most successful religion is devoting to those most serious problems. They would evaluate the religion's effectiveness in tackling these issues (or ignoring them, or making them worse). They might then assess whether the religion was working out well for the planet or not.

If they wanted to get more granular, they might send their researchers to one country with a high percentage of Christians, say, the United States, and then ask, "Which states have the highest church attendance rates?" They would find the following as the top five: Alabama, Mississippi, Tennessee, Louisiana, and Arkansas.[4] They might expect that with so many of their citizens deriving so many benefits of Christian faith, these states would be national leaders in measures of well-being like longevity, education, financial prosperity, and happiness.[5] But they would be disappointed to find (according to recent studies) the following:

Alabama ranks 48th in longevity, 47th in education, 42nd in happiness, 46th in median household income. (It ranks 11th in teen pregnancies.)

Mississippi ranks 50th in longevity, 43rd in education, 43rd in happiness, 50th in median household income. (It ranks 2nd in teen pregnancies.)

Tennessee ranks 43rd in longevity, 33rd in education, 44th in happiness, and 42nd in median household income. (It ranks 9th in teen pregnancies.)

Louisiana ranks 45th in longevity, 48th in education, 46th in happiness, and 47th in household income. (It ranks 6th in teen pregnancies.)

Arkansas is tied with Louisiana at 45th in longevity and ranks 41st in education, 49th in happiness, and 49th in median household income. (It ranks first in teen pregnancies.)

I share these statistics not to propose a simple cause-effect relationship, nor to shame these beautiful states or their good inhabitants, nor to oversimplify highly complex matters, but simply to illustrate that if we want to argue that Christianity has great power to transform people, we might wish that the actual data were a little more encouraging.

If a political party were in power and it kept failing to improve people's lives decade after decade, we would expect party loyalty to gradually erode until people voted it out. That's what's happening in Christianity, in reverse: more and more are voting themselves out the door.

I know what my Inner Fundamentalist is saying right now. He's saying that the point of Christianity isn't to improve the world; it's to help people escape this hopeless world and go to heaven when they die. He's quick to add that the gospel isn't about removing people's sins or even reducing them; it's only about forgiving them. My Inner Fundamentalist knows that I think that's exactly the problem. In its dominant forms, the Christian religion occupies itself maintaining an air-conditioned warehouse in which to accumulate and store forgiven souls until they're shipped by heavenly elevator up to their final destination.[6] I tell my Inner Fundamentalist he is very clever: there's no way to know in this life if his approach is succeeding in the next!

A few years ago, in *The Great Spiritual Migration*, I proposed that the purpose of the Christian faith is clear and simple: it is not an evacuation plan to heaven but a transformation plan for earth, a transformation plan built on the strategy of helping people become loving human beings who build loving societies, following the loving example of Jesus. I noted that in all my years in Christian circles, I was unaware of any well-thought-out Christian curriculum to help people mature in love. After two thousand years, I suggested, it's about time for the Christian religion to get serious about its prime directive.

Shortly after the book came out, a woman came up to me and told me that she had just gotten a cross-disciplinary PhD in psychology and education at a secular university. Her research question centered on how we help educate children to be empathetic. "That's at least a part of what we need, isn't it?" she asked. "If we can train people from childhood to be empathetic, that's one step toward becoming loving people." Then she added, "You know, according to my literature review, I'm the first person in history to write a dissertation on this subject. That's the problem, isn't it? Why are we only now beginning to see how important this work is?"

I came across a powerful video recently of musicians around the world joining New Orleans street musician Grandpa Elliott in singing the old spiritual "Down by the Riverside."[7] The lyric "Ain't gonna study war no more" unexpectedly brought tears to my eyes. The truth is, we're still studying war all the time. But we're doing precious little study in empathy, humility, conviviality, love. The religion that should be leading the way could drop everything it's doing. It could develop a spiritual vaccine—a set of habits and practices that would inoculate people against hate and fear and help them be carriers of love.

It could. But it hasn't on any large and consistent scale for most of its first two thousand years. I'm not surprised that many people are giving up on a failed religion and looking elsewhere.

If speaking of Christianity as a failed religion seems harsh to you, I invite you to step back for a moment of review. Think of Christianity's history of anti-Semitism. Think of Christianity's treatment of its own nonconformists. Think of the Catholic Church's Doctrine of Discovery and what it unleashed on the world, and the unique Protestant appropriation of that brutal doctrine in the American genocide of Native peoples, and the traumatic legacy of white Christian supremacy in slavery, segregation, and their bitter aftermath. Think of the impact of conventional Christian theology on Christian women and gay people and the poor. Think of the privilege Christianity has conferred upon straight white Christian men—especially those with wealth. Think of the impact of Christian theology on the natural world, in the service of money.

If you persist in minimizing these failures of the past and brushing them aside as trivial matters, then please realize: to growing millions of people, *you now represent the contemporary failure of Christianity to transform lives.* To put it more bluntly, *you are a living example of the failure of Christianity, and you are another reason for them not to stay Christian.*

9

Because of Christianity's
Great Wall of Bias
(Constricted Intellectualism)

I was a good student as a kid. It wasn't that I was especially disciplined. It was just that, for a voracious reader like me with inborn curiosity, study came naturally, all the more because my parents encouraged it so warmly. In addition, for a firstborn son with a predisposition toward obeying the rules, paying attention in class and doing my homework were way less stressful than getting in trouble.

As a result, Christianity was a perfect fit for me. One of the first Bible verses I memorized was 2 Timothy 2:15: *Study to show thyself approved unto God.* The King James version I memorized turned out to be a poor translation, I learned from later study.[1] But all the same, the Christianity of my youth valued study, especially Bible study, which generally led to above-average literacy. After all, the Bible is a challenging library of diverse ancient literary texts. Through Bible study I learned about vocabulary, sentence structure, Hebrew and Greek grammar—and English grammar too, along with logical argument, context, translation, narrative flow, metaphor, simile, poetics, typology, rhetoric (the art of argument), hermeneutics (the art of interpretation), and so much more.

Beyond Bible study, church involvement in general taught me a lot of valuable knowledge and skills. I learned to read musical notation intuitively from hymnbooks. I picked up a lot about group dynamics and informal politics just watching my church operate. I gained some proficiency in public communication from public prayers I was asked to offer and youth groups I was asked to lead. I developed a good memory too, in part by memorizing lots of Bible passages, and in part with the help of clever preachers who used mnemonic devices designed to make their main points memorable. (I can't count all the sermons that were titled "The Five P's of Philippians 2" or "The Three C's of Colossians 3." I enjoy alliteration to this day, as you'll see later in this chapter.) I had a special affinity for the Book of Proverbs, which celebrates the value of wisdom and exhorted me to seek "knowledge as gold and understanding as silver."

So you can imagine the shock I felt when the same community that taught me to love learning also taught me to fear it, even mock it. I heard many a preacher jokingly refer to seminary as *cemetery*, implying not too subtly that if you learn too much about your faith, it dies. I remember feeling disturbed by a verse in the New Testament (Colossians 2:8): "See to it that no one takes you captive through philosophy and empty deceit, according to human tradition, according to the elemental spirits of the universe, and not according to Christ." I knew what the text meant, but I could imagine how religious leaders in my community would abuse it to scare us away from the very love of wisdom that Proverbs encouraged.

To be a Christian, I began to feel, was to practice a *tightly constricted intellectualism*: intellect in service of what we already believed. I would later learn that there was a name for this constricted curiosity and suppression of inconvenient truths: *confirmation bias*.

Confirmation bias names our brain's tendency to reject anything that doesn't fit in with our current understanding, paradigm, belief system, or worldview. It's closely related to about a dozen other biases, including:

Complexity bias: our brain's tendency to prefer a simple lie to a complex truth.

Community bias: our brain's tendency to reject any idea that will endanger our status in communities we belong to—to choose tribe over truth.

Comfort/Complacency bias: our brain's tendency to reject information that makes us uncomfortable, is inconvenient, or disrupts our complacency.

Confidence bias: our brain's tendency to believe people who display confidence, rendering us susceptible to those who come on strong even when they're wrong, including authoritarians and con artists.

Conspiracy bias: our brain's tendency to believe stories that exonerate us or portray us as innocent victims or unsung heroes while vilifying an out-group or individual, real or concocted.

Catastrophe/Normalcy bias: our brain's tendency to respond to dramatic catastrophes, but easily miss compounding slow erosions of normalcy.

Cash bias: our brain's tendency to accept information that might interfere with our way of making a living.[2]

I wish that my religion had helped me and others face and confront these biases instead of reinforcing them with religious devotion. I wish that we Christians had taken seriously our founder's words about the truth setting us free—the full and actual truth, that is, not half-truths and group-think. I wish we had learned that the word *repent* means *rethink*, which means *questioning our biases and challenging untested assumptions*. I wish that my religion had taught me to challenge bias by thinking critically, to be curious rather than afraid of the truth, to follow the truth wherever it might lead and whomever it might come through. But instead, I'm sad to say, my religious community held me within a great wall of bias, with a constricted intellectualism that was actually worse than mere anti-intellectualism. (The latter is lazy and easily defeated. The former is always on duty, always vigilant, always at war.)

I have a distinct memory of being about eleven or twelve years old, sitting in church one Sunday, bedecked with a clip-on tie and uncomfortable shiny black shoes, and realizing that I could predict everything the preacher was about to say. "Ah, now I get it," I thought. "I've learned everything I'm ever going to learn here. For the rest of my life, I won't come to church to learn, but to judge how well the preacher did in telling me what I already know."

Christianity was like McDonald's, I concluded: the menu was limited and predictable, but its familiarity felt as comforting as a cheeseburger. What it lacked in nourishment it made up for in convenience.

What I see happening today in much of the Christian world seems to have grown naturally from these realizations I had as a boy. Confirmation bias and its cousins rendered so many of us Christians complacent and overconfident that we didn't realize the degree to which our message and way of life were out of sync with, if not diametrically opposed to, the teachings of our founder. We passed down our delusional self-image from one generation to the next.

When adult Christians whitewash our history, new generations of Christian kids grow up happily within their great wall of bias, enjoying a mythological theme park in which "our people" are always (or nearly always) the virtuous heroes, the innocent victims, and the oppressed, misunderstood minority. Erna Kim Hackett aptly calls this "Disney Princess theology," where Christians vigilantly guard our whitewashed history so we are always the good guys, never the bad.[3]

I see a similar vigilance regarding science. Where science helps our cause, we trumpet it. Where it challenges us in any way, we condemn it as godless, as demonic, as an example of the "philosophy and empty deceit" I was warned about in Colossians 2:8. In the course of my lifetime, my fellow Christians have invested a *lot* of energy in pitting our theology against biology, anthropology, geology, astronomy, physics, psychology, psychiatry, and sociology.

As a boy in the 1960s, I never would have believed that the same literalist, six-day, young-earth, anti-science creationism I was being taught then would still be in circulation when I was a senior citizen. Even then I knew it was silly. But here I am in my sixties, and any number of Southern Baptist, Pentecostal, and "Bible church" children are still being taught the same misinformation in their private Christian schools and by their sincere but misguided parents. My heart breaks for these kids. It feels like intellectual child abuse.

And of course, this same anti-science bias shows up as physical child abuse in the headlines every few years. Pentecostal parents withhold medical treatment for their child because their "name it and claim it" preacher tells them they must have faith in God, not medicine. The child dies, and the parents are left doubly devastated: bereaved by the loss of their child and disillusioned because of their faulty faith. Dr. Darren Slade, a former fundamentalist himself, diagnoses the problem with compassionate honesty: "When we go around saying . . . that miracles happen a lot, we're opening the door for the charlatans to come in and swindle desperate people. . . . [We] prime people to get duped and get hurt."[4]

It's not just contorted history and science that predominate: it's also twisted, constricted politics. Since democracy is never found in the Bible and since it is only applied in very limited ways in the largest denominations, it's held with some ambivalence by many Christians. Recalling our discussions of patriarchy in previous chapters, we can see why Christians might feel that the Christian/biblical God prefers patriarchal monarchy, maybe even dictatorship, and only tolerates democracy as a liberal concession. When given the choice between our side (which is God's side) losing democratically and our side winning non-democratically, the choice for many Christians is easy: it's better for the good guys to win while breaking the rules than for the bad guys to win according to the rules. After all, God as the rule-maker is bound by no human rules. This attitude offers one more explanation for the bizarre levels of support for morally compromised leaders like Donald Trump by a majority of white Christians in America in 2016, 2020, and beyond. Since many Christians see God as an absolute authoritarian, we shouldn't be surprised when they prefer authoritarian leaders to democratic ones.

Mix constricted Christian attitudes toward democratic politics and a shallow political agenda with Christian twisting of history and science, and you have an intoxicating cocktail that renders millions of Christians dangerous actors in a democracy. Having imprisoned themselves inside the great wall of bias, they lose the capacity for critical thinking and become susceptible to the siren songs of conspiracy theories and the seductions of authoritarian leaders. As a result, they put not only themselves but also the rest of us in danger.

I'm writing these words in the aftermath of the coup attempt of January 6, 2021, in which insurrectionists stormed the U.S. Capitol, many raising Bibles and *Jesus Saves* signs and wearing clothing with Nazi slogans. They erected crosses—and gallows—as they shouted to hang the vice president and murder members of Congress, baptizing their violence with prayers "in Jesus' name."[5] This violent outbreak didn't just happen out of nowhere.

For years, ridiculous and dangerous conspiracy theories had been spreading like a Pentecostal revival in churches across America.[6] Having strained out qualified experts, journalists, and scientists, gullible Christians swallowed any number of frauds and fools, rendering themselves susceptible to the actual shallow ideologies and "empty deceit" I was warned about in Colossians 2:8 as a boy.

Beyond its subversion of democracy, what goes on inside the great wall of bias poses two very specific threats to our survival as a civilization, and perhaps as a viable species.

The first and most dramatic is war. If you doubt science whenever it rubs up against your confirmation, complexity, community, complacency, confidence, and other biases, then you're likely to doubt what scientists tell you about the aftermath of a global nuclear war, which, in case you haven't checked lately, is grim.

According to a major scholarly assessment written back in 1986 known as the CRP-2B scenario, after the next nuclear war, society will be permanently reorganized.[7] During normal disasters, say a hurricane or tornado, normal life becomes temporarily abnormal and then returns to normal after the event. But after a global nuclear war, the old normal will never return.

Help will never arrive in devastated areas because local roads, airports, and institutions will have been destroyed. Survivors will be unable to rebuild because, in the absence of any outside help, they will turn on one another in desperate competition for survival necessities. Centuries of accumulated learning, technology, expertise, and institutional development in the direction of equality and justice and human thriving all will disappear in a literal flash, in a big bang of annihilation rather than creation. As if that weren't enough, add to the "traditional" horrors of nuclear war the new nightmares of biological and cyber warfare.

For millions of people to be naive or skeptical about this danger is bad enough. But within the great wall of bias, significant numbers of people are being taught to actually expect it as inevitable, to yearn for it, pray for it, and hope to accelerate it. All their lives, their religious leaders have taught them that this kind of fiery end to history is predestined and prophesied by the Bible and is, therefore, God's actual and inevitable will. It will prove them right, so let it come.

If that sounds absurd to you, you didn't grow up as I did, among millions of conservative Christians who devoured books like *The Late Great Planet Earth* and *Left Behind* and *This Present Darkness*. We saw D-grade movies like *A Thief in the Night*, and we had the hell scared out of us by sermons based on 2 Peter 3:10: "But the day of the Lord will come as a thief in the night; in which the heavens shall pass away with a great noise, and the elements shall melt with fervent heat, the earth also and the works that are therein shall be burned up." If that wasn't predicting a world-destroying mushroom cloud, Adam wasn't legally married to Eve!

Then add one more factor: imagine if significant numbers of people have been guaranteed by their hyper-confident religious leaders that they will be exempt from this grim, hopeless future, being guaranteed safe passage to heaven through a divine skyhook called "the rapture." The absurdity of this scenario surely rivals even the conspiratorial craziness of Q-Anon and the like, but it has been swallowed hook, line, and sinker by millions of my fellow Christians, including many in high places of power in the U.S. government.[8] This doomsday scenario leaves behind all non-Christians to suffer the fate they deserve and is part and parcel of "historic orthodox Christianity" as understood by shockingly high numbers of sincere but misguided Christians.[9]

I share this not as a critical outsider but as someone who was raised within this great wall of bias. I still get emails and social media messages from sincere, true-believer friends and relatives who share this giddy delight whenever there is an earthquake, famine, pandemic, war, or rumor of war, thrilled that these are signs of the end times and that Jesus is coming soon. What's tragic news for everyone else is good news for them, and instead of empathy, they feel elation.

Millions of Christians around the world know, as I do, that this suicidal theology is waiting like a huge cache of explosives in hundreds of millions of Christian hearts and minds, ready to be detonated in a global chain reaction at any moment, a self-fulfilling prophecy of apocalyptic proportions. Sadly, this apocalyptic theology has counterparts in other religions too.[10]

I wish that this was the only grave risk posed by my religious heritage, with its constricted and biased intellectualism. But there is an equal if not greater risk. Instead of a fast nuclear catastrophe related to uranium, this is a slow-motion catastrophe related to carbon.

Make no mistake: it might take decades, perhaps a century, but if the entire human race does not come together to address climate change, sea levels will rise fast and high, reaching catastrophic levels. Droughts, floods, wildfires, and other extreme weather events will intensify. Crops will fail over large areas, causing widespread hunger and economic turmoil. Coastal cities where hundreds of millions of people live will become uninhabitable, causing people to become refugees in unimaginable numbers. A post–climate change world will have more in common with a post–nuclear war world than most people would like to think. In fact, climate change could easily create the conditions that make nuclear war more likely, so we could end up with a compound catastrophe.

It would be nice if we could count on the world's largest religion to be of help in taking pre-emptive action. But I would say the odds are strongly stacked against it, based on my experience as a Christian. There is a lot of money to be made and power to be gained by shortsighted leaders, political or religious, who use confidence bias to tell people the comforting lies and simple untruths they want to hear rather than the complex and uncomfortable truths they need to hear. Community and confidence bias will reinforce the fantasies preached by their leaders. Complacency bias will prompt them to unplug the smoke alarms rather than put out the fire. Conspiracy bias will divert their attention from real dangers to imaginary ones, and it will keep them fighting one another rather than uniting against their common danger and for the common good. Catastrophe/Normalcy bias will keep them oblivious to the slowly deteriorating conditions until it's too late.[11] But it may be cash bias that actually pulls the nuclear and climate triggers.

Most Christians today remain unaware of how Christian leaders since the 1930s have been intentionally co-opted (or, more bluntly, *bought*) by powerful corporate leaders in America (and elsewhere) to provide theological opposition to socialism and support for capitalism. Through this bought-and-paid-for leadership, to be Christian means to oppose socialism, which means opposing any significant regulation of mega-corporations, which means weakening and shrinking government so that it can be "drowned in a bathtub" (to use Grover Norquist's memorable phrase). "Free enterprise" and its sister slogan, "small government," have come to mean blind, fanatical trust in unregulated, unconstrained corporations to do the right thing, leading to blind, fanatical distrust in democratically elected and democratically accountable governments. The "invisible hand" of the market has demanded such trust and obedience that capitalism has become, for all intents and purposes, an idol, a religion, deserving the name *Theo-Capitalism.*[12]

In the United States, and through U.S. influence in many other places as well, the love affair between Christianity and Theo-Capitalism has grown so strong that Princeton historian Kevin Kruse subtitled his important book *One Nation Under God* as follows: *How Corporate America Invented Christian America.*[13]

There are many other areas where I am alarmed about the effects of Christianity's biased and constricted intellectualism, not just on Christians but on everyone. For example, when Christian individuals and organizations resist grappling honestly with scientific findings about sexual identity, they end up doing harm to LGBTQ individuals, and straight people too. When they promote shame-based sexual understandings through "purity culture," or when they uphold gender roles rooted in antiquity (but not biology or psychology), they harm everyone with a gender and a libido. When they resist learning from the best child psychologists, they teach misguided parenting techniques. The more they focus their shame-heavy pseudo-psychology on the family, the more harm they do to both present and future generations.

When Christians resist learning about social psychology, they tolerate or even celebrate toxic masculinity and narcissism in congregational and political leaders. When Christians resist learning from doctors and social workers about the processes of dying, they prepare themselves for the afterlife but not for the long dying process that so often precedes it in contemporary culture. When they resist learning about neurobiology and mental illness, Christians engage in harmful or ineffective therapy, counseling, and teaching. When they don't fearlessly confront the kind of historical whitewashing that we surveyed in previous chapters, Christians allow the racial, ecological, and economic injustices practiced and defended by their forefathers to be repeated by current and future generations.

But however many chapters of however many books are written, they can be ignored, and they will be ignored by Christians who hide within their great wall of bias.

That's true of this book as well.

✌

10

Because Christianity Is a Sinking, Shrinking Ship of Wrinkling People (Demographics)

In the West, the Christian religion is shrinking in size and wrinkling with age. In fact, we can combine increasing average age with decreasing attendance to create a new word to describe the phenomenon: *shrinkling*.

In the United States, Mainline Protestants first sounded the alarm about their shrinkling back in the 1960s. White Evangelicals took great pride in their upward trajectories and their burgeoning youth groups, claiming that their conservative theology made the difference (or perhaps it was their Pentecostal practices, or seeker-sensitive services, or decentralized structure, or something else).[1] Then, right around the year 2000, their curves flattened and started to drop too, as did those of their African American counterparts.[2] Catholic decline was hidden to some degree by large numbers of Catholic immigrants, but I remember a Catholic sociologist telling me once in about 2005 that the demographics among native-born American Catholics were even more alarming than those of Mainline Protestants; they just didn't talk about it.

More recently, the Public Religion Research Institute (PRRI) issued a sobering update: from 2008 to 2019, the number of white Evangelicals in the United States dropped by 6.2 percent to make up 15.2 percent of the population. They had shrunk to about the same percentage of the population as Mainline Protestants (14.7 percent), who, by the way, had actually grown during that period by about two percentage points. (I suspect that the growth in Mainliners is explainable in large part by ex-Evangelicals transferring their membership.) White Catholics had also shrinkled since 2008, from 16.1 percent to 12 percent. As church historian Diana Butler Bass said about these numbers, "Nothing is as it was."[3] Adding to the concern, the Gallup polling organization reported in 2021 that U.S. membership in religious communities (Christian, Jewish, Muslim, etc.) dropped below 50 percent for the first time since their research began nearly a century ago.[4]

In many ways, these Christians in the United States were simply late to a Christian shrinking party that had long been evident in Europe. We are all in the same storm, it turns out, if not the same boat. And forecasters tell us that the storm is about to get a lot worse, because a group's average age can rise slowly and steadily from forty to fifty to sixty to seventy, until the group plunges off the demographic cliff.

Many Western Christians, faced with these dispiriting predictions, take comfort in the fact that in the global south, at least, Christianity is young and growing. But for those of us who have spent a lot of time on the ground and in the pews (or benches or chairs) in the global south, we know the picture is not as rosy as some seem to wish.

I remember back in the 1980s and early '90s hearing stories of "Holy Ghost Revival" catching fire in far-flung places from Cambodia to Fiji, with millions being "saved, healed, and baptized in the Holy Ghost." But time after time, the numbers turned out to be "evang-elastic," stretched to the breaking point to encourage donors in the West to give even more.

Rwanda was an interesting case in point. Rwanda was hailed as one of the greatest success stories in history for both Catholic and Protestant missions, with Christians of one sort or another making up over 90 percent of the population.[5] Then, in 1994, this "most Christian nation in Africa" became the site of a chilling, one-hundred-day genocide that left over eight hundred thousand dead, not counting the raped, maimed, and otherwise traumatized.

I put it this bluntly not to discredit the many truly beautiful and wonderful things being done by Christians in the global south. I've visited churches and Christian leaders in about forty countries, and when I'm asked where I find hope, I always tell inspiring stories of churches in the global south, from Burundi, Uganda, and Rwanda to the Dominican Republic, Mexico, and the Philippines.

But just as years ago the curve of American Evangelicals followed the curve of their Mainline Protestant colleagues, so the curves in the global south may follow those of the north many decades from now, for at least two primary reasons.

First, the same white patriarchal Protestantism and Catholicism that have been losing the confidence of the young in Europe and North America still exert outsized influence if not control over many Christians in the global south, often through colonial missionary organizations that provide funding with strings attached. And Western-style TV preachers make larger-than-life promises of healing and prosperity that poor and vulnerable people find nearly irresistible, even though the promises prove unkeepable. Eventually, young people will tire of watching their parents get poorer while the preachers prosper. Many already have.

Second, as we will see in more depth in Part II of this book, the problems that plague white Western Christianity may turn out not to be uniquely white, Western, or Christian problems. They may not even turn out to be uniquely religious problems. They may simply be *human* problems—problems of greed, abuse of power, fear, institutionalism, inflexibility, apathy, susceptibility to authoritarian con men, and the like. Christianity promised that it had some special divine guidance and protection that would lift it above these human problems to some degree at least, but it's becoming apparent that this promise was on par with those made by Christian leaders claiming to "pray away the gay" or pray in the fast cash.

And so, I suspect that the shrinkling of the Christian religion will likely become a global phenomenon too, eventually, as long as these trends continue:

- more young people learn basic history (not history sanitized by religious censors),
- more young people learn basic science (not science dumbed down by religious censors),
- more young people embrace critical thinking (and refuse to comply with demands that they submit to inerrant or infallible religious authority structures),
- more young people become politically aware, ecologically aware, racially aware, and economically aware,
- more young people have access to professional journalists and citizen journalists who tell the truth about religious scandals and hypocrisy happening now (including but not limited to sex scandals, political deals, and financial mismanagement),

- more young people have access via computers, smartphones, and as-yet unimagined technologies to the internet and a global reservoir of unfiltered information.

This, of course, may sound like a secularist dream coming true: *that pesky Christian religion, with all its superstition and opposition to progress, will finally just fade away!* But I don't think secularists will be happy when they dare to engage in a bit of counter-intuitive thought. First, religious extremists, whether Christian, Muslim, or of other faiths, notice that they're losing ground. As a result, they may become desperate enough to launch theocratic revolutions (like the failed one that rocked the United States on January 6, 2021, or the successful one that has controlled Iran since January 1978). Where those revolutions succeed, you can bet that the teaching of history, science, critical thinking, and journalism will be suppressed, along with political and religious dissent.

Where fundamentalist attempts at theocracy fail, we might suppose that a shrinking and aging religion will have less and less influence in the culture at large. And long range, that might be true. But in the middle range, picture this: More and more young people will leave Christianity, taking fresh thinking and energy with them. More and more middle-aged and older people who share a youthful outlook on life will follow them out the door. That will leave a more uniformly staid and conservative ethos among those who remain, whatever their age. Actually, though, that diagnosis is overly optimistic: deprive an elderly constituency of younger voices, and it is likely to be regressive and extremist, not merely conservative.

We might suppose that this aging conservative/regressive/extremist Christian community will suffer a shortage of resources as it shrinks, hastening its demise. But remember that this shrinkling constituency now has control over a huge array of assets that were amassed over centuries by much larger, much younger Christian communities. Huge bank accounts, pension plans, endowments, and investments are held tight in the hands of this shrinking remnant now. And these assets will only swell as colleges, retreat centers, church buildings, denominational headquarters, hospitals, and other real estate assets that were necessary for a younger and larger constituency are sold off because they are no longer needed by the elderly. This swelling portfolio of assets will grow even larger as members of the old, loyal, conservative/regressive remnant die and leave bequests to carry on the beloved tradition.

Imagine what this wealth can do when used, say, to support a certain brand of politician who loves to promote God and guns, God and country, God and racial "purity," God and patriarchy, God and nostalgia, God and the death of environmental regulation, God and anti-immigrant or anti-LGBTQ hate, God and a quick buck, God and revenge.

Now go a few generations into the future and imagine just three "shrinkled" Christian traditions that have consolidated their wealth and power while intensifying their regressive conservatism—Roman Catholicism, white Evangelicalism, and global Pentecostalism. Then throw a war or two in the mix, or a massive refugee crisis spawned by rising sea levels and droughts, along with a huge rise in economic instability, social unrest, petty crime, organized crime, and political corruption, as we considered in the previous chapter. Then imagine authoritarian populist leaders around the world being able to make deals with these far-right, well-funded Christian groups, promising them protection, privilege, and power in exchange for unified support—both direct and indirect. Can you imagine a moment when every patriotic American, Brazilian, German, Pole, Nigerian, or Russian is expected to be a loyal member of the nationally favored (or legally established) Christian nationalist cult?

Can you see how Christian shrinkling can be a path to a certain kind of grim wealth and power? And even more chilling, can you see that the scenario I just described may not only await us in the future but is, in fact, already unfolding in the present?

Who would want to stay Christian in light of demographic scenarios like these? For many, the answer is *nobody*, apart from a scoundrel or scavenger (recalling Matthew 24:28) hanging around to make a living off a dying organism.

You may feel that these first ten chapters make the rest of this book unnecessary, even impossible. It's an open and shut case: *staying Christian is no longer a viable option for any thoughtful, ethical person.*

As I've written these chapters, especially in the context of recent history, the "magic" or "spell" of Christian authority structures has been broken for me. The curtain has been pulled back on the wizard, and his projections have been exposed as a scam. A sense of disillusionment sometimes washes over me, and I feel like I've lived my life in a respectable yet dangerous cult. I can see why, for many people, leaving Christianity is like entering remission after a social and spiritual malignancy.

But having come this far in this project, I am convinced that these first ten chapters do not foreclose on the rest of this book. Part I actually makes the rest of this book more necessary than ever. So when you're ready, when you've let these first ten chapters settle, I hope you'll take a deep breath, brew a fresh pot of coffee or tea, take a walk outdoors, and then turn the page to Part II.

PART II

YES

By some amazing but vastly creative spiritual insight the slave undertook
the redemption of a religion that the master had profaned in his midst.

—HOWARD THURMAN

❧

11

BECAUSE LEAVING HURTS ALLIES
(AND HELPS THEIR OPPONENTS)

I was speaking at an event in the Rocky Mountains several years ago. A young pastor named Seth introduced himself and asked me to meet with him and some other pastors during free time. I recognized Seth's name: he had planted a new faith community in the Deep South and it was, from what I'd heard, one of the most creative and promising experiments in Christian community happening anywhere.

Seth's community was taking seriously exactly the concerns I articulated in the first ten chapters of this book, so of course I was eager to meet with him and his colleagues. We gathered that afternoon in an outdoor plaza surrounded by mountains, and after we introduced ourselves, Seth spoke first.

"Thanks for meeting with us. I guess I'll start by saying that I am so discouraged," he said. "What we're doing in our new faith community is working. Everything you write about, we're doing it, and it's connecting with people. It's hard as hell, because people are so wounded by religion, so suspicious of it. It's like a corrupted brand. But people still need a spiritual home, what you call a studio of love, and they need it so much. They're finding it in our community."

He leaned forward with his elbows on his knees: "But I feel like I came along five or ten years too late. Just as we're hitting breakthroughs, it feels like all my peers are giving up on the whole thing because of what Christianity represents in the world at large. My peers are just walking away. They're jaded. Disgusted. Exhausted. Some are becoming atheists. Some are becoming 'free range Christians' or 'spiritual-but-not-religious' 'nones' holding onto some core of spirituality but answering 'none' when people ask their religious affiliation. And, of course, I can't blame them, because I'm jaded and disgusted with so much that goes on under the Christian label too, and I think about walking away too. But I just wish . . . I just wish . . . I just wish there was someone left to appreciate the breakthroughs that are happening." Seth swallowed hard and tried to regain his composure.

I got a little choked up myself, in large part out of empathy for Seth, but also out of my own personal pain: I have sometimes felt the same way in my efforts over the last twenty-plus years advocating for a new kind of Christianity. I've done my best, but sometimes it seems too late to matter. This little light of ours, again and again, seems to get blown out by the hot air of a cadre of preachers who line up with an unexamined reprise of the old-time religion we surveyed in Part I.

Since I didn't know what to say, I just nodded and let Seth's pain wash over me, mingling with my own. Then he added some words I haven't been able to forget: "I just feel like people are quitting the marathon when they're only a couple hundred yards from the finish line. And every person who quits makes it a little harder for those of us who are still running the race."

I hold Seth's words now as I reflect back on the first ten chapters of this book. I cannot for one second minimize the seriousness of everything I've written. An unexamined, status-quo Christianity is not worth perpetuating. I cannot and will not stay Christian if it means perpetuating Christianity's past history and current trajectory. The only way I can stay Christian is to do so as part of a creative movement forging a new kind of Christianity, the kind Seth represents.

But when I think of staying Christian, a restless inner dialogue ensues. *If I carelessly throw out the good of Christianity with the evil, I have added to the evil. If I carelessly support the evil along with the good, I have also added to the evil. So how do I affirm and protect the good that happens through people like Seth without also supporting the larger Christian project in which dangerous forces hide like viruses? How can I withdraw my consent and support for the ugliness without also discouraging or destroying the emerging beauty that people like Seth are bringing into the world?*

More than most people, I think, I actually know the Seths out there, thousands of them. They are pastors, church planters, and nuns; friars, priests, and bloggers; bishops, writers, nonprofit leaders, and podcasters; community organizers, migrant farmworkers, urban farmers, and caregivers;

artists, church secretaries, and good neighbors who practice and preach an examined and intentional faith across congregations and traditions.[1] They are laypeople who embody a beautiful faith in their workplaces and neighborhoods. They read my books or hear my talks and reach out to me. They invite me to visit the communities they're forming, whether in person or (as is more the case these days) online. They ask me to endorse their first book or come on their new podcast. There are so many of them, and they are so creative and smart and sincere and dedicated. When I'm with them, I think, *Of course! Of course, I have to stay Christian. How could I abandon these good people?*

I recall Seth's words about quitting the marathon when the finish line is almost in sight. Could he be right? Could the Christian company men be overplaying their hand? Could the house of Old Christianity be about to collapse under the weight of its own hypocrisy, complacency, overconfidence, and decadence? Could those of us who are learning to embody an alternative actually be on the verge of a breakthrough—if we don't lose heart?

Those questions make leaving harder, as does this one: if you and I do not stay Christian, if we give up whatever little voice and influence we have inside the larger Christian community, won't we be an answer to the misguided prayers of the religious company men and their followers, who want the rest of us gone? Won't we be leaving them the keys to the bus so they can keep speeding recklessly down the same road we examined in Part I? Won't we be emboldening them by abandoning our post of creative resistance? What greater damage will the gatekeepers do without prophetic voices "on the edge of the inside" challenging them with an "alternative orthodoxy," as my friend Richard Rohr says?[2]

Won't we be saying to them, "OK. You win. We give up. We quit. The field is yours, beginning with the next generation"?

In this light, it feels like either cowardice or laziness to abandon the Seths and surrender to the Christian company men who currently run so much of the Christian enterprise. You may never have thought of yourself as a fighter. But perhaps the decadence of conventional Christianity is bringing out the fighter (albeit *nonviolent* fighter) in you?

I have to admit something: when I give (or receive) that kind of pep talk and reach a moment of resolve, a question often sneaks up my neck like a chill: *Come on, Brian. Why fight a losing battle?*

I sit with that question for a few minutes, and a memory comes to mind:

one of the rare times I applied for a grant many years ago. The application process included a series of questions, including one that asked for my "theory of change." It was a new term to me, so I began to articulate my theory of change for the first time.

In short, I think that change only happens through failure, repeated failure. A leader names a problem or opportunity and shares an embryonic vision. Most people think he or she is unrealistic if not crazy, so they simply ignore the leader. A few dreamers and idealists, however, are attracted to the project. Most people respond to this tiny team of dreamers in the same way they responded to the original vision: they ignore it. But the team persists and the dream takes shape.

At some point, the majority becomes concerned. *This idea could actually catch on*, they worry. So they criticize the team of dreamers. They may even mock and ridicule them. But the team remains focused nonetheless and makes a bit of progress. Then the majority begins to organize against what is becoming an actual movement, spreading false rumors about the innovators, trying to discredit them and drive them back into the fold—or out of it entirely. That puts the team under stress and some give up. But at least a few remain and keep making progress, demonstrating character and courage in the process. They make mistakes, and progress takes far longer than they expected, which humbles them, but they get up and keep moving forward. At that point, when the opponents of the proposed change see the team's determination, when they fear it actually has a chance of disturbing the status quo, they unite to crush it. Often, the whole project is destroyed.

I realize this isn't a terribly inspiring theory of change. But the story isn't completely over. When the children of those who crush the project watch all this unfold, they make a comparison. Which inspires them the most, they wonder, the fearful vitriol and resistance of their parents, or the vision and persistence of the team of change agents their parents defeated? When the children of the resisters decide to side with the vision of the very people their parents opposed and crushed, that is when change can happen.

I didn't win the grant. But my failed theory does seem to fit a pattern I see when I look back over Part I of this book and review all the good reasons I have for leaving. Failure and success may look like binary opposites. But put them into motion, and they can actually be more like winter and spring, like mass extinction events and post-event evolutionary explosions of diversity. Together they push the process of growth forward. If you want evolution, you have to accept struggle and mass extinction events. If you want birth, you have to go through labor that feels like it's killing you. If you want a new genesis of diversity and beauty, you have to accept that things must look absolutely hopeless first. You have to commit to do the right thing against all odds. Otherwise, the systems maintain their equilibrium and the status quo spins on.

If we re-scan the heartbreaking history we reviewed in Part I, we see this pattern play out again and again. For example, recall the story in the fourth century, when Constantine offered a deal to the bishops of the church: if they would submit to him and turn the church into a compliant chaplaincy to his empire, he would offer them protection and privilege. The majority of bishops jumped at the chance. If I had been alive then, that would have been a great moment to give up, to walk away, to call the Christian experiment a hopeless failure.

But what happened next? A group of spiritual marathon runners did indeed leave the empire, but not the faith. They went out into the wild to experiment with Christianity's rebirth in counter-imperial monastic communities. These intrepid desert mothers and fathers simultaneously cherished the deepest beauty of Christian faith and withdrew their consent from the ugly turn it was taking. The conversion of the bishops to Constantine's agenda created the conditions for a new breakthrough by these creative spiritual pioneers.

Recall another pivotal period, centuries later, beginning around 1100. Criminally incompetent and misguided church leaders in the Western church mustered wave after wave of "Christian soldiers" to venture to the so-called holy land to engage in unholy slaughter of Muslims, promising forgiveness of sins for all who would join the cause. The Crusaders did plenty of slaughtering of Muslims to be sure, all "in the name of Jesus." (In the Fourth Crusade, Western Crusaders also did some serious slaughtering of their fellow Christians in the Eastern church.) Many died in combat, and even more of disease due to their leaders' poor planning for adequate food and sanitation. The Crusades were a holy fiasco.

That would have been another prime moment to walk away from the whole decomposing disaster. But two years after the First Crusade, a baby was born. Her name was Hildegard of Bingen, and over the eighty or so years of her life, she articulated a bold, creative, new kind of Christianity. Two years after she died, around the time of the Third Crusade, a young

Italian fellow we know as St. Francis was born. As a young man, he decided not to give up but to rebuild a Christianity that was in ruins. Like thousands of Crusaders, he went to the holy land, but not to kill Muslims. Instead, he walked unarmed into the camp of Sultan Malek al-Kamil as an interfaith peacemaker. A sister movement of similar spirit emerged under the leadership of St. Clare, colleague of St. Francis and founder of the Poor Clares. Once again, the failure of the many set the stage for the breakthrough of a few.

During the centuries that followed, the peaceful examples of Hildegard, Francis, Clare, and other courageous, creative reformers seemed to be forgotten as the Spanish Inquisition arose and employed the horrific technologies of torture that we outlined in Chapter 2. If I had lived then, that would have been yet another excellent moment to renounce Christianity entirely.

But it also would have been a moment to stand up and stand tall with an alternative vision, to resist and defy the Inquisition, to risk imprisonment, torture, and execution to promote a better way, a nonviolent way, a way of love. That's what Meister Eckhart did in the thirteenth century, along with Julian of Norwich, John Wycliffe, and Jan Hus in the fourteenth, Nicholas of Cusa in the fifteenth, Teresa of Ávila and John of the Cross in the sixteenth, and Brother Lawrence in the seventeenth. Those we honor today as great Christian reformers and mystics chose to stay Christian when Christianity as a whole was a hot, violent, ugly mess.

Then came the Protestant Reformation. The reformers dared to challenge the Roman hierarchy's violent and corrupt religious establishment. But as soon as they left Catholicism, they immediately began creating its mirror image, a Protestant brand of violence and corruption. The Reformers were soon warring against Catholics and persecuting other reformers, including the nonviolent Anabaptists, not to mention the Jews in their midst and thousands of women they accused of being witches.

I can easily imagine being fed up with the whole mess then and declaring myself a "done" and a "none."

But in that ugly time, the Anabaptist minority, instead of giving up, strengthened their resolve to differ from both majorities. They aspired to actually live by the Sermon on the Mount, just as the Jewish minority among them strengthened their resolve to stay faithful to the Law and prophets. Soon, the Enlightenment and Christian humanism arose to advocate for democracy rather than authoritarianism, reasonableness rather than superstition and prejudice, and human rights to protect lives rather than the divine right of kings and religious leaders to take lives.

Meanwhile, the age of the conquistadors and colonizers was unfolding, driven by the Doctrine of Discovery. In the aftermath of those colonial horrors, Black theology, liberation theology, and post-colonial theology arose.

Still, the vast majority of my fellow white Christians lined up on the wrong side of nearly every movement for liberation. But in spite of the ignorance of the majority, wave after wave of theological innovators arose. Feminist, womanist, queer, and mestizo theologians stood up to bigotry rather than submitting to it. Process theologians engaged with science rather than denying it. Eco-theologians confronted the industrial rape of the earth rather than being bystanders to it.

And here I find myself in the last few years. Shockingly high numbers of my fellow American Christians, robed in white patriarchal orthodoxy, pledged their allegiance to Donald Trump and his enablers in 2016, and then when he lost in 2020, they doubled down on extremist conspiracy theories, many supporting a violent coup attempt, dragging the name of Jesus into the bloodshed. That's bad enough, but there are similar examples of regressive and authoritarian Christianity taking similar trajectories in many other countries. Even worse behavior may unfold between the time I write these words and when you read them.

Surely now is the time to consider this Christian project a losing battle, if not a lost cause?

In case after case, when Christianity has faced a fork in the road, the vast majority has taken the broad highway of compliance. They have gone along with their leaders, most without any apparent reservations and some with a literal vengeance.

Sure, a few have had qualms, and they tried to tweak things with all the moderation they could muster. They had to be excruciatingly patient, because if change would come at all, it would come at a glacier's pace—in the era before global warming, that is. But even after a lifetime of staying, would-be reformers found that in spite of their years of patient labors, very little actually changed, except for the worse. So again and again, the status quo would win over attempts at reform. Power won. Corruption won. Money won. Fear won. Complacency and apathy won.

But maybe that's the point: maybe it takes crushing defeat in one generation to create the conditions for the change we need in the next. Maybe death and resurrection, not decline and renewal, is the more accurate model of how change happens.

If that's the case, then I need to tell myself that now is exactly the time *not* to leave Christianity. It's time to keep my skin in the game, to finish my journey, to refuse to conform and refuse to leave, to stay to support the Seths and defy the religious company men.

That doesn't mean that I am committing myself to saving institutions, theologies, liturgies, and other traditions that are unsalvageable. Instead, it means having faith that the good seed will burst out of the old husk and rise after being buried, that the essence, the pearl, the treasure and spark will resurrect on the third day, no matter how bad things get today and no matter how hopeless they feel tomorrow.

Is it a losing battle? I suspect that's the wrong metaphor. This isn't a game or a war that is won or lost once and for all. This is an iterative process, a story that unfolds "through many dangers, toils, and snares," booms and busts, losses and recoveries. It requires heroic persistence. It requires a death to pride, a death to hero narratives, and a commitment to do what's right even when the odds are stacked strongly against success. Truth be told, it's a perpetual process of evolution that unfolds in a time span that makes my little lifetime seem like a lightning bug's flash.

I have to admit: some days I'm tired. I look at the Christian world today, and it appears uglier and more tawdry than when I was younger. Recalling an old proverb (13:12), my hopes for meaningful change have been so long deferred that my heart feels sick.

I think it's important to acknowledge these feelings rather than suppress them.

So I admit it: I'm sometimes tired of staying. I can get out of this struggle, I tell myself. I can let others fight the battles. I can retire, fly-fish for trout in the solitude of the mountains, read poetry, walk among trees, tend my little orchard, and notice the birds.

But then I think of the Seths of the world who need to be encouraged, maybe even by this book.

And I think of the religious company men standing guard on their great walls of bias who need to be challenged, maybe even by this book.

So, *no*. I will not quit. Not today.

Today I will stay Christian.

❦

Because Leaving Defiantly
or Staying Compliantly
Are Not My Only Options

Not long after my conversation with Seth, I was speaking at a different conference, this one in the Appalachian Mountains. Two Catholic nuns were also speaking. To protect their privacy, I'll call them Sr. Ann and Sr. Jean.

Sr. Ann was brilliant and inspiring. I had read her work and admired her from a distance for literally decades. It turned out she had also read some of my work and was looking forward to getting better acquainted. I wasn't familiar with Sr. Jean, but her lectures at the conference were also brilliant and brave.

At the end of the last day's events, Sr. Ann came up to me with a wicked twinkle in her eye. "Would you be interested in joining Sr. Jean and me on the veranda for some very fine whiskey?"

I laughed and said I wasn't enough of a connoisseur to waste fine whiskey on, but I would be happy to join them.

A few minutes later, I was sitting in a rocking chair on the veranda. Ann had retrieved three plastic cups from the bathroom in her room, and she poured a splash of fiery honey-gold liquid into each. I realized Sr. Ann didn't take no for an answer. We clinked our cups in a toast. One tiny sip was all I could take. It made my eyes water, but I could tell it was something special.

Then Sr. Ann poured out her heart. First she told me of the thrill of her vocation back in the 1950s. "Then came the Vatican II era, when," she said, "you could just feel the wind of the Spirit. Change was in the air. Liturgical renewal . . . the Charismatic movement . . . the base community movement from Latin America. What exciting times!"

Sr. Jean interrupted. "I'm telling you the truth, Brian: so many of us sisters were sure that within a few short years, we would be ordained as priests. We felt certain that change was just around the corner."

"But here we are," Sr. Ann continued. "More regressive now than we were in 1970, in many ways. If I had known how effective the anti–Vatican II forces would be at crushing our dreams of renewal, I don't know if . . ."

We each took another tiny sip from our cups and descended into our own thoughts as the conversation took a breath, so to speak, each of us rocking slowly, staring out into the autumn evening.

I felt a wave of discouragement wash over me—the sisters', and my own too—because back in the '70s, when I became part of the Jesus movement and Charismatic renewal, there was a similar feeling of change in the air in the Protestant world. And on one level, a lot had changed. But on another level, our changes were little more than thick layers of makeup on a status quo that had actually consolidated and deteriorated.

My generation of reformers felt radical for using guitars and drums in worship, and now, you might think we succeeded. From megachurches to country chapels today, you'll hear five so-called contemporary choruses for every old-fashioned hymn. Was that success?

We radicals dared to break the dress code, substituting our comfortable jeans, sports shirts, and running shoes for our grandfathers' formal suit coats, ties, and shiny black wingtips. Was that success?

We dared to believe that young people like us could be leaders, and we started new, youth-oriented churches that embraced contemporary culture. We grew beards and long hair and dropped a naughty word from time to time so that our bearded and long-haired peers would feel a little more comfortable among us. And our efforts worked, so much so that now, churches are filled with those previously young baby boomers sporting more gray comb-overs than ponytails. And the younger generation is even more turned off by their parents' religiosity than we were back in the day. Was that success?

We introduced radical new technologies like *overhead projectors* and *cassette tapes*. Now, video projectors and huge digital screens are found in churches across America. Was that success?

I stared into my plastic cup and didn't feel successful at all. In fact, I felt a little guilty for my small part in those years of renewal: our efforts at change had brought tens of thousands of young people into religious communities that later taught them to deny climate change and systemic racial injustice, to maintain the hegemony of arrogant and ignorant straight white men, to support white Christian nationalism and militarism, to continue to look down on people of other religious traditions. (They also swallowed Donald Trump, his toxic patriarchal white supremacy, and his brazen corruption in one big gulp.)

I winced as I pondered all this.

Sr. Ann interrupted my unquiet musings. "But that's not why we asked you to talk with us . . . to hear us complain about the past. I have a more pressing problem. I've been notified that my sisters and I are being investigated by the authorities of the Church. We face the possibility of excommunication."

I told her that I had been a favorite target for heresy hunters. "I empathize," I said, "but I know that a posse of Protestant heresy hunters with websites and YouTube channels is one thing; the Vatican is another."

"That's why we wanted to talk with you," Sr. Jean said. "We knew you'd understand. In many ways, our orders have given us space to lead and innovate, to do creative ministry for the poor and forgotten without the all-male diocesan system controlling everything. But when they begin to flex their muscles over our work, especially with all the mess they've caused with the pedophilia scandals . . . it's pretty hard to take."

Sr. Ann leaned forward: "Now look, Brian, I'm no spring chicken, but I'm not a tired old hen either. So I don't mind a fight." She put her cup on a coffee table and spread out her hands: "But at my age, if I'm kicked out, I have nothing. No possessions. No health insurance. No place to live. No community. At this stage in my life, nearly all my relatives are already gone. So outside my order, I truly have nothing. I wish my faith were stronger, but I have to tell you: I have trouble sleeping some nights. It's . . . frankly, it's terrifying. And it's hurtful. They want to silence us, to pressure us into submission. And that would kill us."

As a Protestant, I think I offered Srs. Ann and Jean a certain safety that would be hard to find in Catholic circles. So I listened and tried to be a pastor, friend, and brother to these dear spiritual leaders. That's all they needed, really. Soon, without me saying anything profound, they had cheered themselves up again. "Well," Sr. Ann said, after pouring each of us one more splash of firewater, "I can tell you this: if I'm getting kicked out, I'm not going quietly. On my way out the door, I'll raise my voice louder than I ever have before!"

We toasted once more, they thanked me for listening, and then offered me a parting blessing that has stayed with me to this moment. I started back toward my room but then decided to take a detour. I found a bench at the edge of a lake and sat under the stars. "There are more than two options," I thought. "I don't have to choose between staying Christian compliantly or leaving Christianity defiantly. I can *stay defiantly*, like Sr. Ann and Sr. Jean. I can intentionally, consciously, resolutely refuse to leave . . . and with equal intention and resolution, I can refuse to comply with the status quo. I can occupy Christianity with a different way of being Christian."[1]

When I say stay *defiantly*, I don't mean *ungraciously*. Srs. Ann and Jean radiate such gentleness and inner calm that accusations of being ungracious simply don't stick. No, with firm yet gracious defiance, they will keep speaking their truths and will continue doing so from the inside as long as they can. If the religious company men eventually do come to escort them from their institutional premises, I know they'll keep speaking boldly yet graciously on their way out too, and then they will continue to do so from the outside.

The word *defiance* is derived from the Latin root *fide*. *Disfidare* meant to break faith or renounce one's faith. It was an opposite to *confidare*, to confide or trust or keep faith. I like the word in this context because it suggests that I can no longer put a naive trust in the structures of the Christian religion, seeing and knowing what I see and know now. But instead of rejecting my religious community, I remain paradoxically present to it, neither minimizing its faults nor hating it for its faults. I may not succeed in influencing it by my example, but it will not succeed in conforming me to its example either. Nor will it tempt me to mirror the rejection it has shown to so many who have dared to differ, dared to ask questions, dared to challenge it.

This is the sweet defiance I saw in Sr. Ann and Sr. Jean. It was rooted in something deeper than the hope of success, because they no longer expected a breakthrough in their lifetimes. In the words of a poem often attributed to Oscar Romero, they saw us as "prophets of a future not our own."[2] In this vision, we aren't addicted to respectability and comfort. Instead, we strive to maintain integrity and remain present, even if doing so causes both us and our faith community some discomfort in the short run.

Perhaps we will be remembered by future generations as heretics. Perhaps we will be remembered as martyrs, heroes, prophets, reformers. Most likely we will not be remembered at all, joining the vast majority of human beings who live good lives but remain unknown to future generations. How one is remembered doesn't matter when one is focused on integrity.

So Sr. Ann, Sr. Jean, and I—and perhaps you too—face the same four options: we can stay Christian compliantly, maybe changing lanes from one denomination to another, maybe advocating for cosmetic reform, but staying on the broad Christian superhighway. We can leave Christianity compliantly (because the company men would rather us go, and we consider the religion a lost cause anyway). We can leave defiantly, shaking our fist as we go. Or we can stay with a good-natured but firm defiance, determined to keep our integrity and speak our truth as best we can, as long as we can, from the outside edge of the inside, staying centered in genuine humility and love.

I know that leaving defiantly has much to commend it. In light of the first ten chapters of this book, it can seem like the only moral pathway. I have many friends who have taken this option, and there are moments when I feel like joining them. Some were so exhausted or traumatized that they needed to get as far away from Christianity as they could, for their own sanity and survival. Others hoped, consciously or unconsciously, that their loud departure would be a kind of revenge. "You won't listen to me? I'll show you: I'll leave!" Still others hoped, consciously or unconsciously, that their departure would so disrupt their faith community that they would be missed, chased, and begged to return: "We were wrong not to listen to you! Please come back!"

But in my experience, once you're gone, you're quickly forgotten. You're less likely to be missed as a beloved sibling than you are to be vilified as a traitor or apostate or sore loser. If anything, your departure makes those who remain be more suspicious of those in the future who raise questions or propose reform. Gatekeepers will wag an index finger and say, "Remember what happened in the past with would-be reformers. They caused a lot of disruption, and then they left anyway. Don't give them an inch. They'll be gone soon enough."

So whether we stay or leave, Christian scholar and professor Kristin Kobes Du Mez says, we need to do so out loud, if possible:

> #LeavingLOUD plays a vital role in revealing dynamics that often remain hidden—dynamics that must be brought into the light. Depending on the circumstances, #StayingLOUD can do the same thing. But silence in leaving or remaining will only allow these patterns to persist. It is long past time for white [Christians] to call out injustice, bigotry, violent rhetoric, disparaging language, racism, misogyny, abuse of power, and the idolatry of Christian nationalism in their own communities, even if doing so comes at a cost. The cost of not doing so is undeniable, and it is a cost largely born by others.[3]

Jesus, of course, counted this cost. He stayed out loud. And it's worth noting where his staying led him. Not to winning. Not to success. It led him to the utter defeat and humiliation of the cross.

Was he a fool to keep faith through his dying breath, to translate his feeling of forsakenness into a prayer? Was he a fool to think that the legacy of the prophets, the legacy of his cousin John, and the legacy of his mother, Mary, were worth staying for, to save that legacy from corruption by the religious gatekeepers of his day?

Was he a fool to stay in the fray with the religious company men of his day, naming their corruption and toxicity with carefully chosen words like "whitewashed sepulchers" and "brood of vipers"? Would he have been wiser to leave quietly for India and become Hindu, or go quietly to China and become Buddhist instead of challenging the status quo of his own religion?

Was he a fool to think that the tiny handful of people who got only a tiny sliver of his message and saw some faint glimmer of what he saw could outlive him and do greater things than he had done?

Are you willing to be that kind of fool? Am I?

Today, at least, inspired by the example of Sr. Jean and Sr. Ann, I am.

13

Because ... Where Else Would I Go?

Since I began reading the Bible on my own back in my teens, I've been drawn to a series of stories told in the sixth chapter of the Fourth Gospel. They both bothered and fascinated me. First, Jesus feeds a multitude by multiplying a small boy's lunch of fish and bread. In so doing, he evokes the story of the children of Israel being fed by manna in the desert. Then Jesus walks on water, crossing over to the other side of the Sea of Galilee, evoking another episode from the Exodus, the crossing of the Red Sea. (For those who see miracle stories as an obstacle, we'll return to this subject in Chapter 15.) Then the crowd finds him and shows how perfectly clueless they are by asking for a permanent supply of free bread.

Jesus tells them they're missing the point. And then, as if to jolt them out of their superficiality, he tells them if they really want to understand, they need to eat something other than bread: *they must eat his flesh and drink his blood.*

Now that sounds strange to our ears, really strange. It must have sounded even stranger to his original audience, whose religious identity included strict dietary restrictions. *Cannibalism? What?*

Jesus makes it clear that he is speaking metaphorically, but many people leave, including some who have been counted among Jesus' disciples up to this point. Some may feel disappointed that the hoped-for lifetime supply of bread is not forthcoming. Others may be looking for a simpler message that doesn't require so much metaphorical interpretation. You can hear them muttering as they depart, "I mean, really, *eating his flesh and drinking his blood?* Who talks that way? Has he lost his mind?"

Then Jesus turns to his remaining disciples and says, "OK. So are any of you going to leave as well?" Peter, always quick to speak, replies, "Lord, to whom can we go? You have the words of the new way of life. We have come to believe and know that you are the Holy One of God."[1]

The whole story resonates with how I have often felt through the years. Truth be told, early on, I wanted my own version of a lifetime of free bread. Sometimes as a student, I wanted to be able to pray my way to A's on tests, whether or not I did my homework, as if the A was the point rather than the learning and growth that come from study. I wanted God to lead me to the perfect woman so I could avoid all the wasted time and effort of dating—not to mention the challenge of becoming a mature man worthy of a good life partner! I wanted God to grant me as much romantic success with as little frustration and risk as possible. In other words, I wanted free bread.

Beyond that, I wanted a simple message that explained away the complexity of life. I didn't want a mysterious and metaphorical message that required me to face life's paradoxes squarely and be humbled by them. I wanted someone who would answer my questions rather than questioning my answers. I wanted someone who would serve up my thinking for me like fresh bread hot from the oven, sparing me the gathering, mixing, kneading, waiting, kneading again, waiting again, and baking process that produces wisdom.

In short, I wanted to be part of a religion that gave me lots of free bread in the form of easy success and free fish in the form of easy answers. I wanted my religion to give me reasons for pride, not shame and struggle. I wanted my membership to mark me as one of the good guys, for all to see. I wanted to be transported instantly to maturity and exempted from the arduous maturation process. And when it didn't turn out that way, I had to ask myself: *why stay when I'm not getting what I was hoping for?*

And then I had to answer my question with another question, Peter's question: *where else would I go?*

I suppose a bunch of us could leave our religions and then get together and start a new religion. But how long would that take to get off the ground? And how much energy would it take, energy that could be better devoted to addressing our most urgent existential threats? And how likely is it that we would be able to avoid the institutional reefs that have sunk every other religion over time? My friends who are serial entrepreneurs tell me a painful

truth: the only thing worse than being part of someone else's failing enterprise is being part of one you founded!

Not only that, but I can't think of anything less attractive than forming,
joining, or promoting *the one church that finally gets it right, the one pure version
of Christianity, the single best denomination ever!* I've been there and done that,
and found out that it was a poisoned apple. Anyone who wants to leave all their
fellow human beings behind on the last flight to heaven, nirvana, the Elysian
fields, bliss, supremacy, innocence, or whatever . . . anyone who wants to be
part of the superior, pure, and elite sect of human beings that separates itself
from everyone else, that person has just become a worse human being.

Perhaps the only answer is to join the ranks of the atheists, agnostics,
and spiritual-but-not-religious, and forge ahead under the auspices of scientific or secular humanism.

I think of a friend of mine, Kat. "I didn't consciously choose to become
an atheist," she told me. "I just woke up one day and realized that's what my
experience as a minister had turned me into." When she realized that faith in
God or religion wasn't coming back anytime soon, she got a secular job and
got involved with the atheist community. "Brian, you think that religious
fundamentalists are mean-spirited and vicious. Wait until you meet some of
the atheist fundamentalists that I've fallen in with. They compare themselves
with all the religious nuts out there and feel really smart. Talk about setting a
low bar. To make matters worse, with God out of the way, some of them act
like there is no being in the universe smarter than they are!"

When Kat was working in a religious context, she explained, at least she
could invite people to engage in spiritual practices that slowed them down
for reflection and contemplation, for self-examination and repentance. "We
spend so much time bashing heads and reacting to each other's egos that
I'm afraid we won't get any farther than you will in the religious world," she
lamented. "Saving the world? We're too busy tearing each other apart and
then blaming religious people for all our problems."

As things stand right now, about 29 percent of humans identify as Christian. Roughly 24 percent identify as Muslim. About 15 percent identify as
Hindu. Another 15 percent or so identify as secular or nonreligious. The remaining 18 percent includes Buddhists (6 percent), members of Chinese traditional religions (5 percent), and all the other religious traditions, including
Judaism, Sikhism, Shintoism, Bahaism, and Jainism, each with less than 1
percent of the world's population.

However we identify ourselves, we find ourselves in at least one of these groups, and each of these groups has real problems.

Again, I do not judge, shame, or criticize anyone who leaves one religion to join another. Nor do I criticize those who, like Kat did, join the 18 percent of secular and spiritual-but-not-religious. People who do so have good reasons for doing so.

But speaking personally, as I reflect on these numbers, I find another reason not to give up my footprint in the planet's largest religious community. If I remain a Christian, I at least stand in religious solidarity with 85 percent of the world's population who identify as religious, be they Muslim, Hindu, Buddhist, Jewish, Sikh, or other. If I identify as atheist, agnostic, or otherwise nonreligious, I lose some of that common ground.

If I am vocally honest about the failures of my religious community, I also stand in solidarity with my nonreligious friends, for whom Christian faults are brutally obvious.

Besides, as Michael Gungor of *The Liturgists* podcast has said, for those of us in the West, Christendom is the water we swim in, especially here in the United States, whether we like it or not. It infuses our history, our culture, our politics. It's on our dollar bills and in our Pledge of Allegiance. Even if we leave Christianity, Christianity doesn't leave us. So we might as well try to challenge it toward positive change.[2]

Maintaining a Christian connection seems all the more important when I acknowledge that Christianity is not only the world's largest religion but also the most heavily armed with both conventional weapons and weapons of mass destruction. In addition, it's the world's richest religion, controlling the largest share of the world's capital and infrastructure. Put its weapons and wealth together, and it is clear that Christianity has more potential than any other single religion to oppress the poor and destroy the planet—or to help the poor and save the planet. The opportunity to influence such a powerful religion as an insider is probably not something to cast away lightly.

I suddenly see why most of my friends of other religions actually prefer me to stay Christian and work for the common good from within. That is exactly how I feel about them. I don't want my progressive Jewish friends to abandon Judaism to its most nationalistic, insular, and least-common-good-oriented constituency. I don't want my progressive Muslim friends to leave Islam to its most theocratic wing. I want them to be faithful Jewish and Muslim examples who are calling their traditions to greater wisdom, love, and big-heartedness. It's the same with my secular humanist friends. I don't want them to abandon secularism to its least humane elements.

In my heart of hearts, I believe each religion and each nonreligious tradition has developed unique treasures, and its greatest honor is not to hoard these treasures or dangle them as an enticement to convert but rather to share them freely with one another. Those gifts, taken together, will help us as humans to make our way forward . . . together.

So here is a way for me to stay Christian: I must try to understand and unearth the greatest blessings of my tradition, just as I face up to its many shortcomings. I must engage in a kind of truth and reconciliation process within my heritage. (This book, I hope, is a contribution to that process.)

Then, simultaneously humbled by my religion's failures and inspired by its treasures, I can find my neighbors—both religious and secular—who are engaging in a parallel process in their communities. In a spirit of humility and generosity, we can confess our shortcomings and share our treasures, working together for the common good of all our fellow creatures on this beautiful, fragile planet.

That process is happening. It is one of the most hopeful signs I see anywhere, and it gains momentum every day. It would take another whole book to tell you the stories of my Muslim, Jewish, Sikh, Hindu, Buddhist, pagan, atheist, and humanist friends and colleagues who share this vision of collaboration for the common good.

Each of us is discovering, deep at the heart of our unique and diverse traditions, a way of inhabiting our traditions that doesn't cut us off from others but rather connects us to them.

It's almost funny when you see it. Religion, at its best, is what re-ligaments or reconnects us to God, one another, and creation. It challenges the stories that pit us against each other: us over them, us overturning them, us competing with them, us isolating from them, us in spite of them, us purifying ourselves of them.[3] It tells a better story, some of us for all of us, a story in which there is no *them*, a story in which we tear down the walls that have divided us and from the rubble build bridges.

That is a way I can stay Christian.

Most days. There are days I feel like my friend Christy Berghoef, a gifted writer, photographer, and advocate for the common good. In early 2021, she wrote in an email to several friends:

Honestly I thought I already had my major crises of faith a decade or so ago. But I am completely and utterly gobsmacked by the current state of christianity's public witness. . . . My faith is a tiny pile of barely lit embers these days, given the extent of the damage done to the world by professed followers of Jesus. I'm in the thick of the chaos here in West Michigan— barely hanging on to my faith, and on many days no longer sure I want to.

Christy and her husband have been outspoken about the issues we ex- plored in Part I of this book. To make matters worse, they vocally opposed the incumbent U.S. president in 2020, when Brian ran for Congress as a Democrat. As a result,

Even the closest family members now believe we're Satan's little helpers on earth—no doubt suspecting we have red pitchforks hidden in the back of our closets, and that it's only a matter of time before Biden summons us to pick them up and fight for the communist, Christian-persecuting country he supposedly desires.

It's painful. It's frustrating to have such ache for people I love but who seem totally out of the grasp of reality, and who no longer seem to love me back. To be surrounded by Trump flags that still (!) continue to be replen- ished after the old ones fade and tear, and "Make America Great Again" banners ripping in the wind behind monster trucks tearing down our quiet country roads while blowing black smoke through their tailpipes, and "All Lives Matter" flags and "Blue Lives Matter" flags waving in the breezes from front porch posts, alongside "Jesus is King" yard signs. It is all just breaking me. I feel sometimes like I'm on another planet where the air is thin and I can't breathe. There is a sense of panic to it all. And I tell myself that no matter what people say or do to our family, I am determined to remain calm and just keep living into the deep and wide love I believe in.

The bolder we live out God's love, the angrier christians around us get, and the more wild their insults grow. I won't be hushed or shy away from bold love. I'm just no longer sure if I'm comfortable proclaiming that my christian faith is the source of this great love. Humanism seems more reflective of Jesus than Christianity does. . . . Anyways, I am tired. I am so very tired.

Someone else in our little email circle replied, "Judaism anyone? Maybe with a side of Buddhism?" Someone else agreed that humanism looked pretty good to her.

Then someone else replied that she had given up on Christianity and looked for another group to find refuge in. But here's what she found: "Every kind of Christian has its equivalent in synagogues, humanist book clubs, ashrams, atheist beer gardens and Comicons." There are in humanist and atheist circles "egomaniacs, charlatans, sadists, misogynists, racists, thieves, liars, idealists, Virgos, procrastinators, flag wavers, book thumpers, exaggerators, drama queens, frauds, pedophiles, addicts, tree huggers, potluck ladies, cat lovers, humanitarians, FBI agents and bores," just as there are in Christian ones.

I have nothing but empathy for Christians who simply cannot bear to remain Christian. But there's nowhere to go that is free from human beings showing their worst as well as their best.

So wherever we go, however we identify, we are going to have to do the hard work of embodying an alternative, of living out loud in "bold love," as Christy said.

Ironically, that is what I believe Jesus was about . . . boldly moving toward the other, boldly drawing a bigger circle, boldly tearing down dividing walls, boldly building bridges of connection and tables of reunion in their place, boldly telling a new and bigger story of bold love that he called *the good news of the kingdom of God*.

If you and I want to participate in this healing and reconciling movement, it would sure help to have a global network to work with. It would even be better if this network had physical, social, and communications infrastructure to assist us. It would be better still if this network had regular gatherings so people could be trained, supported, encouraged, and deployed to be part of this work. Where could we find such a network? If such a network existed, even if it had serious flaws and glaring weaknesses that needed to be addressed, would it make sense to leave it without seriously inviting willing sectors of it to join the movement?

If we left that global network, where else would we go?

❧

14

BECAUSE IT WOULD BE A SHAME TO LEAVE A RELIGION IN ITS INFANCY

The form of Christianity that has any chance of retaining my commitment is not a regressive Christianity, rushing headlong into the sixteenth or nineteenth century. Nor is it a conservative Christianity, change resistant and defensive. It is rather an *anticipatory Christianity*, leaning into the future. Echoing Paul's radical aspiration (Philippians 3:7 ff.), we count everything we have already attained as loss. We write it off. We leave it behind. We forget about it. (I would hesitate to put it this bluntly if Paul didn't use this same stark language himself.) Then, we strain forward to what lies ahead, pressing on toward the goal, responding to the call to love, justice, joy, and peace, as taught by and embodied in Jesus.

Ilia Delio, a brilliant Franciscan nun and scholar, speaks powerfully of anticipatory Christian faith. The Christianity we have known until now emerged in what has been called the first axial period, a time of great intellectual ferment that began around 800 BCE and continued until about 200 BCE. In the first axial age, our species had a kind of internal, individual subjective awakening. As individual thinkers, we began to take both our individual inner life and also a shared understanding of the cosmos more seriously. We wouldn't be where we are if not for the first axial age. But now, like people halfway through a doorway, we are moving beyond it. We are entering a second axial age.

Unlike residents of the first axial age who woke up each day as independent individuals in a fixed and static cosmos, more and more of us today have moved into a new conceptual cosmos. We wake up in an ongoing cosmic story of interdependence and constant dynamic change. Delio explains,

> This new universe story is *radically new* compared to the cosmos of the axial period because our universe is dynamic and unfinished. Since the axial religions, including Christianity and Judaism, emerged in a fixed static cosmos, our new cosmology invites a new story of religion. This new story of religion demands a new theological method . . . one based . . . on anticipation of the future. The cosmic narrative is still unfolding and thus the story is not yet complete. In this respect, we live in an anticipatory universe . . . which means the future is our truest and deepest reality.[1]

The first axial age had remarkable staying power. But step by step over the last few centuries, data accumulated like snow on a roof. Our fixed and static cosmos collapsed under its weight. When spring came, builders of a new paradigm worked in the ruins to create a new vision of the cosmos. Thanks to innovators like Sir Isaac Newton in physics and James Hutton in geology, thanks to Charles Darwin in biology and Einstein and Hubble in quantum physics and astrophysics, thanks to Adam Smith and Karl Marx in economics, thanks to Sigmund Freud and Jean Piaget in psychiatry, thanks to Alfred North Whitehead and Isabelle Stengers in philosophy, thanks to Ken Wilber and Thomas Berry and Michael Dowd in macrohistory, along with many, many others, we have been thrust into a new universe where everything is in motion.[2]

Subatomic particles and waves spin in indeterminacy. Stars and their planets come and go. Continents shift, rise, and fall, as do oceans. Species are not fixed, but in the making, some diminishing toward extinction, others emerging to thrive in new forms. And religions are part of this dynamic process too, as theologians like Monica Coleman, Barbara Holmes, Wil Gafney, Sallie McFague, John Cobb, Rosemary Radford Ruether, Tim Burnette, Tripp Fuller, Philip Clayton, Marjorie Hewitt Suchocki, Thomas Oord, and many others affirm.

As a result, most of us woke up this morning in a universe that was not at its best at the beginning. Nor is it at its best now. It is en route, becoming, in process, always presented with the possibility of evolving into something more beautiful, diverse, alive, and conscious—or stagnating and decaying toward extinction. We do not know what the universe can become, given enough time and enough opportunity, aided by our own faith, hope, courage, and love.

If the Christian faith is to have a creative and constructive future, it will have to undergo its own metamorphosis from a first to a second axial age religion, from a regressive/conservative religion to a progressive/anticipatory one. Like conscious caterpillars in a cocoon, we must imagine life with wings. We must inhabit and tell a new cosmic story.

Here's one attempt: Our adventure begins some 13.7 billion years ago with an expansion, blast, or silent bang of unimaginably hot matter/energy and space/time. From that genesis moment, what we call the universe begins to unfold in all directions and dimensions, known and unknown. As this expanse slows and cools, simple atoms form and converge, creating the components of the first generation of stars. Those original stars burn and burn until they burn themselves out, collapsing in on themselves. Then they explode as supernovas, their unimaginable heat fusing simple atoms into more complex atoms that form new generations of stars and planets, resulting in the physical universe we know today.

About 4.5 billion years ago, around one of those stars, space dust and debris congeal into our little planet. Roughly half a billion years later, some complex chemicals come together and develop the ability to take in energy, first from other chemicals and later from sunlight. Stage by stage, these complex chemicals come together as single-cell life forms. Starting about 3.4 billion years ago, some of these simple life forms start producing oxygen as a byproduct of their existence, and with more oxygen, the planet slowly becomes more hospitable to more kinds of organisms.

Eventually, some of these simple one-celled organisms begin living together cooperatively and reproducing, gradually becoming more complex organisms with diversified parts working together. By 1.2 billion years ago, some of these organisms are identifiable as primitive plants. About 800 million years ago, early sponges become the first examples of what we would call animals. Over the next 250 million years, both plants and animals further diversify.

Then, around 540 million years ago, conditions suddenly change (for reasons we do not yet understand). These changes wipe out many of the first generation of living things. But in the aftermath of this extinction event, a wide array of new organisms develop in what we call the Cambrian Explosion. Over the next 65 million years or so, life diversifies and expands at an unprecedented rate, with sea worms burrowing in the ocean floor, armored trilobites moving across the sand and silt, and primitive arthropods and even finless, jawless fish swimming through the water above them.

As life teems in the oceans, some plants develop the ability to survive on land: first mosses, then ferns, then more complex plants. Meanwhile, as bony fishes develop and diversify, some develop the ability to breathe air through primitive lungs, and soon, amphibians begin living at least part of their lives on land. From there, terrestrial reptiles develop, so that by 300 million years ago, reptiles are spreading across the continents. More extinction events occur around 250 million years ago, leading to the age of the dinosaurs. As the dinosaurs diversify and spread around the earth, birds and mammals also develop.

Yet another mass extinction event occurs around 60 million years ago, wiping out the dinosaurs and leaving mammals and birds space to diversify and expand. Among the evolving mammals, primates evolve, and among the primates, the first hominins emerge about 2.5 million years ago. They soon develop the ability to craft and use tools. Several hominin species diversify— including lineages known to us as *Ardipithecus, Australopithecus*, and *Homo*. Among our genus, *Homo habilis, Homo erectus, Homo neanderthalensis*, and others develop as distinct species.

Then about 200,000 years ago, a scrappy new species emerges in Africa. Around 150,000 years ago, they develop language. These talking hominins, known to us as *Homo sapiens*, spread north through Europe and Asia, gradually displacing or assimilating the other remaining hominins. Between 33,000 and 13,000 years ago, modern humans reach the Americas, completing their planetary dispersion. Only about 5,500 years ago, humans invent writing, making it possible for you to read (or hear) these words I am now arranging.

Obviously, I've constructed this brief history from available data, and as more data emerge, this overview will be improved upon. But whatever the details, in this universe, three things are abundantly clear: first, the earliest form of something is not its pure or original or best or permanent or ideal form. In fact, there really is no pure, original, best, or ideal form. Every form is in process, adapting, evolving, mutating, changing.

Second, over time, the universe becomes more complex, more diverse, more alive, more interdependent, more conscious, and, we might say, more beautiful and good. From simple physics to complex physics, we advance to simple and more complex life, and from more complex life we advance to simple and more complex consciousness. And in the context of whatever degree of complex consciousness we currently possess, more beauty and moral goodness continue to emerge and mature, along with more curiosity to know and articulate what is true . . . and more imagination to envision and create what could be true in the future.

And third, extinction happens on the path of evolution. When conditions change, life forms must either evolve to cope with them or go extinct. When some life forms prove incapable of adaptation, new life forms evolve to fill their niches. That means that no species, including our own, is absolute, invincible, supreme, or ultimate.

So, this is the evolving universe in which I wake up every morning, and when I look to the future, I see two abiding options: evolution and extinction.

But again, as I noted in Chapter 7, Christianity in all its conventional, first-axial-age forms does not allow me to live in this universe, because the first axial age constricted it within a change-averse set of boundary conditions. Since the original form was the highest and best form, diversity is rebellion from that original expression. Creative or progressive change is heresy, apostasy, or corruption. Since a first-axial-age God created and rules this first-axial-age universe, any who dare to evolve and diversify face damnation.

I ask myself: how can a universe like this be anything but regressive and authoritarian? If patriarchy was the earliest form of life we can remember, then patriarchy must be the highest and best form of human society. It is the job of authority figures to clamp down on diversity and change as a threat to their very way of life. Their determination to remain in control is backed by a cosmic Supreme Patriarch behind or above human patriarchy. The Supreme Patriarch will punish all who evolve and reward all who resist change.

Building on the work of Teilhard de Chardin, Karl Jaspers, Ewert Cousins, and many others, Sr. Ilia Delio's diagnosis is helping many of us understand why we are so frustrated with Christianity as it currently stands. Peppier music isn't enough to fix a religion anchored in the first axial age, especially when the only future hope it offers means complete destruction of the existing universe so we can be evacuated to a new heavenly creation where everything is forever and finally fixed (in multiple senses of that word).

It's not that you and I are rebellious infidels who *won't* accept first-axial-age Christianity as it is; rather, we are honest human beings who *can't*. The best we can do is *pretend* to accept it, but that kind of pretense corrupts our conscience and turns good faith into bad faith.

So, where does that leave us? Clearly the jig is up. Christianity's days are numbered. A growing proportion of smart and honest Christians of each new generation will abandon the sinking ship, just as they have been doing for centuries in Europe and decades in the United States. In the not-too-distant future, Christianity will only exist in those enclaves where authoritarian leaders rule over submissive flocks who enfold their religious lives within the assumptions of the first axial age.

Or is it that simple? If we are right, if the universe is actually evolving in a very different story, and if, on our planet at least, human consciousness is still in its early infancy, then wouldn't that mean that Christianity is also in its infancy, and it has another possible option alongside extinction, namely evolution?

And wouldn't an evolving Christianity have an option beyond being forever ruled by authoritarian patriarchs who demand adherence to an outdated conceptual universe? Wouldn't our very understandings of evolution and extinction mean that those gatekeepers and company men who have the futile mission of keeping change at bay are actually one asteroid or climate catastrophe away from an extinction event? Rather than being the faithful stand-ins for our radical founder, might they be blind guides (lacking foresight, however well meaning) who are leading Christianity toward a ditch of extinction?

And if that's true, might we, far from being disloyal heretics, actually have the opportunity to become the evolutionary descendants of Jesus who are called to carry on his radically progressive vision in our brief time on this earth?

In framing our situation this way, I'm not suggesting that these conservative gatekeepers need to be vilified and scapegoated. They are part of the story too, doing the best they can, and most of them sincerely believe in what they're doing. Of course, it would be nearly impossible for people in the first axial age to immediately accept the radical insights of a visionary leader like Jesus. Of course, there would be two steps back after every three steps forward. Of course, there would be evolutionary dead ends before some part of the spiritual gene pool would find a way forward. Of course, old paradigms would need to be preserved until the new paradigms evolved sufficiently to be worthy of trust. And of course, even in their misguided resistance to change, conservative leaders would be preserving some treasures that deserved to be preserved.

This way of thinking allows me to view the authoritarian gatekeepers and religious company men with compassion and empathy. Each in their own way, they all have a part in the story, but nobody has the last word. I must see myself and my colleagues in the same way, with humility, because unless we proceed wisely, our branch on the evolutionary tree of life will also be short. There is more than one way to go extinct.

We are not defined exclusively by who we came from in the past. We can also be defined by what we can become in the future. This is an anticipatory Christianity, and it changes everything, as Sr. Ilia Delio concludes:

> If we take the future as our starting point for thinking about God, creation, and humanity—then *everything* we know must . . . be realigned to an evolving universe, including our theologies, philosophies, economic and political systems, cultural matrices—in short, our planetary life.

In this light, Christianity looks very different to me. Instead of an old, mature, fully formed, maybe even worn-out religion, I see it as a religion still in its earliest infancy. And that raises a new question for me: If I leave the Christian community and conversation, will I be abandoning an infant, speaking in terms of deep evolutionary time?

I remind myself: the universe isn't in a hurry by human standards. It has been unfolding and expanding, diversifying and beautifying in its current form for 13.7 billion years. I remind myself: if we compressed the universe's whole existence into one year, our planet doesn't even form until September 11.[3] The first forms of life don't emerge on Earth until around September 30, but no multi-cellular organisms evolve until December 14. The dinosaurs rule the earth from December 27 to 30, and the first humans don't appear until December 31 at 11:39 p.m. Jesus comes on the scene at 11:59:56, which means that all of Christianity has existed for a mere four seconds. Four seconds!

Or to frame it differently, if we say that modern humans have been around for 200,000 years, Christianity has been around for 1 percent of our species' history. Yes, for better and for worse (as we've seen), the religion made a big splash in a relatively short time. But imagine two scenarios. First, imagine that human civilization, led by its largest living religion, destroys itself in the next century or two. Wouldn't you have to be suspicious, at least, that a species that survived for 198,000 years without Christianity could only last 2,000 years with it? That's not a great reflection on Christianity!

But conversely, imagine that somehow, we reverse our accelerating slide into catastrophic climate change and environmental overshoot. Then imagine that we reverse the accelerating concentration of money, power, and weapons in a tiny group of hyper-elite oligarchs. And then imagine that we manage to keep those super-rich oligarchs from using their growing cache of weapons to plunge us into a mushroom cloud of mutually assured destruction. In that light, imagine that the human race lives for another 200,000 years.

Looking back from that vantage point in the 202020s, the first 2,000 years of Christian history will be to our descendants only 1 percent of Christian history, proportional to what the first twenty years of Christianity are to us. If you're familiar with Christian history, you already know that we know next to nothing about those first twenty years after Jesus' crucifixion, except this: it was very unlike what we call Christianity today. There were no churches, no denominations or celibate clergy (and really, no clergy at all as we know it), no formal creeds or systematic theologies, no organs or Sunday school programs, no annual celebration of Christmas or Easter. It was a twenty-year-old movement, younger to me as I write than the Civil Rights movement and the environmental movement, just twice as old as the Black Lives Matter movement, and a bit older than the #MeToo movement.

So I ask myself again: why should I leave a religion in its infancy? Wouldn't that be like giving up on a baby because after ten months, she still can't walk, talk in complete sentences, read, do basic algebra, or even poop in the potty?

Wouldn't I be wiser to redouble my efforts to help this fledgling religion learn to walk, stop biting its playmates, and feed itself?

Perhaps, then, we should see this tantrum-prone baby's current regressive behavior and temper tantrums as signs of developmental frustration. Perhaps our terrible two-year-old religion is on the verge of a breakthrough.

That's what Sr. Ilia Delio dares us to believe, and I stand with her. She concludes her majestic book *Making All Things New* by offering us six challenges to seize this opportunity. We must *know the earth and our own bodies*, because we have become so obsessed with concepts that we have lost touch with our creatureliness. Second, we need to *see our world religions as sources of energy* that can mature and guide us forward. Third, we need to *understand that thought is a physical reality*: it exists as an emergent phenomenon in brains and can be replicated in other brains, and like any other evolving expression of life, it can lead us forward. Fourth, we need to fully *embrace the idea that something big and beautiful and alive is evolving in the universe*, something that includes individual humans but is bigger than the sum of its parts. Fifth, to thrive in this dynamic universe, we need to *cultivate a zest for living and a spirit of adventure*, to "wildly fling ourselves into the arms of divine Love." And finally, we need to *dare to trust in the process*, the process of evolving life, the process of birth and growth of which we are a small part.[4] Doing so will help us become "artisans of a new future," a "new catholicity," and a "new religion of the world," grasping this moment as "the kiss of God."

If we see our situation in this light, doesn't the earth need at least a few people like you and me to stay Christian—especially in this pregnant, anticipatory moment?

☙

15

BECAUSE OF OUR LEGENDARY FOUNDER

In her warm and insightful book *Freeing Jesus*, Diana Butler Bass writes, "when quizzed why I am still a Christian, I have always responded, 'Because of Jesus. I know it sounds corny, but I love Jesus.'"[1]

I feel the same way.

But neither Diana nor I would ever say, "Because of Jesus, Christianity is fine, and its problems are negligible." In fact, in light of Part I of this book, I must say that Christianity has so much potential for harm that only Jesus can save Christians—and the world—from it. Only Jesus provides a way for Christians to stay Christian, as part of a Christlike resistance to all un-Christlike elements of Christianity and its many mechanisms of domination.[2]

Many of us still call ourselves Christian because, as Diana said, we love Jesus. We "believe in and believe Jesus," and for us, "that comes pretty near the definition of what it means to be a Christian." But therein lies our problem. According to prominent Christian gatekeepers across history, having confidence in Jesus and loving Jesus simply aren't enough.

We must confess agreement with their beliefs, they say, about Jesus, the Bible, the church, the universe, history, the future, and other matters. We must observe their rituals and submit to their authority structures. Above all, we have to take everything Christianity teaches *literally*. True, different traditions have different required teachings. For one, it's literal transubstantiation of the eucharist. For another, it's literal six-day creation. For another, it's a literal interpretation of the creeds. But on a deeper level they agree: "For us to consider you as Christians," they say, "You have to do it *our way—the literal way.*"

Meanwhile, many of our more skeptical friends present us with the opposite problem. To them, Jesus was nobody special, if he existed at all. In all likelihood, they say, the early Christians were duped by a hoax, and a rather far-fetched one at that. In the eyes of our skeptical friends, we too have been duped. I remember an old colleague of mine who said, "What's a nice guy like you doing in a religion like Christianity?"

Speaking to my skeptical friends, I would have to say that if Jesus didn't actually exist, those who invented him as a fictional character were the most brilliant literary and moral minds I've ever encountered. I was a literature major in college and graduate school, and to this day I'm an avid reader of literature, so my literary knowledge is probably above average. I have to say that I have encountered no fictional character with even a sliver of the density and moral brilliance that I find coming through in Jesus.

So I find it highly likely that Jesus existed and that he was a uniquely extraordinary human being. But that does not mean I take every story about him literally.

I think there is an alternative. I would like to explain this alternative in some detail so that both honest skeptics and convinced Christian literalists can at least properly understand what they're rejecting before rejecting it. A few might even be able to see this option as a way for them to love Jesus sincerely *and* to retain their capacities for critical thinking.

Please understand: if you are a committed Christian literalist and you feel you must take literally every story and Christian teaching, I do not want to take that away from you. I was raised as a literalist myself, so I understand your commitment—and your fears about reconsidering it.[3] But I hope you understand that many people, when given the choice between staying Christian and staying honest, feel that honesty requires them to leave literalist Christianity. They simply cannot honestly interpret all biblical stories as accurate accounts. If you demand from them the literalism that means so much to you, you will drive them away from Jesus. My appeal to you is not to let literalism be to today's Christians what circumcision was in the early church: an option that some make an absolute requirement.

I call this alternative to the conventional literalist approach a *literary approach.* If we take the stories seriously as literary artifacts, we do not need to take them literally as absolutely factual accounts.

The literary approach begins with this assumption: Jesus must have been so extraordinary as to become *legendary*.

The Latin root of the word *legendary* means *read*, so the word suggests, "This person is so extraordinary that people will read about him or her in the future."

The word *legendary* can also mean *fictitious*. And many of us feel the tension between *extraordinary* and *fictitious* every time we read the gospels. When traditional Christians tell us that we have to take every word, every detail as literal fact, we find that hard to do, as much as we might like to. But that doesn't mean we must throw out the gospels—and Jesus—entirely.

Instead, we recognize that a legend is a literary phenomenon, and the development of a legend follows a rather common literary process. First, *someone lives a truly extraordinary life* or does something truly extraordinary. Second, *people tell stories* about that life or deed, creating what we call an *oral tradition*. Third, as the stories of oral tradition are told and retold, *details are changed* due to the faulty memory, the vivid imagination, or the dramatic storytelling instincts of the storytellers—something that I understand well as a preacher and writer (who is also a fisherman).

Fourth, *differing versions of the original story spread*. Fifth, when people are confronted with various versions, they have to decide which one to retell, and *people tend to choose the version that fits best with their feelings* about the hero. If they feel the hero is amazing, they gravitate to the most amazing version of the story. If they feel the hero is ho-hum, they will choose the least amazing version. Sixth, as a result of this "natural selection" based on the hero's emotional impact on hearers, the extraordinary person's *extraordinariness is further embellished*. Seventh, *one or more of the stories is written down*, and it is at that point frozen from further embellishment.

Any student of Jesus can see ample evidence for this embellishment process when comparing the four gospels. We find a prime example as Matthew, Mark, and Luke tell of an exorcism taking place, the expelled demons being sent into some swine, and the swine running off a cliff. (Unless you're familiar with the three accounts, you might want to read all three versions before proceeding: Mark 5:1–20, Luke 8:26–39, Matthew 8:28–34.)

Beyond their shared skeletal outline, the three stories differ in fascinating ways. In Mark's and Luke's versions, one man is exorcised. In Matthew's version, two men are exorcised. There are several other details that differ in the three tellings—which city is the setting (Gedara or Gerasa), what happened after the exorcism, etc.[4] Biblical literalists try to reconcile these accounts, but their efforts feel forced at best. I find it much more plausible to acknowledge that legendary embellishment happens. It is a natural process and an interesting one too.[5]

At the end of the day, it doesn't matter to me whether there was one demoniac or two. It doesn't matter which city was the actual setting. It doesn't matter whether the man was naked before and clothed after, or if the clothing motif is simply a literary way of saying the man became socially acceptable again. It doesn't matter if the demons were literal. It doesn't matter if the pigs committed suicide.

That's because if something truly extraordinary happened, I would expect the story to be told widely, and the more widely it was told, the more embellishment there would be. Some differences in details may have arisen accidentally (someone misremembering the name of the village). Other differences may have been intentional embellishments, but even they don't necessarily falsify the story's meaning. Each different detail points to something that was deeply meaningful to the earliest hearers and tellers of the story, so meaningful that they exaggerated or embellished it to draw attention to it.

So, going back to the exorcism and swine suicide story, could it be that demons were the best available explanation ancient people had for what we call mental illness today? Could demons be a metaphor for chemical imbalances, genetic disorders, and trauma-induced breakdowns—conditions that "possess" people and alter their behavior? And could the man in the story have been suffering from what we might call paranoid schizophrenia, PTSD, or a severe bipolar disorder with mania and anxiety? Could it be that everyone else in the village saw this troubled man as detestable, even subhuman, so much so that they wanted to lock him up and throw away the key? And could it have been that Jesus met him, saw his humanity, and showed the man extraordinary kindness? Could that kindness have helped restore the man's mental health (so he was "clothed and in his right mind," as Luke puts it)? And could it be that as a result, the man was welcomed back into the community?

In this telling, the miracle in the story, the magic in the story, wasn't an exorcism. It was love. Kindness drove out shame and self-hatred. Compassion looked beyond troubled behavior and saw not an evil monster to be chained but a fellow human being to be set free.

In this telling, the diverse stories are not flawed historical accounts any more than an icon is a failed attempt at photo-realism. They are stories that have passed through the enhancement of individual and communal imagination to intensify their meaning, recalling the insight of poet-philosopher Owen Barfield, who said, "Mere perception—perception without imagination—is the sword thrust between spirit and matter," or, we might say, between spiritual meaning and the physical reality we experience day to day.[6]

The story, of course, doesn't stop with the man. What about the pigs? Could the pig incident be another example of legendary embellishment? If so, I suspect another literary process is at work as well, a process that emerges among people in rigid, authoritarian, or oppressive social systems. In such settings, certain truths just can't be said directly.

For example, enslaved people in the American South couldn't say, "Black and white are equal, slavery is evil, and slavery must one day fall," or they would be whipped, tortured, maybe killed. A gifted young woman in a strict patriarchal culture couldn't say, "I'm fully equal to a man," or she would be shunned as un-marriageable and banished from her family. Even today, a political candidate running for the U.S. presidency can't say, "I think contemporary capitalism is destroying the environment," or he will lose the election he hopes to win so that he can prevent capitalism from destroying the environment. (Just as the young English major in a fundamentalist church can't say, "I think there may be some *legendary embellishment* and *literature of the oppressed* at work in the Bible," because he'll be quickly excommunicated.)

Now imagine what happens if oppressed people submit to their oppressors' threats and don't speak the unspeakable truth. Something in them dies. Their submissive silence means compliance, rendering them coconspirators in their own diminishment, while the oppressors' power goes unchallenged. So across cultures, people have found ways to, using Emily Dickinson's apt phrase, "tell all the truth, but tell it slant." They use what Søren Kierkegaard called *indirect communication*. When the *literal truth* is too much to bear or too dangerous to speak, they speak *literary truth*. They tell fictional stories that have nonfictional meanings. They speak in parables. They refuse to be silenced by their oppressors or let their oppressors' lies go unchallenged. They speak their truth in the only way they can. They maintain their voice *and their dignity*.

Going back to the story: Jesus, who actually practices the same love for neighbor that he preaches, has treated a deeply troubled man with decency and dignity. The man has been able to recalibrate in the presence of genuine love, and the community has stopped shaming, shunning, and attempting to incarcerate him. People keep retelling this story because it is extraordinary and meaningful and deserves to be told. It's so wonderful, in fact, that they embellish it imaginatively, not as an act of dishonesty but to intensify the story's meaning. Embellishment, we might say, is the sincerest form of flattery.

And along the way, they realize something. The man wasn't the only one healed in the story. The whole village was healed too. A new level of meaning suddenly appears in the story: *All of us were sick, not just that one man,* they say.

We were not behaving well when we banished him and put him in chains. We were all under terrible stress. We were all out of our right minds. We all had been possessed—by the domination of the Romans. We couldn't trust one another. We couldn't trust ourselves. We, the dehumanized and oppressed, began dehumanizing and oppressing one another. How could we have become so cruel?

Maybe our cruelty has something to do with the fact that the Romans invaded us and now occupy us. They've been exploiting us, dominating us, dehumanizing us, and traumatizing us for generations, and asking us to be happy about it. Under their oppression, we have lived with humiliation for so long that we started blaming and shaming one another. Think of it: we raised pigs, which our own religion forbade us to eat, so we could sell them to the pork-loving Romans. We were so compromised by the Roman economy and stressed by the Roman occupation that we scapegoated this poor man, pouring out all our shame and anxiety upon him, as if doing to him what the Romans had done to us would bring us relief. His sickness was related to our sickness, which was related to the Roman mechanism of domination.

This powerful truth, however, is politically unspeakable, so the story is embellished (in two of the three versions) with the name of the occupying demon horde: *Legion.* The name, of course, evokes the Roman legion. And what better way for oppressed, kosher-keeping Jews to defy the Roman legion than to identify Romans with a herd of demonized pigs and tell a story about the herd making a hasty retreat in a suicidal stampede? Isn't this a powerful image to evoke the occupying army packing up in its ships and leaving their shores? Isn't this a powerful way to say, "We are not crazy. It's the oppressive powers who are crazy, and they've been making us crazy!"? Isn't this a truly satisfying way to speak the unspeakable?

By imagining the Romans gone, the villagers get a chance to imagine themselves without a boot (or knee) on their necks. And just imagining that helps them feel human again: liberated, healed, reconciled with the man they had stigmatized, finally in their right minds.

Again, I am not saying that this literary reading is the only true understanding of the story or even the best one. Nor am I saying that I have reconstructed the objective "historical" report. No: that level of certainty about the past is inaccessible to us all. I only have the stories that were told by the witnesses and then evolved in the hands and minds of people who were deeply moved by them. But that is no small thing. Their very act of literary storytelling was an attempt to convey meaning.

I wonder if you can see it: the point of the story is not to tell us what *factually* happened to a man (or two men) in Gerasa (or Gedara) back then. The point of the story is to help something *actually* happen to us right now, so we too can experience healing, liberation, and reconciliation, so we too can break out of suicidal patterns of trauma and harm.

The story isn't intended to convey mere information. It has a higher goal: to convey, through imagination, an experience of transformation so the reader can taste the wonder of encountering Jesus in person. The *experience of transformation* is the point, the treasure hidden in the field, the pearl of great price.[7]

I hope you can see at least the possibility of what seems so clear to me at this moment: Jesus was the kind of extraordinary person who inspired people so profoundly that they told stories about him. As they did, they sometimes embellished those stories in ways that deepened, expanded, and intensified the meaning he embodied, not to mislead or deceive, but so that the *transforming experience* of him could be conveyed. On top of whatever he did in the literal sense, he inspired people to experience something so meaningful that they had to stretch language beyond mere factual reporting to its fullest literary capacities. Their experience felt like liberation. Like love. Like healing and reconciliation. Like good news of great joy for all creation. They wanted us to experience these things too.

When I read the gospels literally, Jesus becomes not less interesting and wonderful but more, not less real and compelling but more, not less transformative and alive but more. The literary embellishments are not facts but neither are they flaws. They are features, part of the way good storytelling works to set people free.

Saving one man from insanity is a good thing, no doubt. Saving two, better. Inspiring a village to tell a story that reminds them to see the humanity of all outcasts and outsiders, that is even better. And inspiring readers and hearers across the centuries and around the world to better understand themselves, their world, and the mechanisms of domination that plague it— isn't that better still? And even more, empowering them through storytelling to speak unspeakable truths in defiance of oppressive systems, so they can stay sane and humane . . . how amazing is that?

Oppressive forces may have left you feeling banished to a graveyard, excluded from your community, stigmatized as crazy, heretical, or whatever, hiding in shame about who you really are, what you really think, how you really feel. Having internalized your rejection, you may find yourself torturing yourself simply for being honest, as if you've done something wrong by speaking the truth as you see it. Perhaps this story about Jesus can help you see and name the oppressive forces that have deranged you and your community, and perhaps in some way, you can take your place in the community again, clothed and in your right mind.

If literalism is your bridge to Jesus, if it is the only way you access Jesus, then I promise you: I am not trying to take it away from you. I just hope that you will not feel you have to impose your literalism on people for whom it is a barrier, not a bridge, to Jesus.

If you feel that literalism chains you rather than liberates you, if you fear that it is part of the mechanisms of domination that have infected Christianity, that only means you need to leave literalism, not Christianity, and certainly not Jesus.

✢

16

BECAUSE INNOCENCE IS AN ADDICTION, AND SOLIDARITY IS THE CURE

As I've been writing this book, I've had the feeling that something has been hovering just beyond my sight. Yesterday, I got a clearer glimpse of it as I read an interview with a Jewish activist and author named Talia Lavin. Her interviewer asked her, "Is it right to say white supremacy is rooted in Christianity?" She replied, "Christianity in the United States has long been entangled with upholding white supremacy." Then she explained that many Christians "are tempted to put Christian in quotation marks" when they talk about Christian white supremacists, or say that white supremacists aren't real Christians. But this distancing, she said, is a convenience that is in itself a privileged option: "I don't get to disavow Jeffrey Epstein as not really a Jew, or Alan Dershowitz, or anyone else I disagree with."

When Christians separate themselves from fellow Christians who do harm, they imply that "Christianity is a front [*sic*] of all moral good and the true interpretation of Christianity is whatever you consider to be personally most moral," because "Christian white people are afforded the luxury of individuality that is denied for religious and ethnic minorities. Each white person gets to be considered on their own terms, and every other group must answer as a whole for the crimes of the one or the few."[1]

If I hold the term *Christian* for myself and deny it to all those I consider wrong and evil, I am upholding Christianity as the "font of all moral good," *which I know is simply not true.*

My idealized conception of Christianity may indeed be such a "font of all moral good" for me. But if I let the idealized conception of Christianity in my head negate the harm Christians are doing out there in the real world, I am deluding myself and letting my idealized form of Christianity (and myself) off the hook for everything we considered in Part I. When enough people do the same, our idealized conception of Christianity can easily become a Trojan horse: a beautiful construct that conceals armed and dangerous people and ideas.

As Talia Lavin made clear, if I try to sequester myself from all evils associated with Christianity, I am exploiting the "luxury of individuality" and white Christian privilege. Not only that, but distancing myself from "bad Christians" absolves me of the responsibility to confront them as my brothers and sisters for the harm they do. It lets me waltz off the stage feeling *superior* and *innocent*.

But to feel both innocent and superior because of my innocence doesn't seem terribly innocent.

Author and pastor Nadia Bolz-Weber has spoken of "the cult of innocence," a useful phrase that bears some exploration.[2] The cult of innocence, as I understand it, works on a simple formula: *an innocent victim to defend plus an evil villain to oppose equals innocence to enjoy.* (If you like: iv2d + ev2o = i2e.)

This formula has a special appeal to those of us who are associated with Christianity, especially the "orthodox" white Christianity we evaluated in Part I. When we continue to support and be supported by that unrepentant religion, many of us feel guilty and, I think, with good reason.

But nobody likes feeling guilty, especially religious people, and most especially Christians who typically reduce Christian salvation to a cure for guilt. We want the fastest and most effective relief possible.

But is reaching for quick and easy innocence an innocent act?

If we are today's minimizers or deniers of the racism, religious bigotry, and other evils of our Christian ancestors—not to mention our Christian contemporaries, aren't we in some way their allies? By excusing ourselves of responsibility because we were not the active perpetrators of evils (racism, environmental plunder, oppression of women and LGBTQ persons, and so on), do we not become tacit perpetuators of those evils—especially if we continue to benefit from them in some way? In the end, how could a person who avoids admitting truths, taking responsibility, righting wrongs, healing wounds, or correcting errors be truly worthy of the term *innocent*?

So much contemporary Christian behavior, it seems to me, revolves around the cult of innocence. I think of a popular bumper sticker you may still see in many a church parking lot: "Christians aren't perfect, just forgiven." No doubt the person who stuck it on the bumper felt pious in doing so, maybe even humble, since he or she was rejecting the pride of perfection and embracing the humility of forgiveness. Now imagine that bumper sticker on the back of an enslaver's horse-drawn cart in Mississippi in 1845. Suddenly that message doesn't look so innocent, does it?

As soon as I acknowledge this, I can't help but think of the pro-life movement that has so mobilized white conservative Christians in recent decades. It has brought Catholics and Protestants together. It has made Calvinists and Charismatics fierce allies. Isn't that a wonderful thing, to see Christians coming together in unity?

Maybe not, especially if the pro-life movement has become a cult of innocence. I speak as someone who marched in the pro-life movement in its early years.[3] I am not saying that a quest for quick and easy innocence was *the only* motivation that drew me into the movement. It wasn't. I am not even saying this was a *conscious* motivation. It wasn't. But I believe it was a *significant unconscious motivation* for me and for many others, perhaps even most, and for that reason, the objectification of the unborn in the quest for innocence deserves some scrutiny.

Here's my hypothesis: when white Christians see themselves as valiant defenders of vulnerable unborn lives, they identify with the innocence of the victim so that *the innocence or purity of the unborn victim is transfused into them.* This idea of transfused innocence has a special appeal to people like me who were raised with an understanding of Jesus as the innocent victim, whose innocence was transfused (*imputed* was the theological term we used) to us through something called *penal substitutionary atonement.* With one "sinner's prayer," we were "born again" and given a new identity card, so to speak. By a divine transaction we were removed from the list of guilty, hell-bound sinners and shifted to the ledger of innocent, forgiven saints, all through association with an innocent victim.

I think it's important to acknowledge: It is only people who want to be moral (or at least appear moral) who would even desire a shortcut to moral innocence. We might say it is an occupational hazard that morally earnest people uniquely face.[4]

It's easy to see how guilt-inducing, shame-based religious communities would put their members under such constant moral pressure that they would be intensely attracted to the cult of innocence formula. They would not only gain transfused innocence from innocent victims, they would also gain an easily identified enemy, namely those evil villains who don't join in the righteous cause.[5] And what an enemy! Their pro-choice neighbors aren't just garden variety bad: they are *baby-killers*.

But even baby-killer rhetoric gradually loses its original potency. So over time it takes stronger terms to get the same effect. The accusation first inflates from infanticide to genocide, a holocaust of the unborn. Then, when even that language loses power to shame, the Q-Anon conspiracy cult comes along and casts non-pro-lifers as pedophiles and cannibals. It's hard to imagine where it goes next.[6]

By joining the anti-abortion movement, the once guilty are propelled from deep moral unease to a secure position of moral innocence and superiority, with the added social bonding that comes from uniting against a shared enemy whom they depict as murderous and vile. That's quite a set of perks for a very low price of membership (namely, agreeing to vote Republican in the United States—or its counterparts elsewhere).

The cult of innocence extends far beyond the pro-life movement. In fact, it's hard to find an arena of public life where the innocence formula isn't a factor, providing a fast and easy shortcut to both purity and superiority.

Shortcuts, of course, are a form of cheating, and when you try to cheat your way to moral innocence and moral superiority, you're already in deep trouble.

Meanwhile, your quest for instant innocence renders you vulnerable to manipulation by clever religious and political operators who promise booster shots of innocence in exchange for votes or donations. These demagogues exemplify an old saying: *the masses see their religion as true; the elites see all religion as false, and the powerful see all religion as useful.*

History gives many examples of cults of innocence being seized by demagogues who transform them into cults of revenge, cults of hate and violence, suicide cults, even death cults of ethnic cleansing.[7] In fact, as a white American I can imagine these dynamics being in play in my own ancestors who participated in my nation's founding atrocities. The Pilgrims, for example, saw themselves as innocent victims of an oppressive Church of England. The American colonists saw themselves as innocent victims of a tyrannical King George. As Protestants, they saw themselves as victims of

Catholic oppression in Europe, just as the Catholic minority in America could see themselves as victims of Protestant prejudice. Could their self-concept as innocent victims have blinded them to their own moral decay as they victimized, dispossessed, and enslaved their fellow humans during the colonization of Turtle Island?

From Stalin to Hitler to Pol Pot, the twentieth century offers more recent examples of demagogues who cleverly used victimization, vilification, and transfused innocence to gain and keep power. By combining political and economic ideology with religious devotion, they converted millions of seemingly normal people into cultish followers. Obvious twenty-first-century examples prove that the scam still works.

People on both the political left and the political right can be seduced into cults of innocence. They just transfuse their innocence from different victims (and project their shame on different villains). The left defends racial and religious minorities, immigrants, the disabled, LGBTQ persons, Native Americans, science, the environment, social justice activists, and the poor. The right defends the unborn, white people, men, straight people, conservative Christians, the rich, traditionalists, gun owners, and those with little education. What Rabbi Danya Ruttenberg said about Jews can be extended to others: when any group is objectified, their full humanity is devalued.[8] Even when defense of innocent victims begins as pure altruism, innocent love, and a healthy desire to do the right thing, it may also be turned into something else and something less, especially when exploited by demagogues.

Demagogues who constantly objectify and commodify victims function as vampires, parasites sucking innocence from a steady stream of victims in whose names they rally support and raise lots of money and votes.[9] Then they stir up their followers with seemingly righteous indignation against the evil villains, all while deflecting attention from their own wrongdoing, whether they be presidents, pastors, or priests.[10] Their fervor for innocence unites their troops into an innocent army.

Imagine yourself in such an army. Your shared euphoria of innocence and your shared outrage at the enemy's vileness easily render you blind to the harm you are doing and the hypocrite you are becoming. Your shared sense of moral innocence and outrage creates an almost impenetrable force field. Inside the force field, you are utterly righteous, good, and on God's side, with no second thoughts allowed. If an insider dares to question the innocence of your in-group, he or she will be called a traitor, defector, apostate, and heretic and will be banished to the enemy out-group mercilessly.

Of course, there really are innocent victims in the world. And there really are dangerous people who victimize them. And there really are good people who defend innocent victims and confront evil-doers.

But good people do not objectify victims as part of a low-cost strategy to transfuse innocence, vilify opponents, unite followers, amass money and power, and distract from their own crimes, thus playing the hungry wolf under the disguise of an innocent sheep.

For those who do not want to take a shortcut to innocence, there is another way to deal with guilt and shame. This alternative is deeper and better, but harder. The old-fashioned word for it is *repentance*: soberly rethinking the past, facing it without minimizing it, grieving over it, feeling the full measure of the pain of victims, seeking to understand the conditions that prompted the victimizers to do what they did, seeking to address those conditions, healing the wounds, righting the wrongs, changing the systems that protected the wrongdoers, and joining with victims in a struggle for mutual liberation. It's only by doing this real work—this soul work, this holy work, this often agonizing labor of personal and social transformation and rebirth—that we redeem the past and actually become better people: not innocent, not perfect, but *good*.

Let's face it: if we're adults, we have moved beyond innocence.[11] But we still have a chance at goodness and decency. We can be done forever with self-excusing attempts to deny, minimize, or suppress the truth about our Christian ancestors and the unjust systems they created. We can acknowledge how those systems still benefit some of us today, even as they harm others of us. We can stop trumping up nationalistic, racial, and religious myths of superiority. We can stop whitewashing the truth in our children's history books and our clergy's sermons. We can stop anesthetizing our guilty consciences with radio and cable news networks that recount history and current events in an unfair, imbalanced, willfully ignorant, and self-aggrandizing way. We can stop erecting and protecting statues to the architects of a slave society and others whose dirty secrets have come out. We can stop trying to drown out the actual facts in order to delude ourselves with "alternative facts." We can stop playing the victim as a ploy for innocence, and we can stop being parasites on actual innocent victims. We can stop feeling superior because we have bought some inexpensive enemies whose evil we celebrate to make ourselves feel better.

We can—we must—seek treatment for and recovery from our addiction to instant, cheap, convenient innocence, so we can deprogram ourselves from the innocence cult.

Which brings me, at long last, to a candid confession: *one of the prime reasons I sometimes want to leave Christianity is to achieve innocence.*

By distancing myself from a discredited religion, I can feel innocent of its wrongs, weaknesses, and failures.

Paradoxically, this confession gives me one of the most compelling reasons yet for staying Christian. *Staying Christian is a way of leaving the cult of innocence.*

✌

17

BECAUSE I'M HUMAN

Staying Christian is a way of leaving the cult of innocence. When I ended the previous chapter with those words, you may have felt a bit confused. The sentence is cryptic, and intentionally so.

If you see Christian identity as a pathway to innocence—as many if not most Christians currently see it, then in identifying as Christian, you are seeking to be clean and separated from the unclean. Christianity for you is a temple, a sanctuary, a destination where good and innocent people isolate themselves from the dirty contagion of their unclean neighbors so they can enjoy the sweet fellowship of their own kind. It is like the waiting room at a train station where those ticketed passengers who have been certified as pure wait to board their train to be transported to their ultimate destination, heaven, where they will be eternally separated from all filthy, unforgiven sinners.

Those sinners don't know it yet, but they will soon be herded into a very different train bound for a very different destination. Instead of singing in heavenly ecstasy among the innocent, those neighbors will soon be crying and groaning in hellish agony among the damned.

When I put it this starkly, this story sounds far from innocent. But I can tell you as one raised within it, as one deeply formed (and scarred) by it: this is the story that millions of Christians have been taught they must believe. It is a story of separation, superiority, and exclusion.

Purity and innocence might sound like good things if you have never read the story of Cornelius and Peter in Acts 10. Peter was raised in a strict purity culture, so he felt it would pollute him to go into the home of an unclean Gentile like Cornelius.

But Peter had a powerful dream or vision in which God repeatedly commanded him to break one of the purity commandments and thus violate his own innocence. The vision shattered his preconceptions, and so he consented to enter the home of Cornelius, the unclean, the Gentile, the other. There Peter made this disruptive statement: "God has shown me that I should not call anyone impure or unclean" (Acts 10:28). He wasn't just changing his definition of what was clean or unclean; he was leaving that binary behind forever.

Peter continued to struggle with this insight (the cult of innocence dies hard), and later, Paul confronted him about his inconsistency (see Galatians 2). Paul understood the struggle, because he had a disruptive spiritual experience that was remarkably similar to Peter's (see Acts 9:1–19). He was what we would call a religious extremist, a violent fundamentalist terrorist going from town to town to arrest, imprison, and kill members of his purity culture who didn't uphold the high standards of the cult of innocence. He was so convinced of his innocence that he felt justified in committing violence.

Through his visionary disruption, Paul realized how he had been blinded by innocence. He went through a deprogramming process to break free from the cult of innocence. In the aftermath of that deconstruction, everything was different for him, so much so that he changed his name from Saul to Paul.

Paul had his relapses into clean-unclean thinking like the rest of us (see, for example, 2 Corinthians 6:17). But he had the audacity to say that the primary contemporary marker of belonging to the community of innocence—circumcision—"didn't mean anything" (Galatians 5:6). To another group, he wrote, "From now on, we regard no one from a human point of view" (2 Corinthians 5:16). In other words, from his new and higher vantage point, instead of dividing the world into us and them, clean and unclean, we participate in a "new creation" in which we seek to reconcile all people to God and one another. To another community, he said that he had become "all things to all people" (1 Corinthians 9:22), leaving his supremacist identity behind. And to yet another community, he described his mission as breaking down dividing walls of hostility and preaching peace to everyone, everywhere, no exceptions (Ephesians 2:14, 17).

Of course, both Peter and Paul were simply building upon the example set by Jesus himself. He touched lepers, those considered unclean. He protected a woman caught in adultery and challenged her accusers by saying, "Let the one without sin cast the first stone." (Which means, if you read between the lines, that if you consider yourself innocent and pure, *you just might become a killer.*) Perhaps most shockingly, two gospel writers share versions of his encounter with a Gentile mother. The woman begs Jesus to heal her daughter of an "unclean spirit," but he doesn't even acknowledge her presence. It's as if, since the mother herself is one of the unclean Gentiles, neither she nor her unclean daughter is worth his attention.

Then, when the woman is persistent, Jesus uses dehumanizing language to dismiss her. His people are *sheep* (albeit *lost* sheep); she is one of the *dogs*, the unclean. When she is undeterred and speaks as a compassionate mother who loves her little girl, he seems to transform before our eyes: "Oh, woman, your faith is great!" The story is as disturbing as it is dramatic, but I read it as a powerful teaching tool, as if Mark and Matthew know that sometimes, a model of growth helps us more than a model of perfection: "Listen, this lesson is hard to learn. Jesus even struggled to come to it. But watch as he models how you can change your mind and see *the unclean* in a new way."[1]

The famous parable of the good Samaritan offers another approach to the same theme (Luke 10). A priest and a Levite, obsessed with their purity, don't want to touch a body made unclean by blood. The Samaritan—a "dirty half-Gentile"—cares more about his injured neighbor than about remaining clean.[2] That, Jesus says, is what it means to live by the greatest commandment.

In my previous book, *Faith After Doubt*, I described an insight I had when I was nearly finished writing:

> The greatest loss I experienced through doubt was the loss of supremacy, and that loss was one of my greatest gains. (By *greatest*, I mean the loss that was deepest, most significant, most subtle, and most wonderful.) The beliefs I held so piously had, for all my life, without my consent or even awareness, contributed to a sense of religious privilege, superiority, and supremacy. Those beliefs deserved to be doubted, and if I had not doubted them, that supremacy would still reign as a covert monarch in my psyche.
>
> The process of doubt not only dethroned that sense of religious supremacy; it took away the taste for supremacy of any kind. . . . I don't want

to be better than anyone. I don't want to win in any way that makes others lose. . . . Harmony is, at its heart, a state and a stage that loves solidarity, not supremacy. If it took the agony of doubt to bring me to this place, then thanks be to God, and blessed be doubt.[3]

I have to be honest about this: in the way I was introduced to Christianity, to be a Christian required supremacy. Supremacy was baked into our doctrines, our practices, our hymnody, our rituals. Let me be clear: *I do not want to stay Christian if supremacy is part of the deal.*

But here's the problem: if I leave Christianity to achieve innocence, won't I just be seeking to be innocent of Christian supremacy, to be purer than Christianity's purity culture by separating myself from it? Won't I be seeking some status of superiority?

That's why the best option I can see (for myself) is to stay Christian while rejecting supremacy and embracing solidarity instead.

Traditional theologians use another word for solidarity: *incarnation*, the belief that Jesus incarnated or embodied the Spirit of God *in human flesh, which means in solidarity with all humanity* (see John 1:14). Through Jesus, God joins in solidarity, not just with religious humanity, not just with enlightened humanity, not just with pure, innocent, idealized humanity, but with the fleshy, messy, mucky humanity of unclean slobs like us—who lost our innocence long ago.

So what is the opposite of a cult of innocence? Not a super-cult of hyper-innocence, but rather a movement of human solidarity. Staying in solidarity with Christianity with all its faults is a way of staying in solidarity with humanity with all its faults. By staying in solidarity with a flawed and failing religion, I stay in solidarity with all flawed and failing religions, and with our whole flawed and failing species.

That means solidarity with victims, yes, absolutely. But it also means a painful solidarity with villains, for they are humans too, and the line between victim and villain doesn't run neatly between humans but jaggedly within each of us. The path of incarnation and solidarity asks me to identify with humanity without discrimination, reflecting God's nondiscriminatory love.

Yes, of course, I'm deeply embarrassed to be associated with so much of Christianity's past, not to mention its present. Yes, I'm horrified by its potential for even greater evils in the future. So part of me wants to get away from it. Far away.

But where would I go? To some isolated mountaintop retreat to form a new cult of innocence?

Where does the quest for innocence stop? If Christianity is the embarrassment that bothers me, what happens after I disassociate from Christianity? I'm an American. What identity is more fraught with self-delusion and unacknowledged wrongdoing than American citizenship? So does that mean that after I separate myself from my religion, I need to renounce my citizenship?[4]

And then, what's next? I'm a big believer in democracy, so maybe I should identify with democracy in the abstract rather than with a specific democratic nation. But tyrants and con artists win democratic elections every year. Besides, what good is democracy if it is owned and operated by megacorporations and super-rich oligarchs? Democracy, like other political ideologies, is looking almost as compromised these days as Christianity.

Maybe I can proudly identify with an economic ideology. I could find my identity in capitalism or socialism or some clever mix of the two. But I know that no economic system offers us all we need in this dangerous moment of ecological and economic reckoning. There is no innocence there.

Maybe I can withdraw into a professional identity, in my case, as a writer or educator. But I turn around and feel like the same problems I face in Christianity are chasing me in writing and education: balancing art and business, figuring out what to say and teach and why, knowing that people may not want to hear what I really feel needs to be written and taught, dealing with the privilege conferred by degrees and book contracts.

If I keep separating from whatever strikes me as flawed, whatever embarrasses me, I will eventually find myself an isolated misanthrope, hating humanity as a failed project. And I'd be ashamed of that too! As Evangelical theologian Francis Schaeffer often said, "If we demand perfection or nothing, we will have nothing."

So at the end of the day, we all face a similar problem: we can disassociate and re-associate with all kinds of groups and identities, but whatever we disassociate from, still, in the end, we are human. The human problem is still with us, and as professor Kate Bowler aptly puts it, there is "no cure for being human."[5] Any religion that promises otherwise is, recalling the Genesis story (3:5), a serpent in the garden.

You and I are two of the approximately 107 billion *Homo sapiens* who have ever lived and the roughly 8 billion alive today. For all our amazing qualities, we humans remain a hot, dangerous mess. We are proud of our brains, but our brains are steered by biases. We are proud of our accomplishments, but we have an ugly side that is all the more dangerous the more it is denied. We can be so kind, but we can also be so cruel. We can comport ourselves with wisdom and dignity one minute and with folly and sleaze the next.

And here's the real kicker: even if some small sect of us were to achieve some level of innocence or goodness or decency, if other humans blow up the world, we blow up with them.

There's no escaping it. We're stuck with each other, and we're stuck with ourselves. We are inescapably, incurably human.

I'm often asked if I have hope for Christianity. These days, I say, "My hope for Christianity depends on my hope for humanity, and we humans are not trending well."

And in that realization, I find a compelling reason to stay Christian.

The New Testament, like the Hebrew Scriptures, is realistic about humanity. It warns of the possibility of self-destruction and it points to the possibility of new beginnings. Staying Christian as an act of solidarity is a way of saying, in the words of songwriter Michael Franti, "This world is so f*cked up but I ain't ever giving up on it."[6]

To quantify our options as humans:

1. There is no way. Humanity is doomed.
2. There is one way, and Christianity (or some other single religion or ideology) is it.
3. There is one way, and it is the rejection of all religion.
4. There may be a way to draw the best resources we can from all our traditions, not to cure us of being human, but to help us become humane, because in the end, we humans are all connected, woven, as Dr. King said, in an inescapable web of mutuality.

The only option I can live with is option 4. So I pick up the work of solidarity in my Christian tradition, and I do so looking for collaborators in other traditions, explicitly religious and not. If we are to avoid self-destruction, it will require solidarity across all our traditions.

Maybe you are beginning to see it now, as if you're coming over the crest of a hill with a new vista in front of you. If you choose solidarity, instead of pulling away from those you once suspected, avoided, vilified, or rejected, you see them as neighbors. You smile. You talk. You try to collaborate for the common good in whatever ways you can. When you disagree, as you must, you do so boldly but also graciously, not burning bridges, not breaking solidarity. They may be your opponents for the moment, but you don't write them off as enemies.[7]

When you embrace solidarity, you embrace humanity, including Muslim, Jewish, Buddhist, Hindu, Sikh, humanist, and atheist humanity, and including the humanity of those Christians whose behavior consistently prompts you to ask if you can stand staying Christian for even one more second. You stop seeking innocence through separation. Instead, you seek love through solidarity.[8]

If you choose solidarity . . . in the way modeled by Jesus, then you don't have to stop being Christian. In fact, you may have just become a better Christian than you've ever been.

As you move forward, you may have to politely pass through a crowd of religious company men who tell you to go away because you don't pass their purity test. You may have some old friends reject you, and you may struggle to keep accepting them anyway. You may have to find new teachers and mentors who can walk with you toward Christianity's deeper, wider heart. If you learn to center there, to dwell there, to rest there, you will find a trap door, if you will, a door that leads into deep darkness. In that darkness, after a long, long silence, you will hear a gentle sound, a faint but beautiful song, a mysterious music that beckons you.

If you dare to follow that summons deeper into the darkness of unknowing, eventually you will come into a new place, a good place, a place not of elite religiosity but of shared humanity.

You will look around and feel that all are welcome here. They have come from different places, but by the same path, the path of love. Muslims have come in their caravan of love. Jews have pursued the Torah of solidarity. Buddhists have followed the noble truth of compassion. Sikhs have learned to see no stranger, and Hindus have descended into essential oneness. Atheists and agnostics have discovered in humanism a path into our common humanity.

In that great space of harmony, you will discover a unity that thrives in diversity and a diversity that contributes to unity, like many instruments and voices coming together to make the same glorious music, full of aching joy and soaring sorrow. In that space, we will call one another family, and words like *Christian, atheist, Jew, Hindu*, or *Muslim* will feel like precious artifacts from our childhood. We will remember those mementos, we will cherish them, for we are who we are because of them. But as adults, we can no longer serve walls that keep us apart. Instead, they are windows, doors, or portals through which we encounter one another, heart to heart. We will "become all things to all people," united in the solidarity of love.

When you find that this option of solidarity is open to you, this option of going to the deepest and most genuine core of your Christian tradition and there finding a love that connects you to everyone and everything, everywhere . . . you don't need to go anywhere else.

Of course, you can if you want to. But here is a way of staying Christian that connects you to others in a quest for solidarity rather than separating you from them in a quest for innocence, dominance, or supremacy.

This feels to me like the way of Christ. This feels like the way of life. This is why I stay and how I stay.

≫

18

BECAUSE CHRISTIANITY IS CHANGING
(FOR THE WORSE AND FOR THE BETTER)

I wish you could see what I see.

It's a story that's been unfolding since long before we were born.

Right at this point where major sectors of Christianity have never looked more misguided or regressive (at least, not in our lifetimes), we are closer to a breakthrough than we've been in a long, long time.

The theological progress we've made is breathtaking. Most of that progress is due to women, people of color, LGBTQ folks, and other previously excluded minorities who have, against all odds, gained a hearing. It's like they've gone out into the fields and harvested an enormous supply of fresh food. They've brought their bounty to a huge kitchen table and generously invited everyone, including straight white men like me who created and presided over the mess we're in, to help cook up a nourishing and tasty feast to enjoy together. Their hospitality is most gracious. It is truly Christian.

I expected them to resent me and people like me. I feared they would bar me from the house just as white patriarchal Christians in the past did to them. But as a wise Black woman once said to me, "No, Brian. We don't want to treat white people the way they treated us. Why would we ever want to behave like white people, after all they've done to us?"

Their gracious welcome, of course, doesn't mean they don't feel a certain suspicion. They have every reason to expect that white Christian men like me will come in and try to take over. They've seen it happen so many times; they know we can't help it. It's how we've been socialized since childhood.

So they have every right to test me, to challenge me, until I prove that I won't ruin the party by dominating the conversation and ordering people around. They have every right to be tough on me and help me see what I have been trained my whole life not to see.

Now imagine if, at this critical moment, under these unprecedented circumstances, I decide to leave Christianity. Right when I'm being welcomed to what my friend John Pavlovitz calls "a bigger table" by the people who have every reason to reject me . . . what if that's when I decide to walk away from the table forever?[1] Wouldn't they have every reason to wonder if I simply didn't want to be a Christian under the new terms of equality?

Howard Thurman, one of America's greatest theologians said, "By some amazing but vastly creative spiritual insight the slave undertook the redemption of a religion that the master had profaned in his midst."[2] If that process of redeeming Christianity is continuing (as I know it is), can you see how tragic—even ungrateful—it would be to leave Christianity now, of all times? Why not give the voices of the oppressed at least a few centuries to heal what the oppressors desecrated for the better part of twenty centuries? Why not join the party they are now throwing, no longer presiding as a master or gatekeeper but humbly and gratefully receiving hospitality as a brother, sister, neighbor, friend, gratefully cutting carrots or washing dishes as part of the family?

Yes, we can, we should, we must withdraw our endorsement of white colonial patriarchal Christianity in all its forms. Yes, we must withdraw every dollar and every minute of attention we can from industrial, Theo-Capitalist Christianity as it sanctions the destruction of the earth and the exploitation of the poor. Yes, we must break free from axial age Christianity as it incarcerates the human imagination. But no, we cannot reject the Christianity being redeemed and reborn at this historic moment through the "vastly creative spiritual insight" of those who saw the underbelly of the old dominant forms of the faith and decided not just to curse the darkness but to start lighting candles and become something better.

The same could be said when we think of Pope Francis. Of course, he isn't saying and doing everything some of us wish he would. He knows he has to bring his people along at a pace that won't blow up the whole Catholic Church, and I can only imagine the threats and resistance he faces behind the scenes. But when you read his letter to the world, *Laudato si*, don't you feel how incredibly blessed we are to have him at a time of ecological and economic collapse? And when you read its sequel, *Fratelli tutti*, don't you see it as a call to exactly the kind of solidarity we dreamed of in the previous chapter?

In light of these remarkable breakthroughs, how could we give up now?

Across every traditional Christian denomination, there are widespread calls for change. Imaginative scholars, liturgists, organizers, networkers, and pastors are creating resources and spaces for beautiful new things to be born. And I've been privy to parallel conversations among Mormons, Unitarians, and other "outliers" to traditional Christianity too.

I introduced you earlier to my Inner Fundamentalist. Now I must bring out of the closet my Inner Cynic. "Nice try, Brian," he's sneering. "But you seem to be forgetting that Pope Francis is opposed by any number of Steve Bannons, Cardinal Raymond Burkes, and other right-wing Catholics who lead powerful universities, think tanks, foundations, and media outlets. Francis is one of the most hated people on the planet![3] And you're not too popular with lots of folks yourself. Right after the wave of creativity you're celebrating, you know there'll be a backlash that will make heads spin. It's already underway."

Then he continues, "And sure, you can celebrate Black, Brown, Asian, Indigenous, feminist, womanist, and queer theologians all you want. But nearly all the money and power are still in the hands of straight, white, patriarchal Christian nationalists who are drunk on the innocence you talked about a couple chapters ago. They won't go down without a fight. You shouldn't be so naive, especially at your age."

Sometimes the only way to respond to my Inner Cynic is by being even more cynical. So I might counter like this: "All the more reason for progressive Christians like me to stay. If the white Christian nationalists gain even more power, if they succeed in recruiting the next couple of generations to their even more virulent forms of combat Christianity, where will we be then?"

My Inner Cynic responds, "No, you should pull away from the whole Christian project. It's unsalvageable. Let it collapse. Let it die."

To which I respond, "Wow. Someone at your age shouldn't be so naive. If Christianity collapses, don't you think that something even worse will fill the void? Don't you realize that white post-Christian nationalism and other extremist ideologies are lined up on the internet, auditioning every day for their role as the successor to Christianity?"[4]

My Inner Cynic can mention the grip that any number of Franklin Grahams, Jerry Falwells, Pat Robertsons, Mike Huckabees, Albert Mohlers, Michele Bachmanns, Eric Metaxases, and Steve Bannons hold over major sectors of Christianity. And I agree: it's past time for us to renounce their combative forms of Christianity and shake the dust from our feet as we do. But how foolish would we be to walk away from the new kinds of Christianity being explored by Wil Gafney, Willie Jennings, Barbara Holmes, Ray Aldred, Kaitlin Curtice, Randy Woodley, Mark Charles, Anthea Butler, Cornel West, Mabiala Kenzo, Emmanuel Katongole, Lisa Sharon Harper, William Barber, Larycia Hawkins, Jacqui Lewis, Michael-Ray Mathews, Traci Blackmon, Yvette Flunder, Jojo Fung, Sivin Kit, Otis Moss III, Claude Nikondeha, Carlos Rodriguez, Bruce Reyes-Chow, and so many other people of color around the world? How stupid would we be to walk away from the Christianity being redeemed by LGBTQ folks, so newly out of the closet? How stupid would we be to walk away from Pope Francis—right when he needs more people encouraging him forward to counteract all those tugging him back?

These redeemers of Christianity are out there, by the hundreds, thousands, and tens of thousands. Catholic and Protestant, Pentecostal and Mainline, Eastern Orthodox and other . . . I know them. Some are heads of communions, bishops, seminary presidents, and professors, with well-known names, with best-selling books and big platforms. Some are pastors and church planters, leading and forming faith communities of all shapes, sizes, and denominations. Some are nuns, friars, Catholic workers, organizing for the common good. Some are podcasters, publishers, bloggers, producing creative content to help in the transition process. Some are artists, integrating needed truth with arresting beauty. Most are quiet people, living ordinary lives of extraordinary love and grace. When they're attacked, they keep moving forward with humble, gracious confidence. When they're discouraged, they find new inner strength. When they think about leaving Christianity, which probably happens quite often, they say, "Not today. Not me." You know this is true, because there's a good chance that you're one of them.

When I think of these people in the kitchen, sharing recipes and ingredients, cooking together, laughing and singing as the house fills with the scent of something fine . . . I can actually imagine significant sectors of Christianity becoming Christian.

It will never be perfect. Of course. It's a human enterprise, and we humans complicate everything. But at least this emerging Christianity could become humble and teachable, curious and self-critical, creative and humane, diverse and harmonious. How could I leave that creative ferment, especially now?

Now: when a gifted team of diverse, multi-generational, transdenominational theologians are engaged in exactly the creative theological scholarship we need, and . . .

Now: when deeply rooted mystics, educators, and spiritual directors are developing and disseminating the powerful spiritual training we need, and . . . [5]

Now: when compassionate workers for justice are doing the brilliant organizing we need to help the poor and vulnerable, not just through charity, but also through political advocacy, systemic change, social entrepreneurship, and both economic and ecological activism, and . . . [6]

Now: when Christian peacemakers are calling us to stop killing and study war no more, and . . . [7]

Now: when musicians, poets, artists, and web developers are engaging in the profound artistic and liturgical innovation we need, and . . . [8]

Now: when creative pastors and church planters are refusing to wait for somebody else to do what needs to be done and are saying, "Well, I'll go first. Let's start a new congregation. Let's add a new service. Let's mentor some new leaders. Let's dream and experiment and do what needs to be done," and . . .

Now: when Christianity's disturbing behavior and vital statistics are getting bad enough that we may be ready for the change we need. As Rev. Stephanie Spellers wisely said: "A church that has been humbled by disruption and decline may be a less arrogant and presumptuous church. It may have fewer illusions about its own power and centrality. It may become curious. It may be less willing to ally with the empires and powers that have long defined it. It may finally admit how much it needs the true power and wisdom of the Holy Spirit."[9]

Now: when millions and millions of Christians are each, in their own families and neighborhoods and businesses and networks, embodying the genuine Christian character and solidarity we need.

Back in Chapter 8, I spoke of Christianity as a failed religion. I was echoing Catholic novelist Walker Percy, who spoke of "the egregious moral failure of Christendom" and especially "the failure of Christendom in the United

States," where "White Americans have sinned against the Negro from the beginning and continue to do so, initially with cruelty and presently with an indifference that may be even more destructive."[10] What do you do when your religion is failing? Do you leave it, like a person running from a crime scene, so you won't be implicated? Or do you stay, bear witness, and help right the wrongs—if you possibly can? What do you do when your nation is failing, or your family is failing, or your company is failing, or your economy is failing . . . or you are failing? Do you give up, or do you find the people working to make things better and work alongside them as long as you possibly can?

Maybe in five hundred or a thousand years we should give up. But surely not now. Surely not *now*, when Christianity is changing for the worse in some quarters—and the better in others.

≥⍥

19

To Free God

Liam was formerly a pastor but left church work—and church attendance—a few years ago. He recently chatted with me by videoconference from his home in the Midwest.

"Funny thing for me," he said, smiling and shaking his head. "I still really believe in Jesus. But God . . . not so much anymore."

"Tell me about that," I replied.

"Jesus, the man, is still absolutely compelling to me," Liam began. "Now more than before, actually. I feel like it took me leaving the church to really see him for who he was. I feel like I'm starting to *get* him now, not as a ticket to heaven and all that, but as a wise and courageous man who used his life to make a difference. I want nothing more than to follow his example in the way I live. But the idea of a Big White Guy on a Throne in the Sky . . . that stopped working for me a long time ago. It's really why I left the pastorate. I'm just not sure if there's any room in Christianity for somebody like me."

Liam explained that his "God problem" wasn't just about how conventional God concepts had caused him personal harm. Nor was his problem only about the harm his parishioners experienced, even though that harm was, he surmised, significant. He also felt that these God concepts pose a credible threat to human survival going forward.

I agree with Liam. If God is entirely separate from the physical world, then the world is just stuff—profane, cheapened, easy to exploit. Besides, if God plans to destroy the world, we humans might as well exploit it all we can while we still have the chance. If God is in control of the world like an engineer controlling a big machine, when we or our neighbors suffer, we can logically conclude that human suffering is God's will. If God dominates the world and everything in it with an iron fist (or rod, as in Psalm 2:9 and Revelation 2:27), we may find ourselves more amenable to authoritarians who do the same, especially if they hold up Bibles in front of churches. If God chooses some for privilege and abandons others for damnation, God sets an example of us/them thinking that only the worst of us will follow. If God likes to save people from predicaments through magic skyhooks, it becomes more spiritual for humans to pray for a miracle rather than to engage in hard work, diligent study, wise planning, and collaboration. These and other understandings might have been problematic in the best of times, but they're downright life-threatening in times of climate change, resurgent autocracy, racist nationalism, gross economic inequality, and weapons of mass destruction.

Liam is not alone in his concerns. For many of us, staying Christian is only possible if we do something about the traditional supreme being concept that has dominated most of Christian theology for most of its first two thousand years. In spite of whatever benefits conventional notions of God have provided in the past, they are outweighed by the costs going forward.

That's why Liam, like several of my friends, says that "most days" he is an atheist.

The truth is, I too am an atheist—in regard to the slaveholder's God, the MAGA-church God of the white Christian nationalists, the prosperity gospel get-rich-quick God, the biblical literalist easy-answer God, the Theo-Capitalist God with the big invisible hand, and the right-wing God who is really upset about abortion but doesn't give a damn about racism, environmental plunder, or authoritarianism. Those are just a few of the many gods I don't believe in, echoing Frank Schaeffer, who describes himself as an atheist who believes in God.[1]

Liam is right: that old Big White Guy on a Throne in the Sky has to go.

As Catholic theologian Hans Urs von Balthasar said, "Atheism can be like salt for religion. It is negative theology posited in the most absolute way. Most of the time, psychologically speaking, atheism represents a disappointment with the narrowness and limitations of a certain concept of God."[2] Even though I share with my atheist friends "a disappointment with the narrowness and limitations" of many concepts of God, I do still dare to believe there is a *You* to address in the universe, a Presence, a Love that loves through all loves, a radiant and holy mystery, the Spirit of life and creativity, the Wisdom woven into the pattern of the universe, the "still, small voice" that beckons creation, including me, toward love and maturity. I can't help but see that *You* shining through in the face of Jesus . . . and through the lives of holy, compassionate, and wise people I meet everywhere. That *You* that I encounter in life is far better than the *He* that many of us were taught in church.

No wonder that, in the primal story of the burning bush, when Moses invited the mysterious presence to reveal its name, the answer was, "I am who I am," or "I will become who I will become"—or, possibly, "I am being itself," or maybe even, "That's for me to know and you to find out."

I am open to the criticism that my use of the personal pronoun *You* may simply be a projection of *me* as a personal being. To some degree, projecting upon God what I know best (my own limited human experience) is inevitable; it's all that I as a creature have to work with. So I give myself permission to do so, expecting some kind of correspondence between my life, consciousness, and relationality and the life, consciousness, and relationality of the *You* whom I have encountered in luminous bushes (and kind faces) everywhere. Even as I reverently dare to address that *You* in prayer, I remember that correspondence is not equivalence. I remember that all theological language is metaphorical—pointing vaguely toward its subject with limping metaphors (as C. S. Lewis said) but never capturing and containing the *You* who is addressed.[3]

So here I am. I find myself in relationship with this insistent *You* that I encounter in the universe.[4] I can't help but be interested in the *You* encounters shared by my contemporaries today and my ancestors through the ages. I don't expect anyone, including myself, to have the final answers. Nor do I expect everyone to use the same language and metaphors to describe their experiences and insights. After all, we inhabit different metaphorical worlds. For example, in one time and culture, it would make sense to talk about God as a shepherd. In, say, the Arctic, where there are no sheep, such language would be meaningless, so perhaps sled dog keeper or seal whisperer would be more appropriate. Each metaphor would have strengths and weaknesses, for God could not be *exactly* like a shepherd or sled dog keeper or seal whisperer in every way.

For people in a culture of dominant patriarchy, of course their metaphorical language for the *You* would be patriarchal. And for people in a prescientific age, an age of magic, of course their descriptions of the *You* would be magical. And if they lived in a monarchy and a shame-based culture, of course their description of the *You* would carry monarchal and shame-based undertones. How could it be otherwise?

If that's the case, why should *their* patriarchal, magical, monarchal, shame-based worldview dominate *our* approach to the *You* in our context? We don't let the assumptions of our ancestors about anatomy, psychology, medicine, or physics dominate our thinking and work in these fields today. Why should we be required to let their theological assumptions dominate . . . especially when some of those assumptions have contributed to the crisis of faith explored in the first ten chapters of this book?

Now, let's flip that line of thinking. Just because our ancestors' views of anatomy, psychology, medicine, physics, or theology have proven insufficient, that doesn't mean we give up on anatomy, psychology, medicine, physics, or theology as failed enterprises. Instead, we honor the efforts of our ancestors by building upon them, which often means moving beyond them. They set an example of thinking creatively within their context. We honor and follow their example, not by endlessly repeating their words and formulations but by thinking and speaking as creatively in our context as they did in theirs. (For this reason, among others, we respectfully yet critically study the work of our ancestors in their context, in hopes that their successes and failures can guide us in our own creative endeavors.) That means that we are not only *free* to adapt and experiment in theology, as we are in other fields; we also have a *moral obligation* to do so . . . especially in light of the harm we surveyed in the first ten chapters of this book.

We may build upon our ancestors' work wisely, in ways that enhance conviviality. We may build upon it foolishly, in ways that reduce conviviality. But not building upon it at all? That seems foolish from the start.

Right now, the old metaphors and notions are holding on like a big white guy clutching at his throne of power. Traditionalists fear that if the old metaphors, categories, frameworks, and language no longer dominate, they will lose the *You* toward which they did their best to point. So, the traditionalists issue this ultimatum: *Either speak of God using old language and metaphors or don't speak of God at all.* (*Quite a fragile God*, I'm tempted to say, *to be so dependent on one set of metaphors.*)

Many atheists issue the same ultimatum as the traditionalists, but they go with the second option—*don't speak of God at all*—in hopes that talk of God will go the way of alchemy, phlogiston, cassette tapes, and landlines.[5]

But I think we have a third option.

The medieval mystic Meister Eckhart famously prayed, "God, rid me of God."[6] Now, seven centuries later, we need to echo his prayer with resolve—to find new names, metaphors, frameworks, languages, and contemplative practices that will help us experience the God who rids us of the God we need to be rid of.

This is a delicate labor that must be entered into with appropriate humility, reverence, and awe.

I know this sounds complicated. It is. I understand why some of my friends want to be done with any talk of God for good, under whatever names or metaphors. And I understand why others of my friends want to cling to conventional notions, using the Bible and Christian tradition as the eternal ceiling for any and all conversation about God. God is perfectly defined there, they say, *in black and white*, so there's no need for new approaches. Just read and repeat, again and again. Stay safely under that ceiling, they warn, or you will lose God, the Bible, the tradition, everything.

But if we dare take a third option—of finding language appropriate to our context to describe the insistent holy mystery that is inherent to our experience of life—we have the opportunity to rediscover the *You* in ways that are as inspiring and liberating in our world as the old metaphors were for our ancestors in their world. We will indeed lose the Bible and the tradition as our *ceiling*, as we were warned. But we will get them back as our *floor*, the ancient foundation to build upon, the soil in which we plant new seeds, the launchpad from which we boldly go where no one has gone before.

When we make this subtle but profound switch from ceiling to floor (or soil), suddenly, before our eyes, the Bible and tradition are transformed into a library of texts that demonstrate the very opposite of what the authority figures told us. These texts and traditions do not reveal one final, ever-unchanging understanding of God. They reveal how notions of God have always been evolving over time, how they constantly grow, relapse, recover, adjust, and grow some more.

It's there *in full color*.

The process begins with hunter-gatherers in a garden, communing with a loving, creative presence in the cool of the day, naked and not ashamed, living a spirituality with no scripture, no temple, no clergy, no creed, no codified beliefs, only an ethical imperative to live in a care-taking relationship with one's environment and fellow creatures, modeling the care of the Creator.

Early humans decide they don't want to live within these creaturely limits, and soon they develop various notions of violent gods that sanction and animate their violent societies.

Faith in a god who loves all people begins to emerge slowly and fitfully, three steps forward and two steps back. In this ongoing conversation, Jesus appears, and he invites his contemporaries to imagine something bigger than God as currently understood.

What could be bigger than God, you ask?[7] Jesus called it *the kingdom of God*, the idea that God and creation are part of one integrated reality that unites all things in one beloved community. In this beloved multi-ethnic, multi-species ecological community, God shares in our experience, in our joys, in our heartbreaks, in the suffering and death of every person, even every sparrow. Finding God with us in our suffering and death robs them of their sting and power to terrorize us. We feel that we are taken up into God's deathless life. God is no longer simply a singular holy *You*, as wonderful as that might be. God is a holy and unbounded *We*, a community or web of life in which we are all included and related, rendered *one another*, and one.

The mystery of the Trinity can be seen as an expression of this three-stage metamorphosis. We begin with *the Father*, the ancient patriarchal understanding of God who rules from above with almighty power. The Father joins with a human mother to give birth to *the Son*, the incarnated expression of God in human flesh and culture, not ruling from above but serving, suffering, and laboring nonviolently among us and with us for a new kingdom, which is a new age, which is the age of love. Then the Son says we are better off not holding on too tightly even to him. He is not the destination but the way. It is better for him to leave the scene so we can welcome *the Spirit*, God blowing like wind, shining like light, flowing like water and wine, incandescent like fire . . . not localized in one human body or group but alive through all the universe and in all our experience, leading us and guiding us into new understandings, world without end. Ironically (or perhaps fittingly), to live in a universe penetrated with Spirit sounds very much like the primal story of people in a garden, walking with God in their day-to-day natural life, without temples, laws, crusades, inquisitions, shame, or fear.

Fr. Richard Rohr often says, "The steps toward maturity are necessarily immature," and he often quotes St. Thomas Aquinas: "Quid quid recipitur ad modum recipientis reciptur (What is received is received in the manner of the receiver)." So if the trajectory of human development starts with interpersonal or group-on-group violence and moves toward universal love, of course the earliest, immature steps would be violent and exclusionary, and people at those stages would see the world—and God—through violent, discriminatory eyes. (No doubt, whenever we regress toward greater violence and exclusion, our concepts of God follow.)

If we walk this path through immaturity, we will come to acknowledge that all our theological language (including the word *God* itself) is poetic. We use words to point to encounters and relationships that those words can never fully capture.

Our language is also poetic in the creative sense: it is an attempt to create something. (The Greek word *poiema* means creation.)

When we argue about God, we aren't simply arguing about an abstract concept. We are also (perhaps even *primarily*) arguing about what kind of life, culture, and world we want to create, which explains why our theological arguments are often so heated. What seems like esoteric debate about highly speculative matters is actually a practical, down-to-earth contest about how we and our descendants will live. Will we conserve the Christian supremacies of the past—male, white, Christian, and human—that helped create the harm we surveyed in Part I? Or will we create new metaphors, language, and formulations that are more humane, more ecological, more generous, just, and regenerative? Every statement about God, every argument, every fine distinction is, in this light, doubly poetic: both highly *metaphorical* and highly *creative*.

When you see it this way, you see that theology, religion, and spirituality aren't just preoccupied with God and mystical esoterica. They are vitally engaged with the creation of the future. They are evolutionary endeavors. By seeking to understand what is essential and ultimate, what is right and good and beautiful, what is wise, what beckons us forward morally, what is, in traditional terms, *God's will*, we are setting the course for our evolution. If our understandings of God do not grow, neither will we. We may not even survive.

It is risky to speak or write about God in fresh ways, building upon the past rather than being boxed in by it. The threat of misunderstanding and censure tempts many of us to participate in a conspiracy of ambiguity, using the word *God* and leaving room for both the Big White Guy on a Throne in the Sky and something beyond it. Perhaps that has been a necessary strategy in the short run. But in light of the ways the Big White Sky Guy has been weaponized to create an unjust and unsustainable world, we need to graduate from the conspiracy of ambiguity into a healing spiritual clarity as we move forward. (This is a theme we'll return to in Chapter 21.) I don't know exactly how we will do it. But I know it must be done.

In this way, we are free, if we so choose, to stay Christian, because we are free to let our old God concepts die and see what rises from the tomb.

Think of a couple in a bad marriage. They gradually come to realize that, if they want to save the marriage, they must set one another free from the dysfunctional roles and expectations in which they hold one another captive, as if in a cage. In a similar way, we can uncage God from at least some of the roles and expectations we have constructed. We can even, if we need to and dare to, free God from the word *God* itself.

That will take faith, of course, perhaps faith we do not yet have, faith that the reality to which we point will still be there if we stop using the same old words to do the pointing.

In this light, whether we're speaking of individuals like Liam or whole communities or even civilizations, we humans may need periods of religious modesty and silence, maybe even atheism—whether for three days or three years or three decades or three centuries. That way, the dust can settle and the familiar god-talk can fade to silence, and perhaps then we can get a fresh glimpse of what is really there.

What will it be? What will we see? On a Throne in the Sky, warning us that if we think a new thought or doubt an old thought, we will be dumped from the frying pan into the fire, forever? *Not so much*, to use Liam's understated words.

As the early Christian scholar Origen said, "Wherever divine wisdom leads us, let us go."[8]

❧

20

BECAUSE OF FERMI'S PARADOX
AND THE GREAT FILTER

Enrico Fermi is best known for inventing the first nuclear reactor. But he is also known for a question he raised casually over lunch one day in 1950.[1]

If the universe is as old and as vast as it appears to be, Fermi wondered, why haven't we been visited by alien life forms? Intelligent species should have evolved on countless planets across our galaxy long before we evolved here on earth. Many should have developed space travel. Where are they?

His question is now known as the *Fermi Paradox*. And one answer to the Fermi Paradox is known as the *Great Filter*. Simply put, if intelligent life has evolved on many planets, perhaps it always self-destructs before it gains the capacity for interstellar travel. Perhaps what we see happening to us on earth—that our technological evolution has outpaced our spiritual or moral evolution—has happened to every other species. Perhaps every intelligent species develops weapons-making skills that outstrip its capacity for peace-making. Perhaps every intelligent species masters the skills of exploiting its planet before it develops the wisdom to preserve its planet. Perhaps every successful species falls victim to overshoot and collapse.[2] Perhaps that's why we haven't been visited. Perhaps that's why we appear to be alone—because we are.

That grim thought, of course, presents us with a chilling question: are we about to follow the normal pattern? Our species, for the first time in our 200,000-year evolutionary history, has the technology to catastrophically de-stabilize our ecosystems and to wipe ourselves out with weapons of mass destruction. Have we reached the Great Filter?

Once you've asked this question, you can't un-ask it.

If humanity destroys itself, religion will likely be the chaplain, providing prayers, blessings, encouragement, and forgiveness to escort the species toward its death. Politics will almost surely pull the suicide trigger or press the suicide button. Economics will likely provide the motive for the crime. And science will have designed the bullet and the gun, or the bomb or the virus, that will do us in. Our problems, once again, are not just religious problems. Nor are they merely political, economic, or scientific problems. Our problems are human problems, expressed in all these different fields of human endeavor.

Here's where I have to laugh, in part, to keep from crying. Having grown up in an apocalyptic religion—obsessed with the rapture, the end times, and heaven, and singing "I'll Fly Away"—I suddenly find myself in an apocalyptic world from which I cannot fly away!

Suddenly, as if I'm experiencing deja vu from my Christian childhood, I find myself thinking in terms of *salvation, repentance, good news,* and *spiritual formation.* If we humans are on a path to partial or full self-destruction, we need *salvation . . .* to be turned around or turned away from our suicidal path. That salvation will require radical *repentance . . .* doubting, rethinking, and turning from the destructive assumptions and worldviews that got us into this mess. That repentance will prepare us for *good news . . .* a vision for a new way of life that is regenerative rather than suicidal. And this good news will require a new kind of *spiritual formation* so that we can develop the personal and social habits of this new, non-suicidal way of life.

With our human predicament in mind, when I survey the biblical library and all the other resources of the Christian tradition, a realization hits me like a bucket of ice water: *I would be a fool to walk away from this incredibly rich treasury of wisdom at this time, when I as an individual—and we as a species—need it so much.*

No, I don't need an evacuation-plan gospel that tells me this world is hopelessly sinking, so I should give up on it and jump into the lifeboat bound for heaven. Instead, I need a transformation-plan gospel, the kind that inspired our ancestors stuck in their own existential threats to seek a way when no way was visible.

No, I don't need the Bible as an inerrant revelation of simplistic answers so I can live in blissful denial about life's complexity and perplexity. Instead, I need it as a library of questions and arguments among communities of people who sought a better way of living in harmony with themselves, one another, the earth, and God.

No, I don't need a comforting spirituality as a tranquilizer to calm my imagination and soothe me into compliant complacency. I need a spirituality that is rich soil in which I can plant new seeds of contemplation from which wise, creative action will arise.

No, I don't need the church as a warehouse that seeks to contain me and entertain me until I can be shipped to my final destination. Instead, I need a community of spiritual activists who share a vision of a bold exodus from systems of oppression, a wilderness journey toward a better day, when we will turn swords and guns into garden tools and musical instruments.

No, I don't need prayers that reassure me that the future is pre-determined, God is in control, and God will fix everything if I keep my head down and stay out of trouble. Instead, I need prayers that transform me and my companions into spiritual revolutionaries who create good trouble, as John Lewis said, building a new world, one brick and garden at a time, in the ruins of this old world that is rapidly falling apart around us.

No, I don't need sermons that interpret the Bible as the biblical literalists do, ignoring its literary depth. Nor do I need lectures that reduce the Bible as cosmological literalists do, flattening it to exclude any spiritual depth. Instead, I need sermons that fulfill Catholic scholar John Haught's sage prescription: providing us not only with *big history* but also with *thick history*, history that not only sees the outside of the universe but also the inside with its rich subjective reality, depth of thought, emotion, value, and relationships, what Teilhard de Chardin called the *noosphere.*[3]

No, I don't need a Jesus whose job is to police the gates of heaven, keeping out all who don't hold the correct beliefs. But I do need the Jesus whose life and message bring unique treasures to earth, treasures that I can share with people of every religion and no religion, just as I remain open to the unique treasures they offer me.

No, I don't need a constricted "Christian worldview" that teaches me to see the world as a machine and God as the almighty engineer who created it and now tinkers with it. The striving I experience in the universe around me, the sense that the whole universe itself is filled with a spirit (or Spirit) that is brooding, gestating, laboring, becoming, yearning, learning, reaching, like plants growing toward light, like salmon leaping up rapids toward a life-giving telos, or like lifeless planets undergoing metamorphosis from hot volcanic hells to Edens full of emerald rain forests and shimmering coral reefs.

When the depths of the Christian tradition help me see the world in this way, I see politics striving for something above the state's ability to govern. I see economics striving for something above return on shareholder investment. I see science striving for something more than information. I even see religion striving for something more than full sanctuaries and overflowing offering plates!

Yes, I could leave Christianity. But would I also leave my spiritual striving? What would be left? Rational analysis that convinces me that life is doomed and meaningless, that we'll never make it through the Great Filter? Desperate action that can too easily become the monster it is trying to fight? Yes, I could reject conventional Christian answers. But would I also reject the questions that have motivated the great Christian saints and sages— questions that keep me striving to grow as a human being? Might I be a truer Christian for striving with the questions than I would be for accepting the answers?

As I write these words, Pope Francis has convened a global gathering called the Economy of Francesco. The gathering was supposed to bring a few thousand people to Assisi, Italy, honoring the vision of St. Francis. But due to COVID-19, the gathering has moved online, which has made it accessible to all of us.

This endeavor is, in my opinion, one of the many truly hopeful projects happening across the planet. The pope is convening a multi-religious group of leaders to inspire young Catholics—and everyone else too—to imagine an economy that supports rather than undermines the vision he shared in his encyclicals *Laudato si* and *Fratelli tutti*. In his contribution to the event, micro-financing expert Muhammad Yunus saw the COVID-19 pandemic's impact on the global economy as an opportunity to create a new normal: "The train that was leading us to death has stopped. It is time to get off and ask ourselves: do we want to go back or is it the right time to go in the opposite direction: a world without pollution, without concentration of wealth, without massive unemployment?"[4]

As I have watched portions of the event online, the irony keeps striking me: what organization has proven itself more disappointing than the Catholic Church over recent years, plagued as it has been (and will be) with pedophilia scandals and coverups, all too often led ineptly by an all-male hierarchy who seem clueless about how little credibility they have left? Yet here is Francis, leader of the planet's single largest religious community, coming along just when we need him, inspiring people to cast a new vision for human civilization!

I see it again: the worst moments can set the stage for the best moments, if we do not give up and succumb to despair or cynicism . . . if we keep striving.

Extinction events are indeed horrific. They can't be minimized as minor inconveniences on the road to further evolution. But so far, in the aftermath of each crash or collapse, new possibilities emerge. Life finds a way. The great question for us is whether we will be wise enough to survive the Great Filter to be part of the continuing story.

The story of Jesus should have prepared us to see our predicament in this way, with all his talk of death and resurrection, buried seeds and new growth, corruption and rebirth, wide highways to self-destruction and narrow paths to life.

It's still not too late, if we dare to see, if we dare to believe, if we can relax our death grip on the past and reach forward into the future with eyes and hearts wide open.

That possibility does not require you to stay Christian. But it does grant you permission—to stay if you feel you can and to leave if you feel you must. In light of Fermi's Paradox and the Great Filter, in light of the available data on our current suicidal trajectory as a species, you'll see that more important than the question of *whether you stay Christian* is the question of *how you will live*, whether as a Christian or as something else.

If you have read Part II and found insufficient resources to overcome the ugliness of Part I, I understand. I am glad that you are not minimizing the danger of a Christian supremacist resurgence, the possibility that smoldering embers of unrecognized evil in Christianity could explode into even worse conflagrations in the future. I am glad you want no part of that. And I hope you can find a better way forward elsewhere.

If you have read Part II and found inspiration to stay Christian, but to do so in a new and better way, that is good as well. I am glad that you take seriously both our predicament and the unrecognized resources held in the Christian tradition, especially in the gospels and centered in Jesus himself.

To some degree, we must all hold both options in tension: *Will we stay Christian?* and *Will Christianity survive?* are less important questions than these: *How shall we humans survive and thrive? What good future shall we strive for? How can we align our energies with the divine energy at work in our universe?* That striving, that pursuit, that transformation project is bigger than Christianity and bigger than not-Christianity. To paraphrase Dr. King, whether we stay Christian or not, we will either learn to live together as family or we will die together as fools. It's a question of survival.

That larger question—of the shape and goal of our life together, whether or not we identify as Christian—will frame Part III of this book. I trust these final chapters will help you savor the amazing gift of living in this unique moment on this side of the Great Filter, in light of Fermi's Paradox, faced simultaneously with existential threats and holy possibilities.[5]

PART III

How

I want to beg you, as much as I can, dear sir, to be patient toward all that is unsolved in your heart and to try to love the questions themselves like locked rooms and like books that are written in a very foreign tongue. Do not now seek the answers, which cannot be given you because you would not be able to live them. And the point is, to live everything. Live the questions now. Perhaps you will then gradually, without noticing it, live along some distant day into the answer.

—FROM RAINER MARIA RILKE'S 1903
LETTER TO FRANZ XAVER KAPPUS

21

Include and Transcend

"It's just a stage." That's what my mother-in-law would say whenever she offered advice about the struggles of parenting. And she was right. Not sleeping through the night? Just a stage. Saying, "No!" or "Why?" to every request? Just a stage. Throwing tantrums? Just a stage. Obsessed with "cool" hairstyles and clothing? Just a stage.

The stages we adults see so easily in children are harder to see in ourselves. The workaholism of our thirties and forties? Just a stage. The obsession with weight or wrinkles of our forties and fifties? Just a stage. Anxieties about empty nesting or retirement savings? Just a stage. Facing death and experiencing denial, anger, depression, or bargaining? Just a stage, and each stage will pass into another.

As I explained in *Faith After Doubt*, about forty years ago I became interested in theories of human development, with their various stage models. Over the decades, I've studied well over a dozen models that try to describe general patterns in the way humans grow. I've seen with increasing clarity how spiritual development is affected by each new stage of our human development. The reverse is also true: our growth (or lack of growth) in spirituality inhibits or unleashes our cognitive, relational, and emotional growth. Their relationship is reciprocal. How could it be otherwise?

Whether or not you choose to stay Christian, here's what I recommend: pay attention to your human development, to the stages you're entering, inhabiting, or leaving.

If you're ready to grow to a new stage but your current form of

Christianity keeps you from doing so, you're going to be frustrated, and rightly so. You may let your current beliefs and practices trap you so you stagnate or even regress. That sense of stagnation or stuckness may eventually drive you to leave Christianity entirely, seeking room to grow elsewhere. That's certainly understandable. But you have another option too: you can leave your current *form* or *stage* of Christianity and enter a new form or stage that allows and even encourages the growth that you desire and need.

A lot of people leave Christianity when really all they needed was to leave a confining *form* or *stage* of Christianity. Some people think leaving Christianity will solve their problems, not realizing that their problems are as rooted in their stage of development as in their religion. The reverse is true as well: some atheists, agnostics, or people of other religions become Christians because Christianity aids in their growth. But eventually, even though a certain form of Christianity solved the problem of one stage, it can become a problem at another, creating a stained-glass ceiling that impedes further growth.

Of all the models of human development I've studied, the simplest is one of the most profound. My friend and colleague Fr. Richard Rohr speaks of "first half of life" and "second half of life."[1] He characterizes the first half of life as developing the basic skills of dualism: dividing the world into opposing categories like good/bad, us/them, safe/dangerous, friend/foe, winner/loser, clean/dirty. This skill of dualism helps us form a container, or moral shape, for our lives, he explains. Then, in the second half of life, we decide how we want to fill that container, and to do so, we develop new skills, especially the skill of non-dual seeing.

Instead of sorting everything into two simple, absolute categories—good and right versus bad and wrong—and thinking that with that judgment our work is complete, we learn to venture further in our understanding. First we learn to see how good and evil are often connected, like light and shadow, or mixed, like metals in an alloy. We see how good intentions can produce unintended negative consequences and vice versa. We come to understand that our judgments about good and evil often say more about us and our vantage point than they do about the person or thing we're judging. Eventually, we learn to see individual things in larger and larger contexts and systems, striving to "see things whole," as the mystics see. We see each thing interrelated, interdependent, and interwoven with others in a larger reality, a reality that defies easy judgments and to which and in which God is present.

Many of us grow older but stay in the first half of life, faithful to one-stage Christianity. We stick with dualism *and nothing more* to the bitter end. It takes "great pain or great love" (often augmented by mindful travel and a great education) to push us into the second stage of faith and life. Richard often augments this two-stage model with a three-stage model: *order, disorder, reorder.* Disorder, we could say, represents the transitional period, the midlife crisis, when the first order of dualism stops working and we haven't yet made our way into the reorder of non-dualism.

Another friend and colleague, the author, podcaster, and performance artist Rob Bell, uses a different three-stage model.[2] In the first stage, we are each preoccupied with *me*; we focus on our individual or personal well-being, in this life and, if we believe in it, the next. We think in terms of my needs, my rights, my freedom, my power, my grievances, my ambitions, my salvation, my perfection, my growth, my future. Then some of us move to *we*; we become concerned for our group, tribe, race, denomination, religion, or nation. Social values like duty, responsibility, and sacrifice become increasingly important to us in this second stage. Eventually, we may expand our *we* to include *everybody and everything*. At this third stage, we begin to see how all humans and all living and non-living things are interrelated and interdependent. There are strengths that we develop at each stage, and if we stagnate in a stage, each stage manifests its own unique weaknesses.

I find both Richard's and Rob's models helpful, along with many other models that propose many more finely nuanced stages. In *Faith After Doubt*, I tried to synthesize what I had learned from a wide array of theorists into a four-stage model: Simplicity, Complexity, Perplexity, and Harmony (or Solidarity).

I use the metaphor of a tree to frame the four stages. Each growing season, a tree adds a ring. The new ring doesn't exclude the previous rings; it embraces them in something bigger. It includes and transcends.[3] Or, to use a metaphor from St. Hildegard of Bingen, surely one of the twelfth century's most interesting people, we all are born with an inner tent of wisdom. When we're born, it's all there, but it is folded so it fits within our infant capacities. As we grow, we unfold the tent and learn to pitch it, so more and more wisdom can make its home within us.[4]

In terms of Fr. Richard's models, Simplicity and Complexity are the *order* of the first half of life. Perplexity is the *disorder* that occurs when the first order is deconstructed—or collapses under its own weight. Then, we may move into Harmony/Solidarity, which is the second half of life and the new, more capacious order. In terms of Rob's three-stage model, Simplicity and Complexity overlap with *me* and *we*. Perplexity marks a transition to *everybody and everything*, which is the focus of Harmony/Solidarity. This table (which I recommend you read column by column first, and then row by row) gives you an overview of the four stages as I've described them:

	SIMPLICITY	COMPLEXITY	PERPLEXITY	HARMONY
PERCEPTION	Dualistic	Pragmatic	Critical/ Relativistic	Integral/ Holistic
FOCUS	Right or wrong	Success or failure	Honest/ authentic or dishonest/ inauthentic	Inclusion and transcendence
MOTIVE	Pleasing authority figures, being right (or considered right)	Achieving goals, being successful (or considered successful)	Seeing through appearances to reality, being honest, authentic, true to oneself	Finding connection, seeing things whole, making a contribution
KEY VALUES	Being right/ clean/good, obeying authorities, staying faithful to tradition, remaining loyal to in-group	Being free and independent, winning, succeeding, achieving goals	Being fair, acknowledging bias and mistakes, facing inconvenient truths	Being compassionate, seeking justice and the common good
ASSUMPTION	Everything is known or knowable	Everything is doable or possible	Everyone has an opinion; every viewpoint is a view from a point	We are all connected, part of a greater whole

	SIMPLICITY	COMPLEXITY	PERPLEXITY	HARMONY
AUTHORITY FIGURES	Leaders who know and teach the right answers, God-like	Coaches who can help me succeed	Manipulators who control the naive and trusting	Fallible people like you and me
US/THEM	Good/Evil	Winners/Losers	Honest/Dishonest	Part of a Bigger Us
LIFE IS . . .	A war	A game or competition	A joke, a quest, and/or a deception	A mysterious gift
IDENTITY	Dependent or co-dependent	Increasingly independent	Counter-dependent	Interdependent
BELONGING	I am part of the good, right, and true group	I am part of the successful, effective, and winning team	I am one of the honest, thoughtful, and independent individuals	I am seeking understanding, connection, and the common good, even with opponents and enemies
GOD IS . . .	Supreme Being, almighty protector, warrior, law-giver, patron, patriarch	Encourager and guide who can help me prosper and succeed	Myth or a mystery	Loving presence, creative wisdom, known through experience and metaphor
CORE QUESTION	What do our authority figures say?	What are the steps to success?	What is the hidden agenda or bias I need to be suspicious of?	What part can I play for the common good?
MISTAKES ARE . . .	Legal infractions, moral failures, disobedience to authorities, ignorance of the rules	Lack of commitment, preparedness, effort, or positive attitude	Failure to question, challenge, think critically	Inevitable, part of learning and growth

	SIMPLICITY	COMPLEXITY	PERPLEXITY	HARMONY
STRENGTHS	High commitment, willingness to sacrifice	Enthusiasm, eagerness to learn, idealism, action	Honesty, curiosity, critical thinking	Integration of previous strengths, with greater depth and wider circle of compassion
WEAKNESSES	Narrow-minded, judgmental, combative, willingness to inflict suffering, false certainty	Superficial, naive, overly pragmatic, excessive confidence	Aloof, uncommitted, cynical, suspicious, elitist, depressed	Susceptible to previous weaknesses
GOOD NEWS	Wrongs can be forgiven	Help is available	You have permission to question and challenge the status quo	Everything belongs, all are connected, all life is sacred
ATTITUDE TOWARD PRESENT STAGE	This is the only correct or orthodox stage	This is the most effective and exciting stage	This stage is tough, sometimes miserable, but more honest than the previous stages	This stage will become a new simplicity, followed by a new complexity, etc.; the growth process never ends
ATTITUDE TOWARD TRADITION	Faith in an authoritative tradition	Faith in a useful or helpful tradition	Doubt in a corrupt or damaging tradition	Faith and doubt in an evolving tradition
ATTITUDE TOWARD DOUBT	Doubt is a failure, weakness, defection, betrayal, or sin	Doubt is a problem to be solved or sickness to be cured	Doubt is a virtue to be cultivated	Doubt is a necessary part of life, a portal from one stage to another
FAITH AND DOUBT	Faith before doubt	Faith managing doubt	Faith in doubt	Faith and doubt in creative tension

	SIMPLICITY	COMPLEXITY	PERPLEXITY	HARMONY
FAITH IS . . .	Assent to required beliefs	Means to desired ends	An obstacle to critical thinking	A humble, reverent openness to mystery that expresses itself in nondiscriminatory love

For a more in-depth understanding, I recommend *Faith After Doubt*. For our purposes here, it's enough to say that if you're frustrated with Christianity, there's a good chance that your stage of development is in tension with the stage of development of the form of Christianity practiced by your current faith community.

You may be frustrated with the judgmental attitudes of Christians in Simplicity, who are always pitting us versus them and judging who's in or out, saved or damned, friend or enemy. You may be frustrated with Christians in Complexity who are obsessed with learning more Bible lore, making more converts, growing bigger churches, gaining more power for their brand of Christianity, and the like. They act as if Christian success is all that matters, and the non-Christian world can go to hell (if it doesn't convert). You may be especially frustrated with what happens when Christians in Simplicity and Complexity team up to create an early-stage hybrid version of Christianity that is not only judgmental and supremacist but also very effective at imposing its judgments and supremacy on others. You may be frustrated to see how susceptible to authoritarianism people in these early stages are, especially because, as C. S. Lewis famously quipped, they may be as willing to kill for their faith as die for it.

In fact, all or nearly all the problems we considered in Part I are exactly the kinds of problems you would expect from early-stage Christianity.

If you're a Christian solidly in Simplicity, I know that it took great moral courage for you to get through Part I of this book, because it challenged all the simple moral categories you are working so hard to construct. If you're in Complexity, you were probably tempted to skip Part I entirely and begin with Part II, since you want to make Christianity work and you're more attracted to a pragmatic *yes* than a critical *no*. But your thirst for information may have carried you through even the hard truths of Part I.

If you're a Christian in Perplexity, you were relieved to read Part I of this book and probably a little suspicious about Part II, worried it would be an exercise in putting lipstick on a pig. You are probably a little uncomfortable right now too, because you're aware of how stage models like this one can become hierarchies that privilege those at the top and oppress those at the bottom. (A concern I share.[5]) If you're in or entering Harmony, you are interested in integrating what you learned in Parts I and II, so Part III is probably the part of the book you've been waiting for.

Speaking personally, I was raised in a form of Christianity rooted in Simplicity. It felt liberating for me as a teenager to discover more nuanced and pragmatic ways of being Christian through para-church organizations and movements rooted in Compexity. But eventually, I knew that I was outgrowing those Stage Two expressions of Christianity as well, which plunged me into Perplexity for many years. Recalling the classic Joni Mitchell song, I felt I had seen Christianity from "both sides now." I had to decide whether Christianity really was nothing more than an early-stage phenomenon, whether it was salvageable after the mess we've made of it, whether there was any room for a perplexed Christian like me if I chose to stay.

But here was my problem: I didn't know if there was anything beyond Perplexity.

From time to time, I'd meet someone whose very presence seemed to radiate *something more*. Or I'd stumble upon a book that conveyed a Christianity that felt more spacious than the versions I had seen. I started to seek out those *something more* books and *something more* people, and in that context, I wrote my first book. It was called *The Church on the Other Side*, and although I didn't use this four-stage language then, I now realize that what I meant by *the other side* was something on the other side of Simplicity and Complexity. I remember telling my wife, "When this book comes out, I'm going to lose all my friends," because I was pretty sure that my peers in Simplicity and Complexity would see my book as liberal, heretical, dangerous, and the like. I did lose a few friends. But so many more people came out of the shadows. "I thought I was the only one who felt this way," they said.

As more and more of us found one another, we gained courage to go public, and soon, as more and more people became part of our emerging conversation, a new coherence began to form. We discovered resources in several Catholic orders, especially in the Franciscan, Ignatian, Benedictine, and other traditions of contemplation and action. We also found needed resources in Anabaptist, Eastern Orthodox, and social gospel traditions. Many of the most liberating resources came from feminist, womanist, Black, Latinx, and Asian Christian traditions, and in queer, mestizo, and Indigenous theologies.[6]

Little by little, more and more of us discovered there was a way to stay Christian beyond the first half of life, beyond *me* and *we* stages, and beyond Simplicity, Complexity, and Perplexity.

That new kind (or stage) of Christianity scared us a little. We had been warned by our teachers in Simplicity and Complexity that anything other than what they offered was dangerous, even damnable. But we experienced a delightful surprise. From this new vantage point, when we read the Bible and especially the gospels, what previously looked two-dimensional, black-and-white, static, and small began popping out into something three-dimensional, full-color, and ever-expanding.

With all this in mind, I'd like to give you permission to make a shift in your thinking. What if you're really trying to change stages, not religions? What if you're really trying to leave not Christianity but Simplicity, Complexity, or Perplexity, or the *me-ism* and *we-ism* of the first half of life? What if your real desire is not simply a way to stay Christian or put Christianity behind you but *a way to be more fully and maturely human*?

Can you see that you could leave Christianity and be no less stuck in some other form of Simplicity, Complexity, or Perplexity, whether religious or secular? Or can you see that you could stay Christian in an early stage but at a great cost to your continuing development as a human being?

You may find that you don't have to leave Christianity; you just have to transcend its early stages and find a Stage Four way of being a Christian.

You may also find that if you inhabit the space of Harmony or Solidarity long enough, it will matter less to you whether others consider you a Christian . . . *or not*. The label simply won't matter so much. You will know who you are, where you've been, what you're becoming, what direction you're going, what you're seeking, and what you value.

Here's what that has meant for me. To the degree I inhabit Harmony, I am able to hold the tensions. I don't have to accept (or reject) Christianity as The One True Religion as I did in Simplicity. Nor do I have to sort through all the complexities to "fix" Christianity, creating my own "successful" form of it, as I did in Complexity. Nor do I have to stay in a state of perpetual skepticism and suspicion as I did in Perplexity, holding myself aloof from commitments because no commitment can withstand the acid of my critique.

From a posture of Harmony, I do not love you any more for staying Christian or any less for leaving Christianity. I realize that some of us will want to stay Christian and others will not, and we will each have valid reasons for our choice. That's why, in Part III, I'm offering ways to hold both the *no* of Part I and the *yes* of Part II together, so we can focus on the *how* of living well. Because whether you identify as a Christian or not, you are still a human being, and you are still passing through life's stages.

I hope you can sit with that simple realization for a while. Maybe take a walk or ponder it over a fresh cup of tea or coffee. Don't turn the page until you let this realization set in: *You're a human being on a human journey of growth and development—whether you stay Christian or not.* You have miles to go before you sleep.

And the same is true of everyone else.

If you can hold that simple realization with empathy for yourself and for others, you may feel walls dropping away and new possibilities opening in all directions.

22

Start with the Heart

Volcanoes and earthquakes, wind and rain, incoming asteroids and jostling continental plates: these forces shaped the earth for billions of years. Then came life with its capacity to evolve, which transformed a barren planet into a world teeming with whales, trees, birds, and bees. Then, over the last few dozen millennia, the earth has been reshaped by another powerful force: *human desire*. Members of our upstart species sculpted stones and arranged them into pyramids and cities. We lit the dark and flattened mountains. We dammed, dredged, and redirected rivers. We deforested jungles and irrigated deserts. We multiplied some species and drove others to extinction. And now, we are rapidly melting polar ice caps, shifting ocean currents, and changing our planet's climate. Who would have guessed that *human desire* would prove no less powerful than volcanoes, earthquakes, and incoming asteroids in shaping the earth?

Our individual human desires are powerful enough, to be sure: for wealth, for pleasure, for power, fame, fun, revenge, play, safety, creativity, belonging, and love. But when our individual desires align and synergize into group desires . . . that's when we can literally move mountains and heal diseases. Or raise sea levels and decimate ecosystems.

The challenge we face is epic: will we shape the world by strengthening wise individual and group desires, or will our foolish desires shape us and, through us, reshape the world?

If religion has a positive role in our future, it will surely involve specializing in desire formation. In fact, for better or worse, *religion is desire formation*.

In terms of the previous chapter, Stage One religions form desires to belong to an in-group and conform to its requirements. Stage Two religions form desires to be successful and advance personal and group interests.

Many of the desires formed by early-stage religions have proven problematic, such as the desire to abandon the common good on earth for individual rewards in heaven, the desire to pit Christians against Muslims or secularists, the desire to stigmatize or scapegoat LGBTQ people or some other minority, the desire to ignore or suppress science, the desire to press rewind and return to a nostalgic past. As a result, many want to leave Christianity and other religions: they can no longer in good conscience desire the desires that early-stage religions are forming. This is understandable.

But it's worth remembering that even if you leave your religion to escape its influence on your desires, unless you are intentional about shaping your desires, *others will do so for you.* In other words, religion isn't the only industry in the desire-formation business.

Anthropologist René Girard and others have helped us see how we humans are hardwired to imitate the desires of our neighbors: we catch their desires like we catch our native language—or a virus. In addition, every day, powerful people spend billions of dollars seeking to mold our desires so we will help them achieve their desires through the fields of marketing and politics, as well as religion.

"Aren't you doing the same thing at this very moment?" you might be asking. "Isn't that why you've written this book? To influence my desires to be more in line with yours?"

In a sense, you are correct. I wouldn't be writing if I didn't desire to influence you. But because of my own passage through the stages we considered in the previous chapter, I find that my desires are changing. They are expanding beyond personal self-interest in this life and the next, beyond the in-group interest of any single religion or nation alone, and even beyond the self-interest of our species alone. When early-stage religion lost its grip on me, I found new spiritual communities that helped me embrace and nurture new desires.

In Stage Three communities, I developed a desire to face and expose hypocrisy, injustice, and bias—not just in *you* or *them*, but also in *us* and *me*. Some of those communities were secular, like the academic communities of graduate school. Some were religious or spiritual, like the Emergent movement in which I have participated. Then, in Stage Four communities, I began to develop new desires, desires to widen my circles of empathy and understanding, desires to experience a sense of connection with everyone I possibly could, desires to welcome truth wherever it came from, not just from my familiar in-group.

So, yes, I would be happy to influence you toward transcending early-stage desires and including them in larger, later-stage desires, whether you stay Christian or not, because if we desire a world and future that are different from the ones we now have, we need to intentionally cultivate a more mature and wise set of desires, individually and in groups.[1]

To describe those desires, desires that take us through Perplexity and into Harmony, I have to begin with a desire that is a matter of survival going forward: a more mature human community will *desire the good of the planet*. Without a healthy planet, there will be no healthy economy, no healthy society, and no healthy individuals, including us. Thus far in our history as a species, the good of the planet has been easy to take for granted. When we spoiled one place, when we took all it had to offer, we simply moved on to another place.

But we've reached the dead end of that project. We have already surpassed the long-term carrying capacity of our planet, and, as the saying goes, we have no "Planet B" waiting in the wings. With more and more of us taking more and more of our planet's resources and pumping out more and more filth, trash, and toxins, we must make a healthy planet a primary desire, a starting line rather than a finish line. For Christians, this means recognizing that the Creator loves creation and desires its well-being—from a spinning galaxy to a nest of barn swallows, and we can join in that holy desire too.[2] People who are not Christians will find their own meaningful and appropriate ways of encouraging this desire.

Then, a more mature humanity will *desire the good of all people*, beginning with the poor and most vulnerable. That means we will strengthen our shared desire for healthy and just communities and societies, from global civilizations to nations to states to cities to neighborhoods to families and circles of friends. So just societies—and economies—in which all people have the opportunity to thrive . . . that can be our second formative desire.

Next, nested within our desire for a healthy planet and a just society, we will *desire our personal or individual well-being*. In our immaturity, we put this desire first. Some of us even naively believed that self-interest would automatically produce a healthy earth and society. Now we know this was a foolish delusion. Going forward, we will learn to take as good care of ourselves as we would want our neighbors to be taken care of. Our well-being won't be above or below theirs but inseparably linked with theirs. This nested approach to self-friendship and self-compassion puts us in a collaborative win/win relationship—rather than a competitive win/lose relationship—with ourselves, our neighbors, and the earth.

Again, the order of these first three desires is significant. Over recent centuries, modern civilization generally started with personal desire and then, as a luxury add-on, may have included social desire, hardly ever even considering a desire for a thriving planet. Going forward, we will recognize a basic insight of systems theory: the well-being of any subsystem depends on the well-being of the larger systems of which it is part. So we start big with a healthy planetary system, and then desire healthy human systems that thrive within it, and then we desire our own individual well-being within those larger human and planetary systems.

Where, you might ask, does the love of God or Spirit fit in?

It doesn't. Love for the transcendent doesn't *fit in* with the others, as one item in the list. Instead, it is inherent in the desire that we experience in the other three desires. Divine love is the nest in which the other desires are nurtured, and it is inherent in all other loves. What I'm suggesting recalls the words in 1 John 4, that "God is love." When we desire the good of the planet, the good of all people, and our own good, we are participating in a love that is bigger than us. As a Christian, I would say we are joining God in God's loving desire for the well-being of the beloved. To love the love that loves the parts is to love the whole. To unify our desires in love is, I think, what Jesus must have meant by purity of heart (see Matthew 5:8).

When we feel in our bones and breath how the first three desires are woven together, how they constitute a permeating holy desire that is wholly benevolent, we don't discover the fourth desire and add it to the list; rather, we find that the fourth desire is already flowing within us, in and through the other loves, and we experience this desire as *divine or transcendent love*—universal, nondiscriminatory, healing, creative, life-giving. We may use many names and words to point to this unifying desire, even though none of them can contain it. It must be lived, experienced, participated in, not simply spoken.

This transcendent love is the one desire that enlivens the striving world, the desire for mutual well-being, for conviviality in Harmony and Solidarity. When this love flows on a planetary (and cosmic) level, on a social (or communal) level, and on a personal (or individual) level, we see it as the one love that animates all other loves. It is the *life* of the web of life—the tree of life, the family of life—of which we're part. When we cut ourselves off from it, we're like a branch that amputates itself from a vine or tree.

For those of us who stay Christian (and perhaps for many others as well), this *web of life* or *tree of life*, this universal flow of love, may be one of our best new metaphors for God, recalling our discussion about freeing God in Chapter 19.[3] Barbara Brown Taylor, who combines theologian and poet as well as anyone I know, captured this insight twenty years ago. Echoing St. Bonaventure, who described God as a mystery "whose center is everywhere and circumference is nowhere," she wrote:

> In Sunday school, I learned to think of God as a very old white-bearded man on a throne, who stood above creation and occasionally stirred it with a stick. When I am dreaming quantum dreams, what I see is an infinite web of relationship, flung across the vastness of space like a luminous net. It is made of energy, not thread. As I look, I can see light moving through it as a pulse moves through veins. What I see "out there" is no different from what I feel inside. There is a living hum that might be coming from my neurons but might just as well be coming from the furnace of the stars. . . .
>
> Where is God in this picture? God is all over the place. God is up there, down here, inside my skin and out. God is the web, the energy, the space, the light—not captured in them, as if any of those concepts were more real than what unites them—but revealed in that singular, vast net of relationship that animates everything that is.
>
> At this point in my thinking, it is not enough for me to proclaim that God is responsible for all this unity. Instead, I want to proclaim that God *is* the unity—the very energy, the very intelligence, the very elegance and passion that make it all go. This is the God who is not somewhere but everywhere, the God who may be prayed to in all directions at once. This is also the God beyond all directions, who will still be here (wherever "here" means) when the universe either dissipates into dust or swallows itself up again.[4]

In this light, to say "I love God" is to say that I give my heart to the divine love that loves in and through all creation. To say, "I have a relationship with

God" is to say that I am joining God in God's desire to relate to all creation as beloved. To say "I believe in God" is to say that I believe in the love that holds and animates the universe. This beloved community resonates with the central message of Jesus (as in Matthew 6:33): *the kingdom and the justice of God*. In this light, Jesus' great commandment to love God, neighbor, and self makes sense as a survival strategy, not just a spiritual aspiration: when we love God, we love neighbor, self, and the creation on which neighbor and self depend. These loves are inseparable. They are, in fact, one love.

In saying this, I'm echoing the six-century-old wisdom of Julian of Norwich, who wrote:

> We are all one in love. . . . When I look at myself as an individual, I see that I am nothing. It is only in unity with my fellow spiritual seekers that I am anything at all. It is this foundation of unity that will save humanity. . . . God is all that is good. God has created all that is made. God loves all that [God] has created. And so anyone who, in loving God, loves all his fellow creatures . . . loves all that is. All those who are on the spiritual path contain the whole of creation, and the Creator. That is because God is inside us, and inside God is everything. And so whoever loves God loves all that is.[5]

Those who do not stay Christian can find their own appropriate language to speak of this all-inclusive desire for universal well-being. Whatever language we use, I do not believe we will be able to sustain the first three desires without a transcendent and inclusive fourth, whether or not we call it *God* and ourselves *Christian*.[6]

With Barbara Brown Taylor, Julian, and many others, I see Christianity as my heart's path into this mysterious and sacred web. But others find themselves on other paths, and I know that each of those paths has its own unique treasures, just as mine does. (That understanding leads to the title of another of Barbara's brilliant books, *Holy Envy: Finding God in the Faith of Others*.[7])

I don't simply desire to hold right beliefs about this luminous web: I desire to enter its fire and flow and let them enter me, to seek and follow its current, to live as part of its story, to experience it personally and intimately, first as *You* and ultimately as *We*.[8] In the words of process theologian Catherine Keller, "What matters, what might matter endlessly, is what we earthdwellers now together embody. Not what we say *about* God but how we *do* God."[9] In that spirit, I want to embody and enact—with you, if you're willing—the cosmic love that breathes in our breath, that animates our own consciousness, that fires the stars.[10]

I imagine a new kind of Christianity—and a new kind of humanity—that instills and strengthens this nested integration of holy, transcendent desires for the beloved world and all it contains. I imagine new curricula being developed so that we are as intentional about teaching children these unifying desires as we are about teaching reading, writing, and arithmetic.[11] For adults, I imagine a parallel creative revolution in both our religious and secular liturgies.[12]

If we desire a thriving world for all as our deepest and most all-encompassing desire, not only will we have everything we need: we will become the kinds of people who help create that kind of world. Healed human desire will re-consecrate what distorted human desire has desecrated.

Because of Christianity's size and power, we need a strong movement of Christians working within the Christian community to prioritize the formation of this integrated desire. As I explained in Part II, this is one reason I stay Christian. But a minority movement within Christianity certainly can't shift our civilization alone. That's why we need parallel movements in Islam, Hinduism, Buddhism, Judaism, Sikhism, and other faiths too . . . along with our noble nonreligious and secular communities.

What will that mean for you going forward? If you can find a community or organization that desires the good of the planet and all its creatures, the good of all people through just and generous societies, and the good of each individual—including you—with a reverence for the sacred love that flows through all these loves, that is a community in which to invest your time, intelligence, money, and energy. That is a community in which to raise your children. If you can't find such a community or organization, perhaps you can create one. To use Christian language, even if it's just two or three of you, that is a community in which the Spirit of God is at work, whether its members use theological language or not.

You may choose not to use the word *God* to describe that transcendent, loving, cosmic desire for the well-being of all. You have reasons not to, I'm sure, and I hope you can make room for those who do. Or you may use the word *God* freely, sincerely, and joyfully. You have reasons to do so, I'm sure, and I hope you'll make room for those who don't. Don't let the language you use to describe the unifying desire distract you from it!

Distractions abound. Ten thousand desires can pull us in ten thousand directions, leaving us stuck and torn. We need to align and unify our desires, as individuals, as communities, as a species. So whatever you do, whatever language you use, Christian or not, strengthen the unifying desire, the desire that desires the well-being of all. That is the Harmony that lies beyond Simplicity, Complexity, and Perplexity.

Everything else flows from there.

23

✿

RE-WILD

Yesterday, I took my kayak out into the Everglades. I paddled across a lake, through a series of mangrove tunnels, and then out into a remote lagoon where I fished for a while and then just sat. My little boat rocked in gentle waves. An alligator surfaced and, upon seeing me, gently submerged and swam away. An osprey hovered, curled like a fist, plunged into the water, and then rose, shivering off spray, a fish wriggling in its talons. Then all seemed still for a while, with only a whisper of wind riffling the lake. A swallow-tailed kite appeared, swooping and soaring in silence just above the mangroves, a graceful miracle in motion. I felt full. I simply needed to be there for a few hours, out in the wild, just to listen, watch, observe, all the more because I've been hunkered down in what I call the "writing cave," a place where I am deep, deep, deep into words . . . the words of this book, in fact.

I felt I needed to shake off words just as that osprey had shaken off water.

I have a theory. When our ancient ancestors developed the capacity for language, words became increasingly all-encompassing. Words became not only our primary way of engaging with others socially but they also became the tool by which we each conduct our own inner dialogue. Language became so powerful, both interpersonally and intra-personally, that the web of words in our heads often felt more real to us than the web of life outside our heads.

Language, we discovered, was a tool we used to describe reality, but it also could become a substitute for reality. We might say it was the original form of virtual reality.

Christianity evolved as, among other things, a language, a set of words pointing to a set of ideas. This language was necessary to liberate people from another language, the language of empire and domination. This liberating language evolved and shaped the inner architecture of generations of Christians, furnishing them with foundational terms like *sin, grace,* and *salvation.* These terms were woven together in stories, and the stories were woven together in a framing story—another phenomenon of language. But like everything, language evolves. Meanings modify. What once was liberating can become a cage in which we pace, dreaming of freedom.

Many people today are pacing the cage. Old Christian words have been emptied of their substance, or their meanings have mutated. The old framing story doesn't fit the reality we experience and feels instead like a conspiracy theory or manic fantasy. We can't help but feel that the language of Christianity creates a make-believe world, a rabbit hole, an alternate reality, where angels and demons are real but climate change and evolution aren't. The gap between actual reality and the Christian linguistic reality stretches our credulity to a breaking point. That's why many can no longer stay Christian, and that's why many of us who choose to stay Christian must deconstruct the Christianity we inherited—and shake off much of its language.

But we can't underestimate the staying power of conventional Christianity. Even if millions of us renounce it, even if we vow never to set foot in its physical architecture again, its language is still encoded in our inner architecture, in our deepest neural pathways and many of our social networks. How can we possibly gain leverage to see, deconstruct, and change something so total, so all-encompassing? To do so, we need something even more immersive and powerful, something capable of disrupting and transforming the vocabulary and grammar that have helped make us who we are. Where can we go for that kind of immersive experience? What can jolt us out of our addictive obsession with the virtual reality of language?

The answer may be as close as our own front doors. If we take our bodies outdoors and into the natural world, if we go far enough and return often enough and stay long enough, we can let our inner beings realign with the original language and architecture of creation. We can get off the theological elevators that take us up, up, and away, into the abstract sky, as Diana Butler Bass puts it, and descend from our heads into our hearts, our bodies, and our bare feet, thus becoming more *grounded*.[1] St. Augustine (Sermon 126.6) put it like this:

> Some people, in order to find God, will read a book. But there is a great book, the book of created nature. Look carefully at it top and bottom, observe it, read it. God did not make letters of ink for you to recognize God in; God set before your eyes all these things God has made. Why look for a louder voice?[2]

Meister Eckhart, who was about fourteen when Aquinas died in 1274, put it no less strongly: "A person who knew nothing but creatures would never need to attend to any sermons, for every creature is full of God and is a book."[3]

When I echo Aquinas and Eckhart by recommending we engage more deeply with creation, I'm not simply talking about going outdoors for recreation or even inspiration, as fine and healthy as those excursions can be. What we need is deeper than that, because so often, we simply bring our old linguistic architecture with us into the outdoors. As we walk through the forest or prairie, our language chatters on, naming, categorizing, and judging everything we see just as we've done before, noticing what we've been trained to observe and missing what we've been trained to miss. Instead, we need to enter the natural world mindfully, reverently, as silently as we can, waiting for the beauty, intricacy, and wonder of what is outside us to overwhelm and hush the barrage of words chattering inside our heads.

In this silent encounter with the natural world, we render ourselves vulnerable to it so that it can impress upon us a new inner architecture, one that is shaped by and in harmony with its wordless patterns and wisdom. We invite natural reality to shape and reshape our inner "civilized" reality. In Christian terms, we let God's original word (or *logos*) outspeak our human words (or *logia*), to transform us into different kinds of receivers, different kinds of Christians, different kinds of humans.

By *God's original word*, I mean the universe itself, the universe that expanded from the original singularity, that point of creation that resonates so beautifully with the "Let there be light" of Genesis 1. If our human words have taken on a life of their own, and if that life is out of sync with the primal logos, pattern, or wisdom of creation, then we need nature to become our teacher. And not just nature but nature as unmodified by human interference as possible. Our name for unmodified nature is *the wild* or *wilderness*.

Of course, these days no part of the wild remains completely untouched by human modification, as attested by global climate change, the global dispersal of microplastics, the spread of invasive species, the extinction of native species, light and noise pollution, and other human interventions. So even the wild becomes less wild every day. That only makes its preservation more urgent as a spiritual priority and as an expression of the fourth desire we mentioned in the previous chapter.

We each have a tiny outpost of the wild that we carry with us wherever we go, namely, our bodies. Like the wild outside us, we constantly try to control and modify our wild bodies. We clothe, tattoo, and sculpt them. We overfeed them; then we starve them. We restrain them from the healthy stress of exercise, or we punish them with the excessive stress of anxiety. We're proud and ashamed of them. We flaunt and hide them. We love them and hate them. And we do all this because of the linguistic architectures and the social constructions in which our bodies live and move and have our being (Acts 17:28). You might say that our linguistic constructions about our bodies are more real to us than our bodies themselves.

Conventional Christianity operates by and large on the "ghost in the machine" model of humanity. We often disparage our physical bodies as "the flesh," fearing them as a temporal distraction and a moral temptation to our nonmaterial spirits or souls. This "spirit in meat" model, rooted in certain schools of Greek philosophy and picked up in parts of the New Testament, puts us at odds with our bodies, as strangers to them.

In the future, those of us who stay Christian will need to make peace with our wild bodies, to listen to them and learn to love them again, to discern God's beloved wildness in them.

This love for our wild bodies seems especially important now, because it's becoming more and more clear that the things we associated with soul or spirit—consciousness, personality, character, morality—are emergent phenomena, arising from our bodies. We are not spiritual ghosts in machines of meat; we are embodied creatures, and consciousness, personality, character, morality, even spirituality arise in our bodies.

I know there is some truth to the statement, "We are spiritual beings having a human experience," but there is perhaps more truth in an alternative statement: "We are biological creatures, wild animals, in which spiritual experience happens." Our bodies are our wildness, a wildness which we are oppressing and driving to extinction as we do with every other wildness. And it is our human social constructions—our ideas, conventions, assumptions, belief systems, cultures, civilizations, religions, and all their words upon words—that drive us to do so.

Rediscovering the wildness of our bodies will help us become more wise in the ways we understand sexuality, eating, illness, and health—including mental illness and addiction, human development and aging, and beginning- and end-of-life issues.[4] (In the words of Hannah Arendt, it will help us take our natality as seriously as our mortality.[5]) Rediscovering the wildness of our bodies will also help us live more wisely with the earth, since every molecule and atom that constitutes our bodies is derived from food, drink, and breath supplied by the sun-warmed earth.

Along with our bodies, many of us keep other outposts of the wild close at hand. Could it be that the dogs or cats that we so love are not just pets but also emissaries of the wild? Could those houseplants we water by the window or the fish we tend in an aquarium also be wild ambassadors who teach us every day to link our well-being with theirs? Could it be that the hours we spend growing tomatoes, peppers, and squash are not simply about feeding our bodies but also about tending to our suppressed inner wildness?

In the wild, under the sun, in the weather, with our bare feet on soil and rock, we can begin to break through to feel the truth: we are not independent ghost-in-machine or spirit-in-meat monads; we are interdependent events that happen here, on and in and with and as part of the earth, which is part of larger solar, galactic, and cosmic systems. Every breath tells us that we are porous. Every meal and every trip to the bathroom tell us the same thing. What was in air and soil was captured in a zesty mango that I ate and that became part of me. Both the mango and I depend on nuclear reactions within the sun to keep us alive. Sun, space, earth, soil, air, wind, rain . . . we are all part of one great, wild web that does not depend on our language to keep functioning.

That is why I took my kayak into the Everglades yesterday. That is why I sat in wordless wonder as the swallow-tailed kite banked, dove, and hovered over the mangroves. I, who love words and make my living by them, need to soar above words, especially my own, out in the wild.

In *The Galapagos Islands: A Spiritual Journey*, I wrote: "In all likelihood, wild theology is the mother of civilized theology. And in all likelihood, civilized theology is in the process of killing its mother and acting as if she never existed. . . . [We need] to be re-situated in the wild, unboxed, outdoor world of creation."[6]

How can we more consciously re-wild our theology and other inner architecture, as Mennonite activist Todd Wynward so aptly puts it?[7] Creative communities around the world are already stepping out to show the way.

For example, churches and secular organizations in New Zealand and Australia have pioneered protocols for honoring the Indigenous peoples of the land, whose cultures still cherish wildness.[8] In these protocols, Indigenous elders might speak and lead a ritual, or Indigenous tribes might be named and their wisdom and stewardship of the land might be honored. I and others have developed additional protocols to honor the land and its creatures, naming local watersheds and locally common—or endangered—species. These protocols become all the more meaningful when congregations build respectful and mutually beneficial relationships with Indigenous peoples themselves, exploring the realities of reparations for the past and partnerships for protection of the land and its creatures moving forward. Protocols like these are only a beginning. But hopefully, they help shape our desires (as we considered in Chapter 22) so we can re-situate ourselves in the wordless language of creation, in all its wildness and wholeness.

To further help us in that process, Ched Myers, Elaine Enns, and their colleagues are shepherding the Watershed Discipleship movement.[9] They remind us that watersheds are our environmental neighborhood, where humans coexist with land, water, fellow creatures, and one another in mutual interdependence. We are not only disciples *in* watersheds; we are disciples *of* watersheds: we learn from them, we become their students, and we seek to live in harmony with what our watersheds teach us. Watersheds are the places where all our grand ideals of regenerative community and economy must be locally embodied, recalling the sage words of author Wendell Berry: "The question that must be addressed is not how to care for the planet, but how to care for each of the planet's millions of human and natural neighborhoods, each of its millions of small pieces and parcels of land, each one of which is in some precious way different from all the others."[10]

Seminaries around the world are offering courses and even whole degrees and other certifications to helps us re-wild our faith. I'm especially grateful for the good people of Seminary of the Wild, described as "a wild seedbed of spiritual and cultural evolution."[11] One of its founders, Victoria Loorz, helped form the Wild Church Network, which is helping outdoor congregations find and encourage one another, to help more and more people move "from isolation to connection, from detachment to immersion, and from dualism to interbeing." In the words of cultural historian Thomas Berry, the Wild Church Network helps people see the world not as "a collection of objects" but as "a communion of subjects." Other seminaries—along with independent spiritual but not explicitly religious programs—are involved in related innovations, offering training not in belief management but in deep transformation.[12]

Sadly, some churches and denominations are shutting down their youth camps and retreat centers as kids take more interest in digital experiences on screens than wild experiences outdoors. But others are rediscovering the importance of summer camps and retreat centers as places to preserve remaining patches of wild. And even urban and suburban churches are realizing that if they own land, they shouldn't see it as a "landscaping expense," but, rather, they should cherish it as a place to heal, preserve, and re-wild.[13] Butterfly gardens, community gardens, and wetland swales are being developed, each one reconnecting us a bit more with the earth. The church I served for twenty-four years, Cedar Ridge Community Church, has become one such example under the wise leadership of Matthew Dyer, Melanie Griffin, and others.[14]

Meanwhile, an amazing array of organizations are working to help us face specific environmental problems, beginning with climate change. Some organizations are explicitly faith-based, others aren't, but we all realize that we need to work together for the common good.[15] And no less important, the descendants of colonizers are finally turning to Indigenous people who survived and resisted colonization, knowing that our mutual survival and well-being now depend upon recovering wisdom that Indigenous cultures still carry, wisdom derived from being wild, a part of the land rather than apart from it.[16]

Obviously, these are important beginnings, and we have so far to go. Imagine every religious liturgy re-wilded and rewritten *from the ground up* (in multiple senses of the phrase). Imagine the same being done with every curriculum in every school. Imagine in every election, leaders teaching their communities that environmental policy is an essential value to guide their voting. Imagine people taking pilgrimages to the wild as seriously as our ancestors trekked to Rome or Jerusalem, echoing our Indigenous sisters and brothers who went into the wild on vision quests.[17] (Jesus, by the way, was an Indigenous man who prepared for his public ministry with a forty-day vision quest in the wild, and he retreated to the wild whenever he could, often to the consternation of his followers.)

Imagine if part of our daily spiritual practice involved reconnecting with the wild earth each day, whether mindfully walking barefoot in a park or garden, or observing the phase of the moon, or noticing birds and learning their songs, or tending one houseplant in an urban skyscraper, or noticing and inhabiting our wild bodies. At the very least, we can imagine letting each meal, each trip to the bathroom, and each look in the mirror become a reminder of our porosity with the wild world.

If the logos of God truly runs through all creation, if creation is actually divine artwork and poetry, if the earth around us and the sky above us truly are preachers, as Psalm 19 proclaims, and if the birds of the air and flowers of the field have essential lessons to teach us, as the Indigenous man Jesus said, then we could learn in theology what we are learning in ecology: that wisdom is biomimicry, and that the way of the wild is the way of life.

I am aware that many people do not enjoy the outdoors. For them, venturing outdoors is an adventure in anxiety, with bugs, unpredictable weather, the fear of getting lost, and other adversities preoccupying them until they get safely back inside their front door. Meanwhile, others have little access to the wild, living in urban or suburban "wilderness deserts." Those of us who love the outdoors, instead of shaming our counterparts and nagging them to join us, can simply let the wild do its work on us, and then bring home a regular dose of it to them, camouflaged in our own wild selves. We can also help them reconnect with wildness in the ways they can, including the oft-forgotten wildness of their own bodies, rediscovering their bodies as wild temples of the Holy.[18]

The prophet's voice, we recall, comes from the wilderness. It takes a wilderness to make a prophet. "In Wildness is the preservation of the world," American naturalist and essayist Henry David Thoreau said.[17] If we are to survive as a species, it will only be through the wisdom that comes from the wild. Whether we stay Christian or not, we need to re-wild, each in our own way.

※

24

FIND THE FLOW

In several of my previous books, I have talked about the importance of movements. But it was only in the writing of this book that I came to see a rather obvious limitation in my previous understanding. I saw movements as coexisting on par with institutions, as peers in an uneasy but necessary dance. In *The Great Spiritual Migration*, I defined the two social realities interdependently: movements challenge institutions to make new gains in human well-being, and institutions preserve the gains achieved by past social movements. (Meanwhile, current institutions tend to oppose the gains proposed by current social movements.)

Now, I have come to see that there are larger movements, like tides in which all institutions and movements rise and fall like individual waves. We might call these larger movements *meta-movements*. (I thought I had coined that term but quickly discovered that there is no new thing under the sun.[1])

Since between 3000 and 4000 BCE, when the first human civilizations were born, we have been part of one meta-movement we might call the old humanity or imperial humanity. (It was preceded by what we might call original or wild humanity, when people lived as hunter-gatherers and primal agriculturalists.) This meta-movement included social and historical epochs that we distinguish with terms like ancient, medieval, modern, and postmodern. Over the course of many centuries, this meta-movement was the context in which thousands of institutions and movements could arise, dance, reform, renew, compete, decline, die, and be replaced. As centuries came and passed, as nations rose and fell, this larger meta-movement carried on.

What happens when a meta-movement runs its course? What happens when the tide begins to turn, when the assumptions that shaped the meta-movement no longer hold, often having been changed by the meta-movement itself? That's when you enter a transition period, a time between the dominance of one way of life and the birth of another. For people whose lives and values were shaped by the old meta-movement, such a disruption feels like the end of an age, even the end of the world.

What would it mean for us if we happen to live during the decline of the old humanity, when a new humanity is in the painful, fragile process of being born? What if some of us are in the process of trying to resuscitate the old, while others of us are conceiving, gestating, and giving birth to the new? What if the growth of the new movement, the new humanity, the new social creation or construction depends on the old one losing its hegemony?

As I write those words, I can't help but feel a flood of resonances with the Hebrew Scriptures. I feel echoes of Isaiah, speaking of God doing a new thing, something fresh springing forth, so that there will be good news for the poor, recovery of sight for the blind, freedom for the incarcerated and oppressed. (Oppression of the poor is one of the hallmarks of the old humanity.) I hear the prophet imagining a promised time when weapons are recycled into farm equipment because nobody studies war any more. (War is one of the hallmarks of the old humanity.) I hear Ezekiel's oracle about a new heart, a heart of flesh that replaces the heart of stone. (The hardening of hearts in the name of self-interest and in-group interest is a hallmark of the old humanity.) I hear Amos envisioning a time when a river of justice rolls down from the heights, filling the lowest places first. (A concentration of power and wealth at the top is a hallmark of the old humanity.) I hear Micah relativizing everything in his religion except doing justice, loving kindness, and walking humbly before God. (Hoarding power, loving money, and walking in racial, religious, or national pride are hallmarks of the old humanity.)

In the Christian Scriptures, I hear Mary envisioning a time when the rich are sent away to feel the hunger of the poor they have exploited and avoided, a time when the poor are filled with the good things previously enjoyed only by the rich. I hear Jesus speaking parables of a new kingdom, of death and resurrection, of God loving the world and wanting to save it, not condemn it. I hear him speaking of coming "wars and rumors of wars" that mark the death of the status quo, but he sees them as birth pangs (Matthew 24:8), not a last gasp. I hear Paul speaking of a new creation and a new humanity in Christ, and John describing a New Jerusalem descending to the earth like a giant cube in a science fiction movie.

And so I imagine: in the middle of the old meta-movement of empires, domination, extraction, and exploitation, what if a long succession of prophets, including Mary, John the Baptizer, Jesus, Paul, and others, were giving us a vision for a new movement being born? And what if the Christian religion, instead of living into that progressive vision of a better future, pretty thoroughly accommodated itself to the old meta-movement? What if the Christian religion married the powers that be and slept more or less comfortably in their arms for nearly two thousand years?

What if part of the restlessness many Christians feel about their faith is disappointment with this accommodation to the powers of the old humanity? What if widespread Christian nominalism isn't only a symptom of the half-heartedness of individual Christians but also of their sense that Christianity in its current forms is not really that big a deal and is unworthy of wholehearted commitment? Would those of us who left Christianity as a religion of the old humanity actually be leaving Christianity? Or would we be setting out to rediscover it as a religion leaning into a new humanity?[2]

Whatever this new emerging meta-movement is, it is bigger than any single religion. In fact, it is bigger than religion as a whole. It issues an invitation, perhaps even an ultimatum, to all religions, all economies, all educational and political systems, all arts and trades, all sciences and technologies, everything. It is, we might say, a spiritual movement that encompasses everything.

Whether or not you stay Christian, I hope you can see what I see: with or without the Christian logo, we must invest in the new spiritual meta-movement that is already emerging within and among us. If it is to liberate us from the dominant meta-movement that has proven itself genocidal, eco-cidal, and therefore suicidal, the new meta-movement we need must go beyond mere sustainability. It must be fully *regenerative*, restoring old balances that have been disrupted and diminished by our current civilizational project and, where that is impossible, finding new balances that make new vitalities possible.

How do we align ourselves with this meta-movement? Here are seven practices that are helping me:

1. **Believe in it.** This may be one of the deepest acts of faith we're capable of: to look at the whole arc of the cosmos and see it not as a meaningless explosion that launches a meaningless process of entropy and ends in a meaningless freeze or crunch, but as a love story. Sr. Ilia Delio captures this vision of a deep faith that inhabits deep time:

> We can read the history of our 13.7-billion-year-old universe as the rising up of Divine Love incarnate, which bursts forth in the person of Jesus, who reveals love's urge toward wholeness through reconciliation, mercy, peace, and forgiveness. Jesus is the love of God incarnate, the whole-maker who shows the way of evolution toward unity in love. In Jesus, God breaks through and points us in a new direction; not one of chance or blindness but one of ever-deepening wholeness in love. In Jesus, God comes to us from the future to be our future. Those who follow Jesus are to become wholemakers, uniting what is scattered, creating a deeper unity in love. Christian life is a commitment to love, to give birth to God in one's own life and to become midwives of divinity in this evolving cosmos. We are to be wholemakers of love in a world of change.[3]

If this language feels too Christian for you, you can find alternative language, perhaps in the writings of Joanna Macy, Brian Swimme, David Korten, Margaret Wheatley, or others. But you will see the resonance, whatever the language, and you will feel the invitation to trust it, to go with it, to follow it.

2. **Go beyond opposition to create positive alternatives.** There is important oppositional and resistance work to be done when so many people and the planet itself are being consumed, as old humanity's suicidal meta-movement enters its later stages of self-destruction. That oppositional work is life-saving, essential, and heroic, like ambulance workers and other first responders rushing to a mass shooting, oil spill, or war. Even as we honor that rescue work, some of us must invest ourselves in other work, the work of creating a healthier way of life in which mass shootings, oil spills, and wars are less and less common. How do we help each rising generation of children "find the flow" of this larger spiritual movement—in a way that

both resists and creates? How do we help their parents help them? How do we influence influencers who will influence others, in arts and entertainment, politics, the academy, business, technology, and other fields of human endeavor? How do we help those involved in resistance and opposition to not become the monster they are fighting? How do we help people who are focused on resistance to appreciate the creative work of their counterparts, and vice versa? How do we recruit people who are part of the problem to switch sides and work with us for the solution? Those are the new questions we must grapple with. To do this, you certainly don't have to be a Christian, but you can be.

3. **Don't expect any micro-movement or institution, including ones you love, support, or even lead, to be the whole answer.** Every micro-movement and institution will be flawed and limited, even as it accomplishes much good. Each one will disappoint and fail, even as it makes its unique contribution. If a micro-movement or institution succeeds, it will change the conditions that made it necessary in the first place, thus requiring some sort of retooling or rebirth. The more we trust any single one to be the magical, long-term solution, and the more we demand it to be perfect, the more likely we will be to sabotage it or hasten its failure. We have to love our micro-movements and institutions, but our deepest trust always needs to be in something larger, a deeper flow, a bigger unfolding of a more potent and persistent desire (recalling Chapter 22). You can hold that deeper trust as part of your Christian identity or as part of another identity. The important thing is not to put too much trust in something that is too small, whether it's a religion, economic system, nation, superpower, or civilization.

4. **Support every positive change in every micro-movement and institution.** In light of the radical change we need, we will be tempted to belittle or even despise incremental positive changes that are achieved in this transition time. But we need to learn that even when the candle is small and flickering, it flickers in defiance of the night. Instead of a *yes, but* response to these positive changes, we can offer a *yes, and*. So we might say, "Yes, it is good to increase efficiency in your internal combustion engines, and it will be even better when we move away from fossil fuel combustion entirely." Or "Yes, it is good to improve traditional educational systems, and it will be even better when these systems are redesigned to contribute to a new way of life." Or, "Yes, it is good to reduce the number of weapons in circulation, and it will be even better when we help people feel that

violence is unthinkable and nonviolence is as habitual as eating or drinking or breathing."[4] You can cultivate this attitude as an expression of Christian identity or of some other identity.

5. **Prepare yourself for turbulence.** The existing meta-movement has thousands of years of momentum behind it. It has amassed wealth, weapons, and the unfathomable power of human assumptions, especially the assumption that *there is no alternative.* The emerging meta-movement has no chance to challenge it—until, that is, the existing meta-movement reaches necessary levels of destabilization and disequilibrium, often through the self-sabotage of overreach. Bible readers will recall Jesus' words about things getting worse and worse, "but this is still not the end." I suggest that Jesus wasn't speaking as a fortune-teller here; rather, he was speaking as a wise man who understood how systems work. He knew that systems are desperate to maintain equilibrium (a.k.a. the status quo), and they often look most successful just before they fall down the steps, so to speak, in phase after phase of decline. In this way, "the end of the world" is not the end of the world, but the end of the current world system, when the current meta-movement runs its course.

6. **Nurture the practices of spiritual resilience.** As the failing machinery of a declining meta-movement strips its final gears, we have to prepare ourselves to live good lives of defiant joy even in the midst of chaos and suffering. This can be done. It has been done by billions of our ancestors and neighbors. Their legacy teaches us to see each intensifying episode of turbulence as a labor pain from which a new creative opportunity can be born. Life will be tough; the only question is whether we will become tougher, wiser, and more resilient. Thankfully, there is a growing body of research and literature focused on the practices we need for surviving the end of the world as we have known it.[5] The communities that learn and teach these essential practices of spiritual resilience will become vital resources for everyone. (We can hope that some Christian communities will take part in this work.) These individual and communal practices will help us dump bitterness, fear, disappointment, and toxicity and refuel with mercy, vision, anticipation, and equanimity. They will help us ignore what deserves to be ignored and monitor what needs to be monitored. They will help us reframe our narratives, so we can mourn, grieve, and lament . . . even as we imagine, celebrate, and labor for the birth of a better future.

7. **Believe in it.** I return to step one because this process is iterative, and

none of us at any moment can see very far into the future. To trust in the process is another way of saying to trust in an intelligence wiser than current human intelligence, to trust in a love deeper than current expressions of human love, to trust in a desire stronger and wiser than current expressions of human desire. Christians refer to this wisdom, love, and desire as God or the Divine or the Creative Spirit, and others can find their own ways of naming it. But whatever name we use, the next step in this process will only become clear when we're pushing through the current step, often at the last possible minute. To use familiar biblical language, we will need to walk by faith through the valley of the shadow of death, always holding anticipative space for something beautiful to be born, especially during the most painful contractions.

Some forms of Christianity will remain desperately loyal to the old machinery, thinking it's as good as it gets. Other forms of Christianity will seek to repair the harm the old machinery has done and participate in the building of a new way of life that is truly regenerative.[6] You can be part of the Christian wing of this regenerative meta-movement if you so desire. Or you can participate as part of some other wing. Wherever you invest your life, I hope it will be in this larger movement laboring for the birth of something new. Embrace the long view and find the deep current, the infinite flow.

When you find that flow, you know it is holy.

❧

25

Re-Consecrate Everything

"There is no away," environmental activist Annie Leonard says. "When you throw something away, it goes somewhere." Once this simple insight hits you, you realize what a myth our culture has built itself upon. The meta-movement of domination and exploitation has told us that if we don't like something, we can simply kill it, banish it, incarcerate it, incinerate it, ignore it, bury it, or otherwise throw it away . . . and it will be gone for good.

But as James Baldwin realized, what is true of things in space is also true of time itself: "History is not the past. It is the present. We carry our history with us. We are our history. If we pretend otherwise, we are literally criminals."[1] We can't, in other words, simply erase the past and throw it away. Similarly, Dr. King realized that we can't throw our enemies away. If we hate and kill our enemies, if we marginalize and ghettoize them, even if we attempt genocide against them, we will create thousands more, as their relatives, descendants, and friends—not to mention our own descendants—forever despise us for what we have done. The only way to get rid of our enemies is to turn them into friends, as Dr. King said: "Love is the only force capable of transforming an enemy into a friend. We never get rid of an enemy by meeting hate with hate; we get rid of an enemy by getting rid of enmity."[2]

So at this critical moment, we have the chance to learn that nothing can be thrown away. That means that everything matters. Every blade of grass, every sparrow, every pebble, every drop of water counts and has value. I see this reality whenever I walk along the beach near my home. The orange shell that the horse conch fashioned remains after the conch dies. The snail itself becomes food and nutrients for other creatures. Soon, a bright red hermit crab has recycled the abandoned shell as her home. Before humans in the meta-movement of domination, exploitation, and extraction, there was no trash. It didn't exist. Every leaf, every bone, every scrap of food was a gift to something else.

That realization provides a sobering reminder to all who decide not to stay Christian. You can leave Christianity, but Christianity won't leave you. No matter how toxic some of its elements, they will still be there in the environment, living on like plastic trash in the minds and hearts and bodies of your neighbors, and through them, Christianity will still influence you.

So Christianity must be recycled, whether you stay part of it or not. Another word for *recycled* is *redeemed*, built on the word *deem*, to give value. And another word for *redeemed* is *re-consecrated*, to make holy again what has been desecrated.

This project of spiritual ecology begins with identifying the elements of our faith that are unholy, unsustainable, and harmful. We need to reduce our trafficking in those elements as we become aware of them. For example, we may need to treat certain harmful doctrines as if they were tobacco, crack, or DDT: we must diligently publicize their negative impacts so people will either use them less frequently, use them only in carefully supervised ways, or stop using them entirely. A doctrine like *original sin* might fit in this category. Many of us have stopped teaching this doctrine at all. In fact, we actively *unteach* it . . . we publicly expose the trouble it has caused. Some of us have kept it, but we only use it after buffering or outflanking it with the term *original blessing*.[3]

In some cases, we can replace harmful elements with less harmful alternatives, just as we replace un-recyclable plastics with recyclable paper. In other cases, we may repurpose old elements, like reusing disposable plastic containers as flower planters or old tires as building materials. This is what some of us are doing with the ideas of heaven and hell. We see how this binary was used to devalue the work of social justice here on earth, so we are repurposing heaven: it is not an escape clause from a doomed and unsalvageable earth but encouragement that even if we suffer for justice in this life and don't see the full results of our labors, our labor will not be in vain, longer term. Similarly, we are repurposing hell: it is not a threat of divine retribution in the afterlife but a dire warning about the inevitable negative consequences of harmful behaviors *in this life*—like war, ecological overshoot, or gross economic inequality. (In other words, we not only say that *war is hell* but also that *hell is war*—or a devastated environment or an unjust economy.) We demonstrate how Jesus, rather than teaching a new doctrine of hell, was un-teaching an existing harmful doctrine; we try to follow his example by unteaching this and other harmful Christian doctrines.[4]

In many cases, we *will* need to bury things, not secretly, to hide them, but publicly and carefully, as we do with radioactive materials or toxic chemicals. For example, when we publicly acknowledge how the Bible has been used to justify slavery, the stigmatization of LGBTQ people, and the inequality of women, we publicly bury those interpretations. We don't forget them, but rather retell them as cautionary tales to guide us going forward. Then we model a better way of interpreting Scripture.

In recent years, we've called this recycling work *deconstruction* and *reconstruction*. I don't know exactly how we will deconstruct and disarm every dangerous element of the problematic past we surveyed in Part I. Nor do I know exactly what a reconstructed Christian faith will look like after its suitably thorough deconstruction.

But I do know that many of us have been working for decades on this project. For example, in my book *Why Did Jesus, Moses, the Buddha, and Mohammed Cross the Road?*, I talked about how baptism has been understood by many as a ritual of cleansing, cleansing the stain of original sin, and so on. As I wrote the book, I was coming to realize that the very idea of being clean carried in it the rendering of the other as dirty, which is the seed of ethnic cleansing. So I dug more deeply into baptism in the New Testament, centering the story of Peter and Cornelius in Acts 10. I saw (as we noted in Chapter 17) that baptism could actually be understood as a rejection of clean/unclean narratives; it could be understood as an immersion into the current of the Spirit running through our world, bringing us into solidarity with all people.

I similarly looked at how common understandings of the eucharist (evoking blood sacrifice), election (being chosen for salvation and leaving others for damnation), foreign missions (which have tended to collude consciously or unconsciously with colonialism in recent centuries), and other elements of inherited Christianity could be radically reimagined and repurposed . . . not just thrown away, but recycled.[5]

So we are recycling *salvation* as liberation, evoking its original biblical meaning in Exodus. We are recycling *the final judgment* as the realization that only time will reveal the full goodness or evil (or mix of both) that flows from any action. As we considered in Chapter 15, we are recycling *demons and the devil* as an early theory or model of mental illness and systemic evil. We are reframing the doctrine of the *Trinity* from a math problem to a profound insight into the dynamic, creative relationality of God and the universe, helping us redefine God not as the cosmic dictator who rules the universe from outside and above but as the relational heart of the universe, enlivening it from within: self-giver, self-gift, and spirit of self-giving . . . poet, poetry, and creative flow of meaning . . . a never-ending circle dance of creative love and harmonious inter-being.

Ultimately, I believe the word *God* itself and the ideas associated with it need to undergo this process in a deep and public way, as I've suggested in several passages in this book. That work is happening and will no doubt continue, with some trying to throw the word away, others doubling down on conventional understandings, still others trying to reduce its use at least until we are clearer about what we mean by it, and others trying to provide sustainable and healthy alternative terms.

All of this can be done. But it will require us to turn our aspiration for progress into a plan of action, not unlike a family eager to convert their household toward environmental sustainability: "In May, we're going to replace our light bulbs. In June we're going to start recycling. In July we're going to improve our insulation. In October we're going to buy an electric vehicle. Next April, we'll go solar," and so on. A church leadership team that wanted to make these changes could create a checklist of desired steps and then schedule each item:

____ Review the prayers that we use in public worship. Diversify the ways we refer to the divine. Specify the desires we want to strengthen. Replace religious verbiage that sounds familiar but says little with meaningful and needed language.

____ Look at the length and structure of our services. Determine the desired outcomes for each element, identify missing elements, and experiment with redesigning our service plan.

____ Determine which song and hymn lyrics are problematic. Where possible, rewrite the lyrics. Where that's not possible, replace that song with a more appropriate one.

____ Assess benefits and liabilities of staying with the lectionary (or current system of sermon planning) or using an alternative plan. Make changes where needed.

____ Determine what outcomes we intend from our sermons. Determine whether longer sermons should be replaced with shorter sermons followed by dialogue, or whether sermons should be replaced entirely with conversations.

____ Rewrite our eucharistic liturgy so that the meanings we intend are clear each time we celebrate.

____ Review our current facilities. Are they necessary? Can they be better used by us and by other organizations to contribute to our larger vision? Should they be sold?

____ Review our foundational documents—creeds, doctrinal statements, bylaws, etc. Do the same with our website. Decide how elements of each can be replaced, clarified, simplified, or otherwise improved, and hold a vote to do so.

____ Remember that we won't get this right the first time. We are embarking on a long-term growth process, so these steps are just a beginning. Plan a celebration when we complete these first steps. Then learn from our mistakes and continue the process.

Any who embark on a process like this should prepare for conflict, because no meaningful change process has ever gone unopposed. When opposition inevitably arises, we need to remember: *even critics and opponents cannot be thrown away.* So we will need to learn how to win their trust when that is possible, a process that always begins with deep and honest listening. And when opponents cannot be turned into allies and friends (or remain present as the loyal opposition, with a vote but not a veto), we will learn to let them depart with our permission, even with our empathy and blessing, because we sincerely have come to understand how they feel. In the process, we will learn to use every criticism or complaint as an opportunity to demonstrate redemptive listening, improve our plan, and clarify our message.[6]

I understand why many want to throw Christianity away. But again: if you throw Christianity away, someone else will have to deal with it, because *there is no away.* So rather than throwing away Christianity—and religion in general—I believe now is the time to rediscover the redeemable, recyclable qualities of Christianity and other religions, to re-consecrate them and appropriately reverence them, even as we tell the inconvenient and unpopular truths of their harmful histories. Beneath the obvious flaws there are still treasures, treasures we would be fools to discard.

A simple thought experiment, I think, can remind us of those treasures. To put a spin on John Lennon's beautiful song, imagine there's no religion. Imagine there's no set of institutions, movements, and communities dedicated to human meaning, human morality, and human imagination of a better future. Imagine there's no set of practitioners who are dedicated to the development of the human capacities for wonder, generosity, repentance, and grace. Imagine there's no set of human traditions seeking to preserve the deepest spiritual wisdom of our ancestors and passing that wisdom on to new generations. Imagine there's no network of local spiritual communities—Catholic nuns and friars serving the poor and forgotten, Evangelical missionaries caring for addicts and the homeless, Mainline Protestants and Eastern Orthodox Christians joining with interfaith groups to seek the common good in this neighborhood, that town, that city.

It may be that we will only see religion's true value by imagining the complete loss of it.

But we quickly need to add another thought experiment, this one about the value of the secular world, the world that operates outside religion's control. Imagine that conventional religion has a resurgence, that what the Taliban have been trying to do in Afghanistan, the religious right and some Trump 2.0 succeed in doing in the United States, or some other political/religious movement succeeds in doing in Brazil or Russia or wherever. Let's imagine some religious politicult crushing the secular domains around the world, so it controls government, business, entertainment, education, and science and tech. Do we honestly think that conventional religion will do a better job with more power than it has done with its current amount of power? Do we really think what's wrong with the world is that religion doesn't have enough power? Seriously?

It may be that we will only see the secular's true value by imagining the loss of it.

When we imagine those scenarios, I think we begin to see that the religious and the secular are not enemies. Like male and female, like day and night, like waking and sleep, like faith and doubt, they need each other. It's not that religion is holy and the secular is profane. It's that both religion and the secular can be holy, and both can be desecrated, recalling again Wendell Berry's wise words.[7] Ultimately, the religious and the secular are not two things, but one: *life*.

Our work is to stop the desecration of life in both its religious and secular dimensions. Our work is to restore both the religious and secular to a creative dynamism that deserves and inspires appropriate reverence. Because business can be truly holy work; in fact, some of the most important spiritual breakthroughs in the world today are happening through people in the world of business.[8] Politics and governance can be holy work; in fact, some of the greatest saints and prophets today are brave activists and political leaders.[9] Entertainment and education can be holy work; in fact, artists, entertainers, teachers, and scholars are filling the spiritual void left by religious leaders who have painted themselves into any number of theological corners. Science and tech can be holy work; in fact, surprising numbers of researchers and inventors are driven by curiosity and love so powerful they invite the adjective *divine*. Yes, even religion can be holy work, though so often it has disappointed us. Every dimension and vocation of life can be holy, even though they often are not.

So the work of spiritual recycling must take place in both religious and secular spheres. In both spheres, we must stop using what is harmful—toxic rhetoric, authoritarian structures, dehumanizing narratives, and the like. Secular and religious atrocities our ancestors have buried secretly and tried to hide—like the Doctrine of Discovery, like the history of American lynching, like the power of oligarchs and their dark money—we must locate, name, publicly lament, and carefully sequester like toxic waste, deriving cautionary wisdom for future generations from our past mistakes. When using things that are potentially harmful, we must take all necessary precautions going forward—redefining our relationship with the Bible or the Constitution or capitalism or mission, for example, knowing that each can be used to harm or to heal. We must recycle and adapt whatever we can—facilities, holidays, ceremonies, institutions, and the like. In these ways, we can reconsecrate everything that has been desecrated, and the hard work of doing so will change us for the better as well.

Yes, change is hard work, especially when the pace of change in every area of life is accelerating. Both changing and resisting change can drain us of our energies. So even here, we need to think ecologically. Just as nature has seasons of rest, seasons of latency, we will need to build pause, rest, and renewal into our rhythms, individually and as communities. Our digital technology may function at the speed of light, but our human bodies and communities can only function at the speed of life. That's why philosopher and activist Bayo Akomolafe says, "The times are urgent. We must slow down."[10]

Those of us who stay Christian must start this truly urgent but also unrushable work in our own household. What we don't redeem, what we don't acknowledge and learn from, will haunt us until we do. As we proceed in this process, we can join with our counterparts in other traditions—including secular traditions and institutions—to become collaborators in a civilization-wide spring cleaning, preparing our species for the new beginning we all need if we are to survive on this beautiful, fragile planet. If we don't learn to re-consecrate everything as holy and spiritual, we will desecrate everything, turning it into trash or burying it in trash.[11]

There is no *away* for anybody, Christian or not.

Everything can be holy, religious or not.

✻

26

Renounce and Announce

I was a senior in high school the first time it happened. One of my closest friends called and asked if we could take a walk. This friend and I had
prayed together, led Bible studies together, been counselors at a Christian
summer camp together. We were about to graduate together. After maybe
twenty minutes of small talk and about a mile of walking, he stopped and
faced me. "Brian, I have to tell you something," he said. "I'm gay."

I knew what conservative Christians thought about being gay, and I also
knew how several of my classmates at my secular school mocked gay people.
And I knew what a good human being my friend was. I had no idea how to
put those facts together.

I wish I had been better prepared to respond to him with the understanding and empathy he deserved, but I recall being flummoxed and stum-
bling over my own words. In the years that followed, especially during my
twenty-four years as a pastor, I would get more and more experience with
people coming out to me, including members of my congregation and my
family. I can't remember how many people would say, "I've never told anyone this before. I'm really scared to tell you. But I need to tell someone.
Brian, I'm . . ."

Their coming out to me eventually led me to come out in my own way:
I had to come out as a Christian who no longer stigmatized my LGBTQ
friends. I had to announce how and why I had changed. There was a price
to pay for that, of course. But the price for staying silent would have been
far, far more damaging. (A pastor who recently piloted his church through

this process captured it succinctly, after losing many members: "We have been bigger, but we never have been better.")

This idea of a *coming out* is one of the many gifts the LGBTQ community has brought the world. "Up until now," a person announces, "you have thought of me in one way. But I have come to understand myself as something different, and I want to let you know."

Whether we stay Christian or seek to leave Christianity in a constructive way, we need to have our own kind of coming out. My friends John Ray and Amanda provide a powerful example of an unplanned but effective coming out to family.

Amanda grew up in a Charismatic Christian family. Her father, in fact, was a well-known pastor with a radio and internet ministry. When she met John Ray, he was a new convert to Charismatic Christianity, doing his best to fit in and learn the ropes. They married young, while still in college, as was encouraged in their church, to avoid "falling into sin." After a few years of marriage, and especially when they went to graduate school, they started reexamining their faith. In the terms we used in Chapter 21, they moved quickly from Simplicity into Complexity and, soon after, into Perplexity. At one point, they were pretty sure they were going to leave Christianity altogether. But along the way, they stumbled upon some books and podcasts that helped them find a way of staying Christian without staying fundamentalist.

In the summer of 2020, they went to visit Amanda's parents at their lake cottage for a weekend. On Saturday afternoon, John Ray woke Amanda from a nap in the guest room where they were staying. He looked miserable, shocked. He explained that Amanda's dad had just literally backed him into a corner out on the dock and asked whom he was going to support in the upcoming presidential election. When John Ray gave the wrong answer, her dad insulted him for about twenty minutes.

"All in 'Christian love,' of course," John Ray told his wife with notable irony. He said he wasn't sure he could stay there for the rest of the weekend, because he felt that he was in the presence of Christian hate.

Amanda had had enough. She marched down to the dock where her dad was working on their boat. It was sunny and warm, but she was shaking with emotion. She took a few deep breaths, and then she let loose what had been building in her for years: "Dad, we need to talk. I'm going to speak, and you're not going to interrupt me. I'm a grown woman, and you need to understand something. You don't control me anymore, and you don't control John Ray either. So here's what you need to know. I am grateful to you and mom for your love and care. But the form of Christianity you taught me stopped working for John Ray and me. We came very close to leaving Christianity entirely, but we have found a way to stay Christian, just not conservative like you and mom. We have changed. I hope you hear that. We have changed. We don't believe everybody who isn't Christian is going to hell. We believe in evolution. We are pro-choice. We stopped voting Republican. We take the Bible seriously, which for us means that we *don't* take it literally. We accept gay people. And we still love Jesus with all our hearts and want to follow him. Just not in the same way as you."

Amanda's heart was pounding in her chest. Her dad started to interrupt. She shouted, "Stop! I'm not interested in arguing with you, Dad! I'm *announcing* something to you!"

Like a lot of preachers, her father wasn't used to anyone standing up to him. She continued, "I'm sure this is a great disappointment to you, Dad. I know it makes you afraid that God will send us to hell. I know you see it as a failure of your parenting. But if you cannot accept us for who we are, right now, that will be your biggest single mistake ever as a parent. Look, Dad, John Ray and I hope to have a child in the next year or two. I would very much like to have a continuing relationship with you, and I would like my child to grow up with a loving grandpa. But if you can't accept us as we are, you will not see us or meet your future grandchildren. Ever. I hope that's clear. That will not be because I am rejecting you. I do not reject you. I love you and I will love you every day of my life. If we have to stay away, it will be because you are not willing to accept and respect me and my husband as adults. That's your choice. I just want you to understand the consequences of that choice."

Her father squinted at Amanda, as if he didn't recognize her. Then he turned and marched up the path to the cottage without saying anything. Amanda waited a few minutes, and then returned to the cottage to report to John Ray what had happened.

Her dad was sitting in a rocking chair on the front porch. He stood and told Amanda she had hurt him deeply and he didn't feel he could ever forgive her, but he eventually would, with God's help. Then he said that he and her mom needed to talk, and then they would get back to her. He started to critique the tone with which she had spoken to him, but she put up her hands and said, "No, Dad. I said what I needed to say in the only way I could say it."

Later that afternoon, Amanda's dad found John Ray and apologized, sort of, and the rest of the weekend was tense, but they got through it. About a week later, her parents called and asked to speak to both Amanda and John Ray. Her dad said he understood why Amanda needed to speak up and he didn't want to drive them away. He repeated two or three times that he didn't approve of the changes they had gone through, but he understood that was the new reality. He didn't like it, and he never would, but he would accept it.

Then Amanda's mom spoke up. "Now just how soon are you planning on having that grandbaby of ours?" Everyone laughed. It felt like they had established a new normal.

What Amanda and John Ray did with Amanda's parents—announcing that they had changed, I've had to do in my own way, as a parent to my adult kids. As I mentioned earlier, I've had to tell them I no longer believe some of the things I believed when they were young. In particular, I've told them that I regret the authoritarian style of parenting that I learned from the Christian community I was part of, that I regret raising them even adjacent to a religious context where there was too much shame. "I did my best as your dad," I've told them, "but you deserved better."

Whether or not we stay Christian, we need to do something similar. First, if we have gone through the kind of deconstruction and reconstruction that we considered in Parts I and II, we need to *come out to* our congregations, denominations, and other Christian associates. I'm not saying we need to *come out from* them, as if we are too good for them. I'm not saying we need to separate ourselves from others as superior and elite. Instead, I'm saying that we need to very lovingly, non-defensively, and non-aggressively be clear about where we are. If others reject us or prefer that we leave, so be it. In the long run, we will find it better to be rejected for who we are than accepted for who we aren't. Whether we have shifted out of Christianity entirely or into a new kind of Christianity, we have to be courageous enough to come out of our closets and go public, not minimizing the change, not feeling embarrassed about who we are becoming, not hiding our light under a bushel of polite ambiguity.

Many of us who stay Christian—but in a new way—are already announcing this "coming out," both as individuals and as congregations. Some of us

204 Do I Stay Christian?

are also reaching out to our Jewish, Muslim, Hindu, Sikh, Buddhist, atheist, agnostic, and other neighbors to let them know we have changed. We find ourselves making deep and heartfelt apologies for ways we hurt people in the past. Wherever necessary and possible, we are following up our apologies with amends or reparations. Sometimes, we create formal rituals of forgiveness and reconciliation.

Our announcement must include a renouncement.

In 2015, a Methodist minister in Paris, Texas, learned that about a hundred years earlier, some members of his congregation had participated in the lynching of the Arthur brothers, two African Americans. That terrorist act led to 3,000 African Americans fleeing the town as part of the Great Migration to the north. The pastor, my friend Rob Spencer, preached a sermon to tell the truth about his city and his congregation's past. A young woman in the area, herself a descendant of the perpetrators, came to him with the idea of organizing a memorial on the centennial of the lynching. Along with two pastors of African American churches in Paris, they helped organize a remembrance service of acknowledgment and healing where descendants of the perpetrators and descendants of the victims gathered to renounce the racism of their town's past and dream together of a better future. They got involved with the Equal Justice Initiative's Community Remembrance Project and have additional plans to work for community transformation.[1] The process has not been easy. Rob has been targeted on social media as a "libtard," and some parishioners have left his church. But again, better to be rejected for who you are than accepted for who you're not.

A similar kind of coming out is happening around the Belhar Confession. During apartheid in South Africa, some Black and colored Christians invited willing white Christians to make a joint statement that called racism a sin. In the years since, several denominations around the world have adopted the Belhar Confession as a way of acknowledging their failure to address racism in the past and their commitment to be different in the future. Several denominations have formally renounced the Doctrine of Discovery as part of this process. I am encouraged by a growing consensus for national and perhaps international truth and reconciliation commissions, building upon the experience of South Africans: first, renouncing injustices done to Indigenous, enslaved, and colonized peoples, and second, announcing a shared commitment to create a common memory about the past and a common imagination for the future.[2]

Many congregations have gone public with other kinds of announcement and renouncement. For example, when they stop stigmatizing LGBTQ persons or when they complete anti-racism training, they may put up a rainbow flag or Black Lives Matter sign. These are ways of coming out, going public, giving testimony: *We've changed. We want you to know where we stand.*

If we take seriously the atrocities we considered in Part I, we can't just move on, keeping our repentance private. We need to engage in public corporate repentance. This repentance will consist not of the least acknowledgment necessary but rather a full, public, and unrestrained accounting. Through renouncement and announcement, our *coming out* can be a *coming clean.*

When some Christians make these kinds of announcements, others will, no doubt, refuse, criticize, and double down on defending their innocence, maybe even their supremacy. That is their choice. When some of us make the announcements we need to make, when we break our silence, come out, and come clean, other Christians will for the first time have a choice: stand with the Christian majority who defend the status quo or join with a growing Christian minority in our ongoing rethinking process. Our renouncement and announcement thus become an invitation.

By renouncing the failures of our past and announcing that we are changing, we commit ourselves to live humbly, justly, and kindly in the present and future. It may just be that if we sincerely follow that path, some Christians who were on their way out of the faith will find a reason to stay—and stay in a new way. And some who have left Christianity may find a reason to return—to embody Christian faith with us in this new way.

Even if you leave Christianity, you will not be exempt from this hard but important work, because it's not just Christianity that has unacknowledged skeletons in its trunk. Nations do too, as do professions, industries, ideologies, races, and economies. You do. So do I. We all have to start somewhere, and that somewhere is with ourselves.

Being human means we have a past to contend with. And it also means that in the present, we can chart a new path into the future, just as Amanda did on that dock with her father, just as Rob did in his city in Texas, just as courageous South African clergy did during apartheid. Christian or not, coming out is full of challenge.

Your coming out may happen spontaneously, as it did with Amanda. You might prefer to write your coming out statement or organize a public event as Rev. Rob Spencer did. Even if you don't share it publicly, the act of crafting an honest and intentional statement might have value simply in helping you articulate where you've come from, where you are, and where you're going. (In a sense, each of my books has been an extended coming out statement of this sort.) I crafted a few examples of statements of renouncement or announcement that echo messages others have shared with me over the years:

Many of you know I've been going through a faith crisis recently. I have decided to stay Christian, but I must renounce all forms of Christianity that claim or defend supremacy, privilege, domination, and violence, and I must announce my aspiration to follow the path of solidarity embodied and taught by Jesus.

I want to let you know that I no longer want to identify as a Christian. It's not that I left my faith; rather, it has left me. I intend no disrespect to those of you who remain Christian, and I hope you will respect my decision to continue my life outside the Christian faith.

Dear Family and Friends—I want you to know I am no longer a Christian. Last year I realized that Christianity was smothering me and subjecting me to constant condemnation because I am gay. Since leaving, I feel free and honest and alive. If my decision upsets you, instead of criticizing me, you might consider how you can make your church a less damaging and more healing place so people like me don't need to leave to save their lives and sanity. Be assured that I love you as always.

Many of you know that I was on my way out of Christianity, but I recently found a new congregation that welcomed me and is on the same journey I am. It's enabling me to rediscover the good things about my faith and let go of the things that I felt were harming me and others. I just wanted to let everyone know that I have found a way to stay Christian, but in a new way.

An announcement: My commitment to follow the life and teachings of Jesus is stronger than ever, but for my own health and sanity, I can no longer remain associated with Christianity. I have tried to be an agent of change from the inside, but I am battle-scarred and worn down. Each of you who attacks me for this decision—please understand that you are only confirming this decision's wisdom and necessity. For all of my Christian friends who understand why I need to make this choice, please know that I am not rejecting you and hope our friendships can continue and maybe even improve because I am being honest and you are accepting me as I am.

Professor Jones, I have spent a lot of my life preaching against liberal or progressive Catholic faith, just as you taught me to do in seminary. I want to let you know that I have become what we both have criticized for so long. Much of my preaching, I now see, was an effort to persuade myself not to go where honesty and integrity were leading me. I cannot leave Christ, whom I love and serve, but I can no longer remain a supporter of what conservative Catholicism has become. Progressive Catholicism offers me a way to maintain honesty and integrity in good faith. I will always be grateful for all I learned from you, and I'm sorry to disappoint a mentor who invested so much in me twenty-five years ago. Please be assured that even if you are no longer comfortable seeing me as a friend, I will always see you as one of my most influential mentors.

Self-reporting statements like these can help you renounce and announce both clearly and graciously, and your doing so will help others in the long run, even if it upsets them in the short run. Remember, as the sage pop star Taylor Swift has said, that haters gonna hate, so don't be surprised when they do. I can only hope that you will receive positive responses that outweigh the inevitable negative reactions that come from those who feel they must prove their loyalty to the in-group by casting you into an out-group. When they constrict their circle to exclude you, you can expand yours to include them.

✢

27

Stay Loyal to Reality

In 2004, American journalist Ron Suskind recounted a conversation with a White House aide (widely believed to be Karl Rove):

> The aide said that guys like me were "in what we call the reality-based community," which he defined as people who "believe that solutions emerge from your judicious study of discernible reality." . . . "That's not the way the world really works anymore," he continued. "We're an empire now, and when we act, we create our own reality. And while you're studying that reality—judiciously, as you will—we'll act again, creating other new realities, which you can study too, and that's how things will sort out. We're history's actors . . . and you, all of you, will be left to just study what we do."[1]

The term *reality-based community* was born into public consciousness that day.

This aide's claim to create reality reeked with the kind of imperial pride that precedes a well-deserved fall. It set the stage for the rise of Trump, that lover of conspiracy theories from birtherism to Q-Anon to the Big Steal. As Hannah Arendt explained in *The Origins of Totalitarianism*, decoupling politics from reality has a long history: "Before mass leaders seize the power to fit reality to their lies their propaganda is marked by its extreme contempt for facts as such, for in their opinion fact depends entirely on the power of the man who can fabricate it."[2] No wonder Dr. Timothy Snyder said, "Post-truth is pre-fascism."[3] And no wonder sage author and religious educator David Dark said, "Sin is active flight from a lived realization of available data."[4]

Christianity, especially since Galileo and Darwin, has had an uncomfortable relationship with available data. But people can easily jump from the Christian frying pan into a secular fire with its own unreality, discovering that there is a fine line between ideologies and conspiracy theories, and that secular ideologies from communism to capitalism can function much like post-truth religions, teaching their adherents to reject available data and cling to ideological purity.

So whether we stay Christian or not, we need to aspire to be part of the reality-based community as we move forward. As I said in *Faith After Doubt*, we must be more loyal to reality than to our current beliefs about reality.

My studies of bias and authoritarianism have reinforced my commitment to remain a loyal member of the reality-based community.[5] But they have also helped me see how tenuous our grasp of reality is, even on our best days. Because our brains evolved for survival, deep-seated survival mechanisms can easily interfere with our aspiration to know the truth. These fight, flight, freeze, fawn, and flock mechanisms render us vulnerable to con artists who use fear and shame to manipulate us, seducing us with what we want to hear so they can manipulate us for their advantage. Because con artists come in both religious and secular flavors, we all are vulnerable.

Our evolutionary wiring leaves us vulnerable not only to the con artistry of others but also to our own self-deception. Going forward, we're all going to have to be on guard for the ways our own inner mechanisms can conspire to keep us from the truth . . . whether that truth is scientific or spiritual. Yes, those who stay Christian urgently need to practice all due diligence so that we don't repeat the failures we considered in Part I. But so does every other community susceptible to group-think: scientists, educators, Democrats, Republicans, conservatives, liberals, everybody. Nobody is exempt from self-delusion, so nobody is exempt from the need for vigilant self-examination.

Of course, the question remains: How do we know that we're aligning with reality or a false narrative constructed by a con artist, demagogue, cult leader, or fool, including ourselves? While there is no surefire trick for avoiding being fooled or being foolish, there is a spiritual practice that can help us: *the practice of unknowing*. Policy analyst and author Jamie Holmes literally wrote the book on uncertainty. *Nonsense: The Power of Not Knowing* argues that in "an increasingly unpredictable, complex world, it turns out that what matters most isn't IQ, willpower, or confidence in what we know. It's how we deal with what we don't understand."[6]

When we learn to acknowledge our unknowing, when we learn to sit humbly and in a relaxed way with uncertainty, when we learn to restrain ourselves from jumping from ambiguity to premature closure, we gain some protection from self-deception. If we are willing to sit with unknowing long enough to examine evidence, consult wise counselors, think critically, and keep our hearts and minds non-anxious and open, we will increase the likelihood that we are moving forward in sync with reality.

Prayer, in my experience, can be an anxious attempt to gain control (with God's help) over the unknown. But prayer can also be a healthy practice of relaxation, of settling into quiet confidence and "peace that passes understanding," of learning to acknowledge and hold our unknowing, our un-control, our un-closure. Since I understand prayer as the intentional formation of desire (recalling Chapter 22), and since I desire to remain receptive to reality beyond my current understanding, I have written a prayer that I return to often these days. It is derived from the list of biases we considered in Chapter 9. I use it to help me break down my great wall of bias so I can live more wisely with unknowing, so I can remain part of the reality-loyal community:

I do not know everything. I do not even know how much I do not know. Nor do I know how much of what I know is impartial, faulty, or false. So I pray:

Source of all truth, help me to hunger for truth, even if it upsets, modifies, or overturns what I already think is true. Guide me into all the truth I can bear, and stretch me to bear more, so that I may always choose the whole truth—even with disruption—over half-truths with self-deception. Grant me passion to follow wisdom wherever it leads. [Confirmation Bias]

Spirit of wisdom and understanding, help me not be seduced by simple lies or repelled by complex truths. Instead, teach me to seek out understanding as if it were hidden treasure, digging deep beneath surface appearances to discover what is real in the depths. [Complexity Bias]

Inspirer of holy boldness and humble bravery, give me the humility to learn from my community along with the courage to differ graciously from my community, seeking truth even when my companions are unwilling to see it or accept it. Help me remain humbly loyal to the truth even when I am misjudged and rejected by my community for doing so. [Community Bias]

Revealer of insight, do not let me be satisfied to see only what is visible from my limited perspective. Grant me insatiable curiosity to understand what my neighbors can see from their different vantage points. Help me draw near to them, to walk with them, to see through their eyes, hear through their ears, and feel through their experiences, so my horizons will be broadened through empathy. [Contact Bias]

Spirit of wisdom, protect me from being misled by those whose words are full of flattery, familiarity, and false promises, and keep me humble enough to learn from those whom I am tempted to dismiss as strange, difficult, or unfriendly. [Complementarity Bias]

Wellspring of all self-knowledge, give me humility so that I do not overestimate my competence. Save me from both excessive confidence and a lack of confidence; instead, please grant me proper confidence, to see myself, my abilities, and my limitations with a clear eye and sound mind. [Competence Bias]

Voice who beckons me toward growth, help me see what I am mature enough to see right now, and not only that: help me to know now how little I can know until I grow more mature. Grant me the curiosity and awe so that I may honor the bottomless, limitless wonder, beauty, and mystery of this world. [Consciousness Bias]

Spirit of truth who sets us free by the truth, do not let my desire for comfort blind me to truths that will inconvenience me. Grant me resolve to welcome the pain that often comes with wisdom. Help me choose empathy over apathy and courage over complacency, and to abhor the bliss that accompanies ignorance. [Comfort/Complacency Bias]

Holy source of both surprise and consistency, help me never to be held captive by rigid ideology on the one hand or addiction to novelty on the other. Do not let me be blinded by conformity or loyalty to any political party or economic arrangement. Whatever is changing around me, help me always to do justice persistently, love kindness cheerfully, and with unflagging sincerity, to walk in humility with you, my God. [Conservative/ Liberal Bias]

Cosmic witness who cannot lie, keep me vigilant against con artists for whom lies and truth are spoken with equal confidence, and who tell me what I want to hear so that I will do what they desire. Protect me from surrendering to others my responsibility to think for myself. [Confidence Bias]

Holy light who illumines what is real, help me to see danger that is all the more threatening because it unfolds gradually and, likewise, help me to see possibility that is easily missed because it emerges slowly and subtly. Grant me, I pray, the long view. [Catastrophe Bias]

Beloved One who loves me, help me to hate money in comparison with you and help me see in the love of money the hidden root of all kinds of evil, so that I may see and cherish what has true value, freely giving what I cannot keep to gain what I cannot lose. [Cash Bias]

Companion who walks with me in light, help me guard my heart from stories and theories that cast me as an innocent victim or virtuous hero, while simultaneously casting someone else as villain or enemy. Instead, help me join your cosmic conspiracy of kindness, justice, joy, and peace for all, seeing myself and all my neighbors as equal beneficiaries of your boundless, merciful love. [Conspiracy Bias][7]

If you do not pray, you might adapt these aspirations into statements for meditation, each beginning with, "May I . . ." Whatever language we use, knowing what we know about ourselves as human beings (Christian or not), we find ourselves in need of intense desire formation focused on the preciousness of truth, wisdom, insight, hindsight, foresight, and understanding.

This individual discipline is necessary, but it's not always sufficient. That's why we need communities of kindred spirits of diverse perspectives who, rather than reinforcing group-think, help us rest in unknowing and engage in self-examination, desire formation, and shared conversation across disciplines, religions, cultures, and professions. The "positive peer pressure" of groups like these can help us strengthen not just our openness to the obvious truth that comes knocking on our door but also our hunger and thirst for the subtle truth that beckons us out into the world with childlike curiosity. In the words of Jamie Holmes, these communities can help us "push back against our own mind's need to reduce and simplify and dispel all remaining doubts."[8]

Our critics, we will eventually learn, can be valuable to us in this regard. Sometimes, they're just working out their own biases at our expense. But sometimes, they are trying to tell us that we're missing something.

As I see it, to be loyal to God is to be loyal to reality, and to be loyal to reality is to be loyal to God. But that's only true when we remember that reality isn't simply what is. Reality also contains within it the seeds of what can be but is not yet. In other words, part of the reality to which we must be loyal is the future possibility that is subtly present in the present moment. (Richard Rohr says it like this: "Saying yes to 'What is' ironically sets us up for 'What if?'")[9]

Imagine looking at the universe in its first several billion years: swirling gases, surging energy fields, nothing solid. Or imagine looking at the earth when it was a lifeless planet of rock, water, ice, and volcanoes. Even then, rain forests, coral reefs, savannas with elephants and giraffes, cities with stand-up comics, and Latin jazz were inherent in the possibilities—they just weren't visible yet. To see that possibility is what faith is about: not merely seeing the seeds in the apple but seeing the million apple orchards waiting to spring from those seeds.

Loyalty to reality does not feel like certainty. It feels more like humility. It feels like awe, wonder, curiosity, patient attentiveness. It evokes Jesus' calls to the perpetual rethinking of repentance, to lifelong childlikeness, to the cultivation of the born-again or beginner's mind. It renders you less a pundit and more a contemplative. And so we must keep our eyes, ears, and hearts open, tending the fire of desire for truth in our innermost being. For without a sincere loyalty to reality (pregnant as it is with unknowable possibilities), we will be lost, Christian or not. With a humble, teachable loyalty to reality, we can survive and even thrive, inside the Christian religion or out.

❦

28

STAY HUMAN

When I start to write a book, I wonder when they will come: those surprising moments of discovery that have animated every writing project that I have ever undertaken, moments when I realize, "Ah, so *that's* what has been trying to be said!" There have been many such moments in the writing of this book, but four stand out.

As I finished Part I, I couldn't stop thinking of the little dog Toto in *The Wizard of Oz*. When Toto pulled back the curtain, the little wizard and all of his mechanisms of intimidation suddenly seemed pathetic, shabby, comical. Similarly, the more I looked back over Christian history—including recent history—the more I felt that the white male authority structures of the past and present had lost their magic. They were rendered almost weightless. Yes, our ancestors did the best they could with what they knew, and for that, they should be studied and appropriately honored. But knowing what we know now, we have a new responsibility: not simply to carry on the tradition but to challenge and improve it, and our descendants will have the same responsibility when we pass the baton to them. In light of what we now know, to carry on a deeply flawed tradition without improving it feels like a grave infidelity.

A second realization—a rather obvious one—came as I began Part II, when it dawned on me that *Do I Stay Christian?* points beyond itself to a second question, a very personal one: *how do I stay Christian?* I've been wrestling with that question in every single book I have ever written. In my first book, for example, *The Church on the Other Side*, I considered what it would mean to identify as a Christian on the other side of the modern/post-modern divide, a divide I knew I was crossing. The intentionally ungainly subtitle of *A Generous Orthodoxy* demonstrated my attempt to expand the definition of Christian identity by complexifying it: *Why I Am a Missional, Evangelical, Post/Protestant, Liberal/Conservative, Mystical/Poetic, Biblical, Charismatic/Contemplative, Fundamentalist/Calvinist, Anabaptist/Anglican, Methodist, Catholic, Green, Incarnational, Depressed-yet-Hopeful, Emergent, Unfinished Christian.* That broader definition, I hoped, would have room for me. I began making more concrete proposals about Christian identity in the *A New Kind of Christian* trilogy, and, almost ten years later, in *A New Kind of Christianity.* I focused on the spiritual formation that nourishes a new kind of Christian identity in *Finding Our Way Again* and *Naked Spirituality.* I grappled with Christian identity in a multi-faith world in *Why Did Jesus, Moses, the Buddha, and Mohammed Cross the Road?* I described the transition processes of leaving an old identity and moving toward a new one in *The Great Spiritual Migration* and *Faith After Doubt.*

You would think after all that writing, I would have Christian identity all figured out.

And I do.

Of course, I'm kidding. Which brings me to the third moment of discovery, perhaps the most dramatic. As I was completing Part II of this book, I realized that *I really don't care if you stay Christian.* Quite an admission after all these years! Yes, I would be happy if you decided to stay Christian in the ways we've considered in Parts II and III. Yes, I want you to experience the fullness of life, the life abundant that Jesus taught and embodied. But no, I won't be disappointed or feel that this book has failed if you can't stay affiliated with the Christian religion as expressed in your context. Christianity may have already wounded you too deeply for you to stay, or you may feel that it has become so infected with toxic elements that you must, in good conscience, quarantine yourself from it. My goal in this book has never been to push you toward a predetermined answer to the title's question but rather to help you find your own answer, an answer you can live with honestly, with integrity, with open eyes and deep intention.

Which leads me to the fourth *aha* moment. By the time I began Part III, I realized that a new question of human identity now overshadows old questions of religious identity: *what kind of humans do we want to become?* All our models of humanity are as contested these days as our models of Christianity. In fact, the divisions among Christians reflect the divisions among Muslims, Jews, Hindus, atheists, Republicans, Democrats, capitalists, and socialists. Under the same label, some are arrogant and others humble. Some are selfish and others generous. Some want to conserve their own privilege and power and others want justice and joy to be more widely distributed to all. Some are motivated by fear or greed and others by curiosity and grace. Some are afraid to let go of the past and some are afraid of bringing too much of it along into the future. Some care about the global common good and others care more exclusively about their individual or in-group interests.

The turmoil in so many of our identities comes back, again and again, to this very human question: what kind of humans do we want to become? So: *To be or not to be better humans: that is the question.*

Will we be wasteful, consumptive destroyers of this earth?

Will we be hateful, competitive warriors, battling in-group against in-group, religion against religion, nation against nation, ideology against ideology until the bitter end?

Will we fail to learn from the hindsight of history? Will we refuse to exercise the foresight of imagination? Will we succeed only at being short-sighted, living for the next paycheck or next election? Will we be addicted to certainty and blinded by our unchallenged biases?

Will we think that converting everyone to be Christians just like us—or converting everyone to be *whatever* just like us—will solve all our problems?

Do we really think that any of us have being human figured out? Might all our other identity struggles simply be proxy battles about this deeper question of what kind of humans we should become?

Several passages from the Bible quickly come to mind as I ruminate over this most basic of questions, this question of our humanity.

First, I picture a scene from John's Gospel (chapters 7 and 8), where Jesus and the religious leaders of his day get into a series of arguments. Dropped in the middle of these arguments comes the dramatic episode where Jesus protects a woman from being executed by stoning at the hands of these religious leaders. In the process, he gets them to admit they have their own sins to worry about. (Quite a moment of self-discovery!) Then he says he is the light of the world, to which they object: he can't be anything special because he's illegitimate, a bastard, which is, in their minds, an unforgivable blemish on his identity (8:19). A few verses later, they ask the question of identity more directly: "Who are you?" (8:25).

Then, as he often does, Jesus turns the question on them. *Who are they?* Of course, they say they are descendants of Abraham . . . a lot like folks today saying, "I'm Christian," or "I'm Roman Catholic," or "I'm a Reformed, Bible-believing, Spirit-filled, Conservative Protestant Evangelical Charismatic Christian," or whatever. Then Jesus goes to the heart of the matter: *Sure, you call yourselves descendants of Abraham. But you're plotting to kill me!* (8:37–40). If I can paraphrase slightly, Jesus is saying: *What does "descendant of Abraham" even mean if it is your camouflage for hate and violence?*

Jesus' words here recall those of his cousin John, who had said a few years earlier (Luke 3:8 ff.), "You brood of vipers! . . . Do not begin to say to yourselves, 'We have Abraham as our ancestor'; for I tell you, God is able from these stones to raise up children to Abraham." Again, to paraphrase slightly: *You're descendants of Abraham? Big deal. Want to know what really is a big deal? It's how you live, how you treat people, what kind of humans you are.*

Then I hear Micah, the great Jewish prophet. He too lives in a time of ferment and controversy, full of arguments about God and religious identity. Micah (6:8) asks the bottom-line question: *what does God really desire of human beings?*

It all boils down to this, Micah says: *O human being, this is what God desires for you. That you do justice. That you love kindness. That you walk humbly in the presence of your God.*

Micah turns a religious question into a human question.

Christians like very much to call Jesus the *Son of God.* Jesus much preferred to call himself the *Son of Man* (or *son of humanity*). There are many layers of meaning to the term. But the simplest and most obvious is this: a *son of humanity* is a *human being*. If you want to put a finer point on it, *son of* means *the essence of* or perhaps *a new generation of.*[1] Jesus is saying that he represents the essence of humanity, a new generation of humanity, a new kind of human being. In this light, his constant invitation, *follow me*, means *imitate me* and *join me on my journey toward a new way of being human.*[2]

Then I hear Mary add her voice to the voices of Jesus, John, and Micah. In her socio-political poem known as the Magnificat (Luke 1:46–55), Mary magnifies the Lord because God upsets the status quo, scattering the proud, bringing down the powerful from their thrones, lifting up the lowly, filling the hungry with a feast, and giving the rich a taste of the hunger the poor have long known. In this flipping of the social script, Mary asserts what really matters: simply being *human*, humble enough to receive mercy.

And so I think Jesus, John, Micah, and Mary should have the last word. I close my eyes and imagine them surveying the Christian landscape today and saying, "You say you're Christians? Big deal. Evangelicals, Mainline Protestants, Eastern Orthodox, or Roman Catholics? Big deal. You recite creeds or speak in tongues or both? Big deal. You say you aren't as bad as the other guys? Big deal. You're conservative? Liberal? Big deal." Right then, when a group of atheists and secularists start applauding, happy to see the religious hypocrites exposed, I can imagine Jesus, John, Micah, and Mary having some choice words to say to them as well.

What can we do but humbly seek to know ourselves for what we are? Naked of our religious labels, we are fragile human beings who were born but a moment ago, who are here for maybe seventy or eighty circuits around the sun, and who will surely die. Surely we don't think we've figured everything out so quickly! And so too for our species: we are a newly evolved and highly vulnerable population, living on a thin, fragile film of suitable habitat on a tiny planet orbiting an average sun on the rim of an average galaxy that is just one of over a hundred billion other galaxies. Yes, we are capable of wisdom, beauty, and tenderness, yet we are still an ignorant and violent species overall, shockingly cruel at times. The dinosaurs lasted for 165 million years, but after just 0.125 percent of their time on earth, we humans are on the verge of destroying our civilization and devastating the biosphere in the process. And we dare to call ourselves *Homo sapiens, the wise ones*! If we want to be certain of something, it should be this: we are not very wise.

In that light, whatever you choose to call yourself, Christian or not, I hope you will aspire to be a *humble* human being . . . *religiously.*

Not only that, but however you answer the *Do I Stay Christian?* question, I hope you will desire to be a *kind* human being, because that person next to you, that person you think is so stupid or so wrong or heretical or narrow-minded, that person you call your enemy . . . that person is part of your family, part of your species, part of your story, part of your kind, and more like you than you would like to admit. You are woven together in one fabric. As foolish as that person looks to you, you look to someone else. So if you want others to be kind to you, be kind to others.

And not just other humans. Remember that if bees and other insects stop pollinating fruits and vegetables, you won't eat. Remember that if phytoplankton in the oceans and trees in the rain forests stop producing oxygen, you won't breathe. Remember that if prevailing winds stop bringing clouds to rain on your land, you won't drink. So be kind and gentle to the earth, to all its creatures, to all its nonliving systems, as well as your fellow humans. I hope you will desire to be a kind human being . . . *religiously.*

And in addition to being a humble and kind human being, I hope you will aspire to being a *just* human being. Don't seek power over others to control them or exploit them or harm them. Instead, use whatever power that comes your way for the common good, so that all people everywhere can share equal justice and equal dignity. Seek justice. Love justice. Do justice. Be a just human being . . . *religiously.*

When I say *religiously*, I mean *intentionally*, seeking out practices that promote justice, kindness, and humility. And I mean *collaboratively*, joining or building communities or networks that promote those practices. And I mean *reverently*, knowing how precious this heartbeat and this breath really are, and feeling every moment how much danger and opportunity are held in these human hands. *Religiously*, as I'm using the term, means *with a sense of the sacredness of everything* and a commitment to reconsecrate everything.

Having read this book, you understand why I could not stay a Christian if my only option was the old way, the old way of white Christianity, the old way of patriarchal Christianity, the old way of Theo-Capitalistic Christianity, the old way of violent, exclusive, and authoritarian Christianity with its suppressed but real history of cruelty. I do not judge others who feel at home in that kind of Christianity. How can I, having lived there myself for much of my life? I understand its many comforts.

But learning and experiencing what I have, the old way is no longer an option for me.

You have seen how I have found the permission and freedom to be a new kind of Christian, a progressive Christian, a contemplative-activist Christian, a Christian humanist, or whatever you want to call me.[3] I am learning to be content whatever I am called, as long as I remain passionately eager to embody a way of being human that is pro-justice, pro-kindness, and pro-humility.

You have that permission too, if you would like it.

In this space, we can ask previously un-askable questions, make previously forbidden confessions, imagine previously impossible possibilities, and form previously un-formable communities so we can continue our spiritual quest.

What is that quest? To become the most just, kind, and humble version of ourselves that we possibly can, day by day . . . to practice a faith that expresses itself in love . . . to lean with others into a new humanity, a new generation or new kind of humanity, open to every good resource that can help us, explicitly Christian or not.

This doesn't sound easy, you say. *There's not much certainty in what you offer.*

Ah, that is so true. But are either *ease* or *certainty* even options for us, being who we are, living when and where we live?

In the absence of ease and certainty, what amazing things can happen!

Life can happen.

Wonder can happen.

Faith, hope, love, unspeakable joy can thrive in difficulty and uncertainty.

A new humanity—humble, just, and kind—can be born.

Can you imagine that, fellow human?

AFTERWORD

✤

There once was a bird who lived in a tree. The bird was named Faithful. From the time she was a tiny hatchling, her parents used to sing a song every morning. The song was called "Home," but Faithful thought Home was the name of her tree.

Even after her siblings fledged and flew away, Faithful never ventured far from the nest. It was all she had ever known through the spring and summer of her life. To her, it was Home.

Fall came. The leaves changed from green to amber, rust, pumpkin, and scarlet. "Home has never been more beautiful!" Faithful thought. "I'm so glad I stayed."

One day, gusty winds blew and a hard, cold rain fell. One by one, the leaves flew off the tree. After the storm, Faithful became worried. "Home has never been so ugly," she said.

She looked up and saw other birds flying. She wondered if she should join them. Would it be safe? Would her tree survive without her? Would she survive without the tree? What would her parents think, after providing such a beautiful nest in this tree called Home?

To stay or to leave . . . it felt like the biggest choice she would ever make.

One morning, one of her brothers, Adventure, flew in and perched on a branch beside her. "I've been looking everywhere for you," he said. "It's time to migrate."

"I don't know what to do," Faithful said. "I don't know if I should stay Home or leave."

Adventure cocked his head. "Faithful, I think you're confused," he tweeted. "Home isn't the name of your tree. Home is the name of your song. Wherever you sing your song, that is your home."

For many of us, Christianity is the name of the tree in which we were raised, or it is the tree in which we sought refuge later in life. But the season has changed. The tree has changed. We have changed. The longer we stay, the more disappointed, disillusioned, frustrated, and even trapped we feel.

Perhaps we need to discover that Christian faith wasn't meant to be our tree. It was meant to be our song. Wherever we sing with love, joy, peace, and patience, wherever we sing with kindness, gentleness, generosity, and justice, there we manifest what being human means to us. Our song is our gift to the world.

Trees grow. Trees change through the seasons. They mature, decline, and die. Then new trees grow where the old trees once cast their shadows. What matters most isn't staying faithful to the tree but staying faithful to the song, our song, the song only we can sing.

Perhaps you will sing your song from the old familiar tree. Perhaps you will leave the tree but keep singing your song.

Perhaps you will stay in the tree but give up singing entirely.

Perhaps "Do I stay Christian?" isn't the kind of question you can answer with a simple *yes* or *no*, because perhaps what Jesus was about wasn't which tree to perch in but how to sing your song in the symphony of creation.

If you began this book wondering if you could or should stay Christian and have found a way to do so in good faith and with a whole and undivided heart, I am happy for you. May you embody a form of Christian faith that will reverse rather than perpetuate the problems we considered in Part I, while embodying the aspirations of Parts II and III. May your life sing with joy and resilience wherever you go. May you find or form a flock of kindred spirits so that your voice and theirs will fill the earth with the music of conviviality. And may hundreds, thousands, millions, even billions find their voice and sing their song in the symphony of creation across future generations.

If you have reached the end of this book and now understand more clearly why you can no longer identify as a Christian, I am happy for you as well. Knowing what you're not (and why) is an important dimension of discovering who you are and can be.[1] May you become an even better human being outside the Christian religion than you ever were within it. May you bring with you whatever good things you gained from your Christian experience and leave behind all extra baggage. May the song of your life inspire others—including your Christian neighbors—toward a better way of being human, of being alive.

If you have read this book and still aren't sure whether you can stay Christian, I am also happy for you. The fact that you are taking great care with this decision means you are approaching it with the seriousness it deserves. As your decision process unfolds, may you focus more on the *how* question in Part III of this book . . . the question of how you want to live, what kind of human being you want to be, how you want to sing. Whatever your decision about staying Christian, you will be better off for taking the *how* question, the *human* question, seriously.

Do I stay Christian? In the end, the answer that really matters is not the one you or I give with our words, but the one we give with our lives. That's what the great Austrian poet Rainer Maria Rilke wrote in a letter to a conflicted young protege in 1903. (You'll find it on page 157.) "Love the questions" and "live the questions," Rilke counseled, and hold patience "toward all that is unsolved in your heart." Only by loving and living the questions can we "live along" them into a meaningful answer.

As I have lived the question that frames this book, I've had to occupy *yes*, *no*, and *I don't know*. For the rest of my life, I will feel deeper empathy and solidarity with people in each place. I hope you will too. We're all in this together. We really are. May our lives sing.

ACKNOWLEDGMENTS

I wrote most of this book during the COVID-19 pandemic, during which I never ventured far from my home in southwest Florida. I honor the Indigenous peoples of this land, especially the Seminole and Miccosukee, and before them, the Calusa and the Muspa, and the peoples whose names we do not know who preceded them. I honor the land and waters that surround me, and the resilient creatures who are my neighbors here. This book took shape in this land.

Thanks to Rev. Jeffrey Petersen and Rev. Paul Nuechterlein (http://girardianlectionary.net/about-paul-nuechterlein/), who read a late draft of this book and offered invaluable feedback. Thanks also to Rabbi Jill Jacobs for her advice on Chapter 1.

Thanks to my agent Roger Freet and to the publishing team at St. Martin's Press, and especially to my editor, Elisabeth Dyssegaard. They helped this book come alive. Thanks also to Young Jin Lim for the cover art, which inspired the afterword.

Thanks to all the people over these many years who have shared with me their struggles of Christian identity. Thanks also to people of other faiths who have shared their parallel journeys.

Thanks to my children and grandchildren, who inspire me, and to Grace, for her partnership in parenting and grandparenting.

And a final thanks to you, dear reader, for what you will make of this time we have shared, thinking together, dreaming together, in the presence of holy mysteries that all religions try their best to honor and that no religion can ever fully contain.

❧

HOW TO GET THE MOST OUT OF THIS BOOK

There are two practices that have always helped me get the most out of a book: first, *underlining and compiling quotations*, and second, *reading as a team sport*.

As you read, I encourage you to underline words, sentences, or paragraphs that stick out to you. Write in the margins and blank pages. At the end of each chapter, write a sentence that summarizes what in the chapter was most important to you. As you go along or when you've finished the book, copy the underlined or highlighted quotations and your additional insights by hand in a journal or type them into a special document. Add additional reflections as they come to mind. In this way, make this book *your* book. If you're reading on a screen, you may be able to highlight and annotate, take screenshots, or cut and paste quotes and save them in a separate document. If you have an artistic flair, compile those notes on a poster and hang it in your home or share it on social media.

Reading mindfully, not in a rush, with a pen in hand (or using other technology) takes you out of the passive mode, where you say, "I wonder what the author is going to show me?" It puts you in a more active mode, where you're like an explorer, asking, "I wonder what I'm going to find here? I wonder what connections I will find to my current situation? I wonder what will challenge what I currently think? I wonder what will bother me, upset me, or otherwise disturb me . . . and why I will react this way?" When you write or type significant quotes and your reflections, you engage your mind and body, further activating your reading process. Then, each time you reread your notes, you reinforce and enhance what you've learned.

To take your reading experience to the next level, you can join or form a team of readers, in person or online, following or adapting these steps.

1. *Choose a schedule.* You might do a chapter a week, or five or seven chapters a week, or whatever you think best. At two or three chapters a week, the book's twenty-eight chapters (plus introduction and afterword) could be covered in a thirteen-week quarter.
2. *Choose a leader or rotate leadership.* Rotating leadership has a number of advantages, and leading a group like this is fun and not burdensome at all. At (or before) the first gathering, a leader can say something like this: "I think it would be helpful for us to establish some shared values or guidelines. Here are three I've found helpful: a. No interrupting or dominating the conversation, b. No "fixing" (correcting, arguing, etc.), and c. Listen and speak from the heart. Do these make sense, and do you have any additional values or guidelines we should consider adding?"
3. *Invite leaders to do the following*: a. send a reminder to participants about what chapters you'll be discussing at the next meeting, b. begin and end the meeting on time, c. keep things moving so everyone can participate at least once, and d. perhaps use an opening and closing ritual or prayer. (You might find the prayer in Chapter 27 to be helpful, perhaps using a stanza or two each week.)
4. *Read the assigned chapters before you gather*, underlining or copying sentences or paragraphs that stand out as especially relevant, interesting, meaningful, confusing, disturbing, or helpful.
5. *Begin with a welcome or opening ritual*: light a candle, read a quotation, share a few minutes of silence, say "Our simple goal is to speak from the heart and listen from the heart," or something similar. Then the leader goes first (to set an example) or invites someone else to go first. That person reads something they've underlined or otherwise selected, explains why it was meaningful, or raises a question about it. The group takes a few minutes to respond. Then that participant chooses a person to go next. If someone isn't prepared or doesn't want to participate, they can pass. There's no pressure.
6. *Repeat the process* until everyone has had a chance to share a selection. If time remains, you can go around the circle multiple times.
7. When you near the end of your time, *remind participants of the chapters for the next meeting.* You might also introduce a closing ritual or practice. To close, you might simply go around the circle and invite

each person to share a word or a sentence to summarize a takeaway or gratitude from the session. End by thanking each person for their participation.

Here are some specific suggestions you may wish to use or adapt for your group:

You could gather in a home, coffee shop, classroom, or restaurant. You could gather in a circle in a forest or park, or talk two by two along a trail. You could gather online, seeing one another in "gallery mode." You could experiment with different settings from week to week. You could combine some or all of your meetings with a meal, snack, drink, or dessert.

At the beginning of each gathering, to acknowledge that readers of this book may be in very different places, you can read a welcome like this:

"We are all friends around this table. All equals. All unique. All welcome. Who we are is who we are. There is no need to pretend. Some of us have a lot of beliefs and very few doubts. Some of us have a lot of doubts and very few beliefs. Some of us love God, but we're not sure about Jesus. Some of us love Jesus, but we're not so sure about God. Some of us aren't very sure about anything, and others feel very sure about almost everything. Some of us gladly call ourselves Christians. Some of us barely call ourselves Christians. Some of us once were Christians, but not anymore. Some of us aren't sure we ever were Christians, or aren't sure what that means, or whether it matters. But this we share: we welcome one another to this circle just as we are, for we all are part of one web of life on this precious planet in this amazing universe."

You may want to include a time of contemplative silence at the beginning or end of your gathering. Holding silence may feel awkward at first, but people quickly learn how to rest into silence if it is properly introduced, perhaps with words like the following:

"We will observe a few moments of silence, to breathe deeply, to listen to what arises in our hearts, and to feel the presence of unconditional welcome and liberating love among us." It's generally better, especially at first, to make the silence too short rather than too long, perhaps one to three minutes. You can extend it over time as doing so feels appropriate.

APPENDIX II

☙

IMAGES YOU CAN'T UNSEE
(ADDENDUM TO CHAPTER 2)

I originally included in Chapter 2 the following material detailing the use of torture against Christian nonconformists, especially during the Spanish Inquisition. But early readers told me they found it too graphic, implanting images in their minds that they couldn't "unsee." I relocated this material here for those who can handle it, because it is important not to let this part of Christian history be forgotten, minimized, or covered up. Sensitive readers should read no further, because some of these descriptions are deeply disturbing.

The Red X: Many targets of the inquisitions had to wear a patch of red cloth in the shape of an X on their clothing whenever they were in public, a mild punishment in comparison to others, but one can imagine the social impact of being publicly marked in this way. (One also sees later echoes of this practice in Hawthorne's *The Scarlet Letter* and in the Jewish stars required in Nazi Germany.)

The Hair Shirt: More odious, those who confessed to heresy (sincerely or to avoid further torture) had to wear, as an act of penance, a heavy shirt with animal fur turned in toward the skin. The physical discomfort was real; so was the impression made on others who witnessed the penitent in public pain and public humiliation.

Branding Irons: Red-hot irons applied to various body parts caused immediate excruciating pain, lasting tissue destruction, and permanent scarring of the flesh, marking the nonconformist for life. (We see a more recent version of permanent branding in the Nazis' use of tattoos in Auschwitz and elsewhere.[1])

The Strappado: Individuals suspected of doctrinal nonconformity would be hung by their wrists, with their hands tied behind their back usually resulting in dislocation of the shoulders and, if sustained long enough, death.

The Judas Cradle: Upping the agony of the strappado, the Judas cradle was a stool with a pyramid-shaped seat. The victim would be suspended naked by the limbs above the apparatus, with the point of the pyramid touching the anus or vagina. As the victim lost the strength to uphold the body, the point of the pyramid would enter the orifice, expanding it and ripping it open by degrees. If the victim confessed and was released midway through the torture, the resulting infection would often prove fatal. Other forms of impalement were also employed to punish religious nonconformists.

The Spanish Boot: A wooden or iron casing would surround the victim's foot or lower leg. Wedges would be hammered between the casing and the body, causing dislocation of bones, crushing of bones, and, needless to say, excruciating pain. Another related torture involved placing the feet in iron or copper boots and filling the boots with boiling water, oil, or molten lead, or filling the boots with cold water and then bringing the water to a boil. Other forms of foot torture included presses and screws.

The Brodequin: The victim, in a seated position, would have boards applied to the inside and outside of each leg, bound by strong ropes. Then wedges would be hammered between the ropes and the wood, gradually putting the legs under such pressure that the bones of the leg would burst and the bone marrow would ooze out.

The Heretic's Fork: Imagine a slug of metal with two sharp tines pointing upward and two pointing downward. Then imagine this double-sided fork being strapped to the front of the neck by a collar, with two tines touching the chin and the other two touching the sternum. The victim must look upward (toward heaven, if you will); any movement of the head or jaw, including any attempt to speak or even swallow, would result in piercing pain. To make matters worse, the slug of metal was positioned to compress the Adam's apple, creating a sense of suffocation. After hours of straining the neck muscles to avoid bodily penetration, with no hope of escape, the victim would have powerful reasons to recant their heresy and submit to "the truth."

The Rack: The victim's hands and feet would be tied to chains or ropes that would be gradually tightened, dislocating joints and rendering the victim incapable of defending himself or herself from hot iron pokers, screws, and other instruments of additional torture. The shockingly loud sounds of snapping tendons and separating joints produced strong reactions in those who witnessed torture on the rack, as did the screams of the victims, not to mention the victim's loss of bladder and bowel control in the presence of excruciating pain.

Suspected nonconformists were also forced to ingest excessive quantities of water with a funnel and subjected to various other water tortures. They were strapped to an apparatus called the knee splitter. They were silenced with the use of tongue screws. They were imprisoned for long periods without sufficient food, light, or sanitation. They were put in the stocks or pillory. They were burned at the stake. During and even after the Spanish Inquisition, these and other tortures were intended not only to break or punish the nonconformists themselves but also to terrorize the general public so they would remain compliant, fearing that they might be the next victim if they did not.

✄

DO I STAY IN MY DENOMINATION?

The general question "Do I stay Christian?" is often complicated by the more specific question of staying Catholic, Evangelical, Orthodox, Pentecostal, Methodist, or whatever. Sometimes, a person can't stay Southern Baptist but could possibly stay Episcopalian, or a person can't stay Episcopalian but could possibly stay Quaker. If that's your question, although I don't think it's appropriate or even possible to offer one-size-fits-all advice, I can offer a few stories. You'll recall from Chapter 12 the story of Sr. Ann and Sr. Jean, who decided they would stay in their church and speak their truth until they were forced out, demonstrating the option of staying both defiantly and graciously.

That's the advice I received when I was a young pastor. An older pastor must have sensed that I might get myself in trouble, so he approached me with this unsolicited counsel: "Try not to leave your denomination. Stay as long as you can. But if it becomes clear they don't want you, then it's time to leave, because love is not rude, and staying where you are not wanted is rude."

I followed that older pastor's advice and stayed in my denomination as long as I could, but eventually moved on when it was clear I was no longer welcome.

Several years later, one of my mentors called me out of the blue. He had progressive leanings but worked as a theologian within a more conservative denomination. He said, "Brian, if I had to do it over again, I wouldn't have stayed in my denomination as long as I have. I now see that they were never going to be open to what I had to say. I could have accomplished so much more if I had found a more hospitable environment to work in. I wish I had seen that long ago, because life is short, and now, at my age, I think it's too late for me to find a more open context to work." Neither he nor I could have known that a few weeks later, he would die suddenly, marking that unexpected call as our last conversation. Looking back, I sensed he was giving me a parting gift of hard-won wisdom: *take into consideration whether your current context will allow the highest and best use of your gifts and time.*

Perhaps the question of *whether to stay* in your denomination should be reframed as *how to stay* while you're in it, followed by the question of *how to leave* when you discern it's time to move on. Drawing from my experience, I can offer the following suggestions.

1. *Find kindred spirits and raise a flag.* That's what gave birth to the Emerging Church/Emergent Christianity conversation that I have been part of. A few individuals spoke up and found each other, and we raised a flag so others could find us. These days, raising a flag might mean setting up a website, hosting some gatherings (online or in person), starting a podcast and building a community of listeners, and so on. Network widely with other groups that seem to be going in a similar direction. See one another as colleagues rather than competitors.

2. *Recast your identity.* Just as Part II of this book has offered a way of recasting Christian identity so you can stay Christian in good faith, you can find ways of articulating a new Methodist, Catholic, or Pentecostal identity (or Mormon, Jewish, Muslim, or Hindu identity).

3. *Expect critique and use it wisely.* Gatekeepers will almost always criticize outliers who organize and speak up, threatening them with exclusion so they will quiet down and conform. Don't take this critique personally or respond defensively; these loyal traditionalists are simply doing their jobs. Use every private and public criticism as an opportunity to graciously, patiently clarify your message. In this way, your critics will help draw attention to your fledgling movement, and each new critique will help you further clarify your message and proposals.

4. *Determine your goals.* Do you simply want the freedom to gather and exist as a minority voice in your denomination? Or do you want more—to be respected, empowered, enfranchised? Do you hope that your departures from the norm will be accepted in the mainstream, and if so, how likely is that to happen within the next five, ten, or fifty years? Do you expect, in the long term, to be expelled or shunned,

while in the short term, you want to gather as many as possible to be expelled or shunned with you, so after your expulsion you become a viable alternative to the dominant group?

5. *Be flexible.* My friend and colleague Cameron Trimble says, "You can always have your way if you have enough ways." It's wise advice. That means that the goals you set (#4 above) will need to be revisited as conditions change.

6. *Find clear language for ambiguous situations.* For example, when people ask me, "Are you still Evangelical?" I can answer with clarity: "I'm from an Evangelical background and spent the first half of my life Evangelical. But over the years, I changed and Evangelicalism changed too. So although I love my Evangelical neighbors and I am who I am because of my heritage, most Evangelicals would consider me an outsider, and I don't try to impose myself upon them." Catholics might say, "I'm a Catholic in the spirit of St. Francis and Pope Francis, but that leaves me feeling alienated from a lot of the Catholic hierarchy today." A group of progressive Seventh-day Adventists or Latter-day Saints might say, "We grew up in this community and love much of our heritage, but our status is unclear because we aren't sure how much the church will be able to change to accommodate people like us."

For many, the question is even more specific: do I stay in my congregation? Some of what I've said about staying in your denomination should apply to your congregation, but I would add this: when your continuing participation in your local congregation becomes unhealthy for you, your family, or the congregation itself, it's probably time to leave. I recommend you leave with a letter to the church leaders, in which you do the following:

1. Say thanks for all the blessings you've experienced in their company and be specific about those blessings.
2. Explain why you can no longer stay. Do so with clarity and honesty, but without hostility of any kind. Show the courage to differ (and leave) graciously.
3. Express your desire to stay on good terms, if possible. In other words, part as neighbors, not enemies, and keep friendships intact whenever possible.

If you leave with bitterness and harsh criticism as you walk out the door, be assured that you will make your congregation glad to see you go, and you will harden them against any of your desires for change. If you leave with both clarity and charity, they may wish they had been able to keep you involved, which may stretch them in a positive direction in the future.

Sometimes, leaving a group is so traumatic that you won't have the energy to find a new spiritual home, at least for a while. That's understandable. Long term, I would hope that you could either find or form a spiritual community where you can practice the values we considered in Parts II and III of this book.

✌

A LETTER TO PASTORS
(ADDENDUM TO CHAPTER 26)

Dear Pastors, Priests, and others in Christian Ministry,

Because I was a pastor for twenty-four years, every word I write is, in some way, intended to help you and others in this important though challenging calling. One pastor friend, after reading a draft of Chapter 26 and its theme of "Renounce and Announce," asked me this question: "Is it fair to a congregation for me to 'come out' as a new kind of Christian, knowing the painful disruption that causes, or is there more integrity in simply stepping aside to allow them to continue growing in a framework in which I can no longer remain? Is it fair for me to drag them along for a ride they didn't sign up for? Is there more integrity in simply stepping away because I don't feel the old wine skin can handle the pressure of new wine?"

I'd like to offer a few very brief responses to this question.

My friend is right: some congregations are not currently able to handle "the painful disruption" of grappling with the content of this book. (His question makes me wonder if some sort of warning label should be applied to the cover.) It may be better to start something new and fresh, or to find a congregation that is ready or even eager for a new beginning.

But whenever possible, I hope you can bring your leadership team into the process and, eventually, the whole congregation too. (This book could be a resource in that process.) Share with those you trust most what you're thinking, what you're struggling with, how you feel, how you're changing. Only do so if you are prepared for the worst possible reaction; that way, you are more likely to be pleasantly surprised rather than shocked. Tell them that you would very much like to stay and help the congregation go through a rethinking process with you, but you're aware that the process may be beyond the congregation's current capacity.

By doing so, you are honoring your leaders as partners rather than fore-closing upon a decision without them having a say. You may discern together that it's best for you to move on, but they may commit to an attempt to move forward with you into a process of change. If the latter, I encourage you to find a church consultant who understands a. the transformation you're seeking and b. the polity within which you work. Having the wisdom of someone "outside the system" can make the difference between a successful change process and a self-destructive one.

This is what I experienced as a pastor. My leadership team (thanks to one intrepid lay leader) framed and faced this question: *Is this road that Brian is walking only his journey, or is it our journey too?* The leadership team agreed (with a minority dissenting) that this was *our* journey. "There are many churches that can meet the needs of traditional Christians," one person said, "but very few that can help the people we're trying to help." That meant that we had to get comfortable letting more traditional Christians go so they could find a place that was in line with "what they signed up for." That wasn't easy, but it was essential.

In between you leaving and staying in your current pastorate, there are other options. Perhaps you can find a way to continue to serve the main congregation in its current form while creating a "side congregation" where there is freedom to experiment. Again, it's wise to bring in a church consultant whenever possible.[1]

Whatever you do, I encourage you to find at least a few non-utilitarian friends to be your support system as you move forward, friends who sincerely care about you, want what's best for you, and have nothing to gain or lose based on choices you make. Whether you call these relationships spiritual direction, soul friendship, peer mentoring, or something else, they can provide you a calm center in the eye of the storm.

These friends can also remind you to be a friend to yourself, to join God in loving and caring for you as a person and a Christian as well as a pastor.

The truth is, pivotal times like these are fraught with difficulty and conflict, and it's easy to see yourself as part of the problem when you're actually trying to be part of the solution. If you are worn out, exhausted, and wounded in the fray, then by all means, take the time away you need to heal and restore your soul.

If you have the inner fire to stay in the struggle, may you know that you are walking a path that reformers, prophets, mystics, and sages have walked before you, including a fellow who grew up in Nazareth of Galilee and died just outside Jerusalem.

✒

ADDITIONAL RESOURCES

1. Podcasts (and similar resources on Facebook, YouTube, Instagram, etc.) come and go, but here are several (in alphabetical order) that have invited me as a guest in recent years (plus a few others), all grappling with Christian identity in ways that readers should find helpful:

Another Name for Every Thing (Richard Rohr), *Beached White Male* (Ken Kemp), *Beloved Journal* (Rob Lee), *The Bible for Normal People* (Pete Enns, Jared Byas), Brandan Robertson (Instagram Live/Brandan Robertson), *Caleb Mason* (Caleb Mason), *Can I Say This at Church?* (Seth Price), *The Church Needs Therapy* (Kevin Sweeney), *Compass* (Ryan Dunn), *Cooperative Baptist* (Andy Hale), *The Confessional* (Nadia Bolz-Weber), *Drop the Stones* (Carlos Rodriguez), *DTALKS* (Joe Shaw), The Enneagram Journey (Suzanne Stabile), *The Eternal Current* (Aaron Niequist), *Faith Conversations* (Anita Lustrea), *Faith Matters* (Tim and Aubrey Chaves), *Faith Without Fear* (Nick Quient), *For the Love* (Jen Hatmaker), *Freedom Road* (Lisa Sharon Harper), *Future Christian* (Loren Richmond, Jr.), *HomeBrewed Christianity* (Tripp Fuller), *Ideas Network* (Konrad Michalski), *In Conversation with Frank Schaeffer* (Frank Schaeffer), *Innovating Church* (Rachel Stout), *Irenicast* (Bonnie Rambob), *Jesus Never Ran* (Matt Kendziera), *John Dear's Peace Podcast* (John Dear), *Kate and Colby Show* (Kate and Colby Martin), *Learning How to See* (Brian D. McLaren), *The Liturgists* (Michael Gungor), *On Being* (Krista Tippett), *On the Way* (Dominic Fay), *Open Circle* (Matt Laidlaw), *A Pastor and a Philosopher Walk into a Bar* (Randy Knie), *Pastor with No Answers* (Joey Svendsen), *Peacing It All Together* (Randy Woodley, Bo Sanders), *A People's Theology* (Mason Mennenga), *Randall Worley* (Instagram Live/Randall

Worley), *(Re)Thinking Faith* (Josh Patterson), *The RobCast* (Rob Bell), *Seekers and Speakers* (Jonathan Merritt), *Speculation* (Nick Vargo Fiedler), *There's a God in My Closet* (Ben DeLong), *Turning to the Mystics* (James Finley), *Vicars' Crossing* (Kevin George), *What If Project* (Glenn Siepert), and *The Zeitcast* (Jonathan Martin).

2. Here is a short list of authors whose work should be especially helpful to readers of this book:

Diana Butler Bass, Kaitlin Curtice, Brian Zahnd, Jacqui Lewis, Jonathan Martin, Anne Lamott, Doug Pagitt, Lisa Sharon Harper, Rob Bell, Sarah Bessey, Philip Clayton, Nadia Bolz-Weber, Steve Chalke, Tripp Fuller, Fr. Richard Rohr, Sr. Joan Chittister, Doug Pagitt, Sr. Simone Campbell, Fr. James Martin, Sr. Ilia Delio, Fr. James Alison, Mike McHargue, David Dark, Pete Enns, Frank Schaeffer, Glenn Siepert, and Wil Gafney.

3. Of my own work, if you found this book helpful, you may also enjoy:

The *A New Kind of Christian* trilogy. These fictional books tell the story of Dan Poole, a pastor who goes through a period of questioning whether he can stay Christian. *A New Kind of Christian* (Fortress Press, 2019) launches the series, as Dan finds a friend with whom he can speak freely about his questions and doubts. *The Story We Find Ourselves In* (Fortress Press, 2019) focuses on a fresh way of reading the biblical story. *The Last Word and the Word After That* (Fortress Press, 2019) challenges traditional Christian teaching on hell.

A New Kind of Christianity (HarperOne, 2010) picks up the issue of Christian identity in a nonfiction format by focusing on ten questions that are unsettling the status quo for many. *We Make the Road by Walking* (Jericho, 2014) offers an overview of the Christian faith from a fresh perspective.

Why Did Jesus, Moses, the Buddha, and Mohammed Cross the Road? (Jericho, 2012) explores Christian identity in a multi-faith world. If you are seeking a meaningful Christian identity that respects rather than resents other religious identities, this will be a helpful resource.

Faith After Doubt (St. Martin's Press, 2020), as we saw in Chapter 21, presents a four-stage model of Christian faith that may help readers who feel that they have outgrown Christianity, or who may be seeking to stay Christian but in a broader or deeper way. *Naked Spirituality* (HarperOne, 2011) also explores this four-stage model as a framework for spiritual formation.

NOTES

✿

Introduction

1. You can read the transcript here: https://www.nytimes.com/2007/08/05/us/politics/05transcript-debate.html. You can read Rep. Tancredo's responses here: https://www.ontheissues.org/Archive/2007_GOP_Iowa_Straw_Poll_Tom_Tancredo.htm.

2. See, for example, *Politifact*'s list, "Latest False Fact-Checks on Donald Trump": https://www.politifact.com/factchecks/list/?speaker=donald-trump&ruling=false.

3. For more on this comparison, see the short documentary film *God $ Green*, available here: https://filmfreeway.com/GodandGreen.

1. Because Christianity Has Been Vicious to Its Mother (Anti-Semitism)

1. I was referring in particular to James Dobson, founder of Focus on the Family and author of *Dare to Discipline* (Tyndale, 1970), and Bill Gothard, founder of what was then called the Institute in Basic Youth Conflicts.

2. See Robert P. Jones, "The Unmaking of the White Christian Worldview," *Time*, September 29, 2021, online here: https://time.com/6102117/white-christian-americans-sins/.

3. On Copernicus, see Wyatt Houtz, "John Calvin on Nicolaus Copernicus and Heliocentrism," *BioLogos*, October 28, 2014, https://biologos.org/articles/john-calvin-on-nicolaus-copernicus-and-heliocentrism/. On Galileo, see Dava Sobel, *Galileo's Daughter* (Bloomsbury, 2009). See my discussions of Darwin in *The Galapagos Islands: A Spiritual Journey* (Fortress, 2019). On Carson, see http://www.environmentandsociety.org/exhibitions/rachel-carsons-silent-spring/ and https://rachelcarsoncouncil.org/faith-science-action/.

4. For two literary explorations of colonialism, see Chinua Achebe, *Things Fall Apart* (Penguin, 2017), and Barbara Kingsolver, *The Poisonwood Bible* (Harper, 1998). For theological reflection on colonialism, see the works of Emmanuel Katongole, especially *A Future for Africa* (University of Scranton, 2005). See also Chapter 3 of this book and *Evangelical Postcolonial Conversations*, edited by Kay Higuera Smith et al. (IVP, 2014), to which I was a contributor.

5. Many New Testament scholars have noted the anti-Semitism in the Fourth Gospel, presumably written before AD 100. In 1941, during the Nazi reign, Walter

Sikes addressed the issue in a *Journal of Religion* article, "The Anti-Semitism of the Fourth Gospel" (vol. 21, no. 1, p. 23), available online here: https://www.journals .uchicago.edu/doi/abs/10.1086/482664. An early factor in the anti-Semitic turn in Christianity was the second Jewish revolt against Rome, known as the Bar Kokhba Revolt (132–135). When the Roman emperor Hadrian crushed the revolt and punished Jews harshly for their attempted independence, it became a matter of personal self-protection and group self-interest for many Christians to separate themselves from the traditional Jewish community. See https://www .jewishvirtuallibrary.org/the-bar-kokhba-revolt-132–135-ce/. See especially James Carroll, *Constantine's Sword: The Church and the Jews, a History* (Mariner, 2002).

6. Roge Karma, "Coronavirus Is Not Just a Tragedy. It's an Opportunity to Build a Better World," *Vox*, April 10, 2020, https://www.vox.com/2020/4/10/21213287/coronavirus -covid-19-pandemic-epidemic-society-historian-nationalism-globalization. Note: the article contains an apparent typo, listing the population of Jews in Strasbourg as 200,000 instead of 2,000. The correct number is given in this interview: "HNN's Robin Lindley Interviews Medical Historian Frank Snowden," historynewsnetwork .org, April 12, 2020, https://historynewsnetwork.org/article/174985.

7. René Girard offers a powerful theory to explain this process. See *The Girard Reader*, edited by James G. Williams (Crossroads Herder, 1996). I also summarize Girard's mimetic theory in my book *Why Did Jesus, Moses, the Buddha, and Mohammed Cross the Road?* (Jericho, 2012).

8. "The Plague and the Jews of Strasbourg," *Jewish Currents*, February 13, 2018, https:// jewishcurrents.org/the-plague-and-the-jews-of-strasbourg/.

9. "Antisemitism in Christianity," https://en.wikipedia.org/wiki/Antisemitism_in _Christianity.

10. Only now are documents being unsealed that reveal the anti-Semitic silence of the Catholic Church in the Nazi years. See Sylvia Poggioli, "Records from Once-Secret Archive Offer New Clues into Vatican Response to Holocaust," NPR.org, August 29, 2020, https://www.npr.org/2020/08/29/907076135/records-from-once -secret-archive-offer-new-clues-into-vatican-response-to-holoca.

11. See https://newsadvance.com/news/local/liberty-university/liberty-university -launches-think-tank-to-promote-traditional-judeo-christian-beliefs/article _396a7545-9df3-5162-984f-de930ef16a87.html.

12. Tweeted August 28, 2020: https://twitter.com/TheRaDR/status/12994489886309 49888?s=20.

13. Thanks to tour leaders Jeff and Janet Wright. More information on their tours is available here: http://www.footstepsofjesustour.org/.

14. See Lesslie Newbigin, *The Gospel in a Pluralist Society* (SPCK, 1991).

2. Because of Christianity's Suppression of Dissent (Christian vs. Christian Violence)

1. See Geoffrey S. Smith, *Guilt by Association: Heresy Catalogues in Early Christianity* (New York: Oxford University Press, 2015), pp. 59–62.

2. See James Carroll, *Constantine's Sword* (Mariner Books, 2001).

3. For a more sympathetic reading of Constantine, see Peter Leithart, *Defending Constantine: The Twilight of an Empire and the Dawn of Christendom* (IVP Aca-

demic, 2010), p. 287. For a rebuttal to Leithart, see *Constantine Revisited: Leithart, Yoder, and the Constantinian Debate*, edited by John D. Roth (Wipf and Stock, 2013).

4. See "Thomas Aquinas: *Summa Theologica*, First and Second Part of the Second Part on Interior Will, Unbelief, and Heresy," January 1, 1265, Berkley Center for Religion, Peace and World Affairs, https://berkleycenter.georgetown.edu/quotes /thomas-aquinas-em-summa-theologica-em-first-and-second-part-of-the-second -part-on-interior-will-unbelief-and-heresy.

5. Both religious supremacists and white supremacists have been highly successful in minimizing or covering up their crimes. (Often, the two overlap.) See Michael S. Rosenwald, "At Least 2,000 More Black People Were Lynched by White Mobs Than Previously Reported, New Research Finds," *Washington Post*, June 16, 2020, https://www.washingtonpost.com/history/2020/06/16/lynchings-report-equal -justice-initiative-reconstruction-racial-terror/.

6. We'll return to the subject of the Great Migration in Chapter 26.

7. See Becky Little, "How Medieval Churches Used Witch Hunts to Gain More Followers," History.com, September 1, 2018, https://www.history.com/news/how -medieval-churches-used-witch-hunts-to-gain-more-followers.

8. Directorium Inquisitorum, edition of 1578, Book 3, pg. 137, column 1. Online in the Cornell University Collection; quoted here: https://en.wikipedia.org/wiki /Inquisition.

9. For readers with a strong stomach, I've included a brief description of these tools of terror in Appendix II.

10. A June 19, 2004, *Washington Post* article by Rich Preheim summed it up like this: "Protestants and Catholics . . . had one thing in common: Anabaptism had to be eliminated." The article, reporting on recent steps toward formal apology for two centuries of violence against Anabaptists, included this quote from a Catholic bishop: "We all have black sheep in the family." This kind of admission sidesteps the fact that those who committed atrocities like these were not betraying group values, beliefs, and official policies: rather, they were being faithful to them. See https://www.washingtonpost.com/archive/local/2004/06/19/atonement-for-2 -centuries-of-persecution/7d724d0f-5e13-4c2c-b1f1-880f6e10f120/.

11. The strange story of Ananias and Sapphira in Acts 5 of the New Testament, I must admit, seems to set the stage for some of these atrocities. For a serious engagement with this troubling text in light of René Girard's mimetic theory, see Agnieszka Burakowska, *A Deadly Covenant: Mimetic Interpretation of Acts 5:1–11*, available here: https://www.ceeol.com/search/article-detail?id=415103.

12. Adapted from Mirabai Starr, *St. John of the Cross: Devotions, Prayers and Living Wisdom* (Sounds True, 2008), 1–4. Also available here: https://cac.org/prayer-in -captivity-2020-04-22/.

13. Southern Baptist megachurch pastor Robert Jeffress, for example, said seeing children in cages and separated from their families by the Trump administration was "gut-wrenching" but justified. See Stephen Young's *Dallas Observer* interview, "Bonus Jeffress: The Pastor Talks to the Observer about Trump's Child Separation Policy," June 19, 2018, available here: https://www.dallasobserver.com/news/first -baptist-dallas-robert-jeffress-on-child-separation-10811842.

14. See J. Porter Harlow, "A Case Against Torture," April 8, 2017, available here: https://world.wng.org/2017/04/a_case_against_torture; and Eric Gorski, "An Evangelical Divide in Debate over Torture," *Seattle Times,* May 14, 2009, https://www.seattletimes.com/nation-world/an-evangelical-divide-in-debate-over-torture/.

15. To touch the pain of that period in Irish history, and to feel the pathos of those who sought to heal that pain, see Pádraig Ó Tuama's collection of poems, *Sorry for Your Troubles* (Canterbury Press, 2013).

16. See Mary Papenfuss, "Steve Bannon: I'd Put Anthony Fauci's Head on a Pike as a 'Warning,'" *HuffPost,* November 5, 2020, https://www.huffpost.com/entry/steve-bannon-anthony-fauci-christopher-wray-head-on-pikes_n_5fa47a2cc5b64c88d3fe9d67/. See also this piece on Rick Joyner, by Nicholas Kristof: "He's a Famous Evangelical Preacher, but His Kids Wish He'd Pipe Down," *New York Times,* March 27, 2021, https://www.nytimes.com/2021/03/27/opinion/sunday/evangelical-rick-joyner-family.html.

17. See, for example, *The Rise and Fall of Mars Hill* podcast (https://www.christianitytoday.com/ct/podcasts/rise-and-fall-of-mars-hill/) and Jessica Johnson, *Biblical Porn: Affect, Labor, and Pastor Mark Driscoll's Evangelical Empire* (Duke University Press, 2018). See also Rob Collingsworth's summary of recent events in the Southern Baptist Convention: https://threadreaderapp.com/thread/1442877974307614722.html/.

3. Because of Christianity's High Global Death Toll— and Life Toll (Crusader Colonialism)

1. Charles the Great (748–814) led an earlier series of wide-ranging military campaigns to subjugate or re-subjugate Europe under Christianity. He forced conversion of Saxons at sword point and once massacred 4,500 Saxon rebels. He also fought Muslims in Spain. But the term *Crusade* is usually reserved for incursions focused on the Eastern Mediterranean, beginning in 1093.

2. See Frank Pastore's article here: "Why Al Qaeda Supports the Emergent Church," *Townhall,* July 22, 2007, https://townhall.com/columnists/frankpastore/2007/07/22/why-al-qaeda-supports-the-emergent-church-n752344/. The article appeared a short time after I appeared on Pastore's radio show, where he challenged me to join him in encouraging the United States to go to war with Iran, and I refused.

3. Thankfully, there have been exceptions, many of them chronicled in David Bosch's book *Transforming Mission* (Orbis, 2011). But the exceptions are exceptional: in most cases, Western Christians have not treated non-Christian minorities well. In places like Palestine, Egypt, Ethiopia, China, and Malaysia, non-Western Christian minorities have approached their majority neighbors in a very different way. See, for example, *Christianity in East and Southeast Asia,* edited by Kenneth Ross, Francis Alvarez, S.J., and Todd Johnson (Edinburgh University, 2020).

4. For a doubly disturbing account of Columbus's beliefs, see Joe Carter, "How the Eschatological Views of Columbus Changed the World," *Gospel Coalition,* October 9, 2018, https://www.thegospelcoalition.org/article/eschatological-views-columbus-changed-world/. The theological assumptions behind Columbus's voyage are shocking enough, but the bizarre acceptance of them as "God's providence" by the author provides evidence that essential elements of colonial Christianity—double

predestination, Christian supremacy, biblicism, and divinely sanctioned violence, for example—have yet to be interrogated for their dangerous ongoing impact. Like plagues, those deadly beliefs mutate, occupy new host bodies, and live on.

5. This "permission slip" was originally articulated in the papal bull *Dum Diversas* (1452) and then reiterated in *Romanus Pontifex* (1454). *Dum Diversas* was translated into English from the Latin in Frances Gardiner Davenport, ed., *European Treaties Bearing on the History of the United States and its Dependencies to 1648* (Carnegie Institution of Washington, 1917), 20–26. For more on the Doctrine of Discovery, see Mark Charles and Soong-Chan Rah, *Unsettling Truths* (IVP, 2019), and http://www.kingscollege.net/gbrodie/Timeline%201452%20-%20Pontifex%20Romanus.html/.

6. See Zack Beauchamp, "500 Years of European Colonialism, in One Animated Map," *Vox*, January 16, 2015, https://www.vox.com/2014/5/8/5691954/colonialism-collapse-gif-imperialism, and Adam Hochschild, *King Leopold's Ghost* (Houghton Mifflin, 1998).

7. Quantifying or even estimating the death toll of Christian colonialism is difficult at best, in part because many deaths came through germs carried in white host bodies that decimated local populations. Smallpox alone was estimated to have decimated 80 to 90 percent of many of the Native peoples it encountered in the Americas. Those who weren't killed directly by European diseases were often casualties of starvation, the result of crops not being planted or harvested in times of social chaos, when people had to flee their homes to avoid being murdered or enslaved by European Christian colonizers. Scholar Andrés Reséndez has noted that most populations rebound after a plague; those in the Americas did not. For that reason, he concluded that "slavery was the major killer." In the Caribbean, he judged, "between 1492 and 1550, a nexus of slavery, overwork and famine killed more Indians . . . than smallpox, influenza or malaria." See *The Other Slavery: The Uncovered Story of Indian Enslavement in America* (Houghton Mifflin, 2016).

8. See Edward Baptist, *The Half Has Never Been Told* (Basic Books, 2004), and Chinua Achebe, *Things Fall Apart* (Holt McDougal, 1999).

9. One of the best chroniclers of this trauma on descendants of both the colonizers and colonized is Resmaa Menakem, *My Grandmother's Hands* (Central Recovery Press, 2017).

10. The whole text of the speech is available here: https://teachingamericanhistory.org/library/document/what-to-the-slave-is-the-fourth-of-july/. I have updated masculine nouns and pronouns.

11. See Robert Jones's *White Too Long* (Simon & Schuster, 2020), quoted in Michael Luo's *New Yorker* article, "American Christianity's White-Supremacy Problem," September 2, 2020, available here: https://www.newyorker.com/books/under-review/american-christianitys-white-supremacy-problem/.

4. Because of Christianity's Loyal Company Men (Institutionalism)

1. See https://brianmclaren.net/dear-white-christian-pro-life-friends-1-4-compiled/.

2. As organizational psychologist Tomas Chamorro-Premuzik has written, we live in "a deeply flawed system that rewards arrogance rather than humility, and loudness rather than wisdom." His book, *Why Do So Many Incompetent Men Become Leaders?* (Harvard Business Review, 2019), answers the title's question in three ways. First,

we don't do well in distinguishing competence from confidence; we assume the most confident are the most competent. Second, we are attracted to charming and entertaining leaders rather than humble ones, even though humble leaders perform better than charismatic ones. Third, grandiose and megalomaniacal narcissists attract more attention than people of integrity; the latter, as a result, are often passed over in searches for leaders. According to research, Chamorro-Premuzik reports, women score higher than men on measures of competence, humility, and integrity; as a result, organizations that exclude women from leadership predispose themselves to have overconfident, arrogant, and narcissistic leaders. Will Roman Catholic, Eastern Orthodox, and Southern Baptist patriarchs take note?

3. See Luke 10:25–37.
4. See Mark 7:11.
5. See Matthew 23:23.
6. See Matthew 5:17–48.
7. Luke 6:46.
8. Matthew 23:24.
9. Matthew 5:43–48.
10. For more on what I call Confidence Bias, along with other biases, see Chapter 9. Also see *Why Don't They Get It?*, a short e-book available at brianmclaren.net, along with seasons 1 and 2 of the podcast *Learning How to See*, available here: https://cac.org/podcast/learning-how-to-see/.

5. Because of Christianity's Real Master (Money)

1. See "Income Inequality in the United States," inequality.org, https://inequality.org /facts/income-inequality/.
2. See Brian Terrell, "Dorothy Day's 'Filthy, Rotten System' Likely Wasn't Hers at All," *National Catholic Reporter*, April 16, 2012, https://www.ncronline.org/news /people/dorothy-days-filthy-rotten-system-likely-wasnt-hers-all. Dorothy Day may indeed have been thinking about capitalism when she said "this lousy rotten system." The problem was that the Christian enterprise had degenerated into a capitalist enterprise. Terrell summarizes: "Clearly, in this interview Dorothy expressed her conviction that it is the *church's* 'acceptance of this lousy, rotten system,' its accumulation of wealth, its blessing of usury and industrial capitalism and the wars that support it, from which the *church's* problems stem. She was speaking specifically here of the church, not of society at large."
3. In the fourth gospel, the money changer incident happens at the beginning of Jesus' ministry, so he does return to the Temple thereafter. Not so in Matthew, Mark, and Luke.

6. Because of the White Christian Old Boys' Network (White Patriarchy)

1. "Homicide Statistics by Gender," https://en.wikipedia.org/wiki/Homicide _statistics_by_gender.
2. Several of the following paragraphs are adapted from a book I co-wrote and published with my friend Gareth Higgins: *The Seventh Story: Us, Them, and the End of Violence* (self-published in 2017), available here: https://theseventhstory.com.

3. From the essay "Understanding Patriarchy," published as Chapter 2 of bell hooks, *The Will to Change* (Washington Square Press, 2004).

4. The Cold War between Russia and the United States in the twentieth century could be seen as a battle between white Christian male supremacy and white atheist male supremacy. In the decades since the Cold War ended, Vladimir Putin has discovered how useful the church can be to his ambition. His gambit has worked. In recent years, white Evangelical and Catholic leaders in the United States like Franklin Graham and Pat Buchanan made it abundantly clear that they preferred White Putin to Black Obama. To many key leaders of the white patriarchal Christian right, Putin became the "lion of Christianity," along with, of course, Donald Trump and other cartoonishly macho figures. See https://www.politico.com/magazine/story /2017/02/how-russia-became-a-leader-of-the-worldwide-christian-right-214755 and https://www.ncronline.org/news/politics/russian-connection-when-franklin -graham-met-putin/. The groundbreaking book by Dr. Kristin Kobes Du Mez, *Jesus and John Wayne: How White Evangelicals Corrupted a Faith and Fractured a Nation*, makes this case powerfully and artfully (Liveright, 2020).

5. Elaine Weiss, *The Women's Hour* (Penguin, 2019). See also Elizabeth Eisenstadt Evans, "Faith Played a Complex Role in the Battle for Women's Right to Vote," *National Catholic Reporter*, June 8, 2019, https://www.ncronline.org/news/justice /faith-played-complex-role-battle-womens-right-vote.

6. In 2020, 29 of 195 countries had women heads of state (about 15 percent). Since 1950, 75 countries have elected a woman as head of state at least once (about 38 percent).

7. Again, for more on this subject, see Kobes Du Mez, *Jesus and John Wayne*. See also Brad Jersak, *A More Christlike Word* (Whitaker, 2021), and Jessica Johnson, *Biblical Porn: Affect, Labor, and Pastor Mark Driscoll's Evangelical Empire* (Duke University Press, 2018).

8. For more on authoritarianism, see my extended essay *The Second Pandemic: Authoritarianism and Your Future*, available here: https://brianmclaren.net/a-new -online-resource/.

9. For "spiritual movement of equality, emancipation, and peace," see Matthew 23:8. For "women were among his inner circle," see Luke 8:1–3, Luke 24. For "Jesus defended Mary of Bethany's place," see Luke 10:38 ff.

10. For "spoke all languages," see Acts 2. For "Gentiles in general were welcomed as equals," see Acts 8. For "there was neither Jew nor Greek," see Galatians 3:28. For "people of every tribe and nationality united," see Revelation 7:9 ff.

11. The situation becomes more complex when we acknowledge that some faith communities of color uphold male dominance and LGBTQ stigmatization and label movements for equality as the work of liberal white colonizers.

7. Because Christianity Is Stuck (Toxic Theology)

1. Simone Weil is often quoted in this regard: "In the Church, considered as a social organism, the mysteries inevitably degenerate into beliefs." From *The Notebooks of Simone Weil* (Routledge, 1984), p. 284.

2. For incisive insight on this subject, see the work of Sr. Ilia Delio, exemplified here: "Evolution Is Our Fundamental Reality," Center for Chistogenesis, July 15, 2019, https://omegacenter.info/evolution-is-our-fundamental-reality/.

3. This image of being legally bound to a dead spouse, by the way, is employed by Paul the apostle in Romans 6.

8. Because Christianity Is a Failed Religion (Lack of Transformation)

1. Michael Luo, "American Christianity's White-Supremacy Problem," *New Yorker*, September 2, 2020, available here: https://www.newyorker.com/books /under-review/american-christianitys-white-supremacy-problem/.

2. I first encountered a Christian admitting that Christianity has failed in the writings of Walker Percy, especially in his essay, "Notes for a Novel About the End of the World," in *The Message in the Bottle* (Farrar, Straus and Giroux, 1975). Percy says, "Christendom seems in some sense to have failed. Its vocabulary is worn out" (p. 116). Then he speaks of "the egregious moral failure of Christendom" and especially "the failure of Christendom in the United States," where "White Americans have sinned against the Negro from the beginning and continue to do so, initially with cruelty and presently with an indifference that may be even more destructive" (p. 117). He asks, "What is the task of the Christian novelist" who has "cast his lot with a discredited Christendom and having inherited a defunct vocabulary?" In many ways, that question (expanded from the Christian novelist to the Christian in general) frames Part II of this book.

3. For more on this subject, see John Pavlovitz, *If God Is Love, Don't Be a Jerk: Finding a Faith That Makes Us Better Humans* (Westminster John Knox, 2021).

4. See "List of U.S. States and Territories by Religiosity," https://en.wikipedia.org /wiki/List_of_U.S._states_and_territories_by_religiosity.

5. For longevity, see https://www.beckershospitalreview.com/rankings-and-ratings /states-ranked-by-life-expectancy.html. For education, see Brett Ziegler, "Education Rankings," *U.S. News and World Report*, https://www.usnews.com/news/best -states/rankings/education. For financial prosperity, see https://en.wikipedia.org /wiki/List_of_U.S._states_and_territories_by_income/. For happiness, see Cory Steig, "List of U.S. States and Territories by Income," https://www.cnbc.com/2020 /09/26/survey-which-us-states-have-the-happiest-residents.html.

6. Thanks to Diana Butler Bass for the elevator image, from *Grounded* (HarperOne, 2015).

7. See "Down by the Riverside feat. Grandpa Elliott," YouTube, October 23, 2014, https://youtu.be/nQ1gHm8v3ek.

9. Because of Christianity's Great Wall of Bias (Constricted Intellectualism)

1. The Greek word rendered as *study* in the old King James version would be better translated *be diligent* or *do your best* in contemporary English.

2. For more on biases, see Chapter 27. Also see my short e-book *Why Don't They Get It? (Overcoming Bias in Others—and Yourself)*, available here: https://brianmclaren .net/store/. Also see episodes 1–12 of the podcast *Learning How to See*, available here: https://cac.org/podcast/learning-how-to-see/.

3. White Christian readers of the Bible, Hackett says, tend to "see themselves as the princess in every story. They are Esther, never Xerxes or Haman. They are Peter, but

never Judas. They are the woman anointing Jesus, never the Pharisees. They are the Jews escaping slavery, never Egypt. For the citizens of the most powerful country in the world, who enslaved both Native and Black people, to see itself as Israel and not Egypt when it is studying Scripture, is a perfect example of Disney princess theology. And it means that as people in power, they have no lens for locating themselves rightly in Scripture or society—and it has made them blind and utterly ill equipped to engage issues of power and injustice. It is some very weak Bible work." Erna Kim Hackett's full post can be found here: "Why I Stopped Talking About Racial Reconciliation and Started Talking About White Supremacy," feistythoughts.com, August 23, 2017, http://feistythoughts.com/2017/08/23/why-i-stopped-talking-about-racial-reconciliation-and-started-talking-about-white-supremacy/.

4. From an online conversation, "The Case Against Miracles," available here: "Miracles! Atheistasis with Darren Slade," YouTube.com, June 15, 2020, https://youtu.be/uaZhhMkJQPo.

5. One of the most graphic first-person reports can be found here: Luke Mogelson, "Among the Insurrectionists," *New Yorker*, January 25, 2021, https://www.newyorker.com/magazine/2021/01/25/among-the-insurrectionists. The transcript of one prominent prayer can be found here: Hemant Mehta, "There's Video of Christian Terrorists Praying to God Inside the U.S. Capitol," friendlyatheist, January 17, 2021, https://friendlyatheist.patheos.com/2021/01/17/theres-video-of-christian-terrorists-praying-to-god-inside-the-u-s-capitol/.

6. In the days leading up to the insurrection, Evangelical figures like Eric Metaxas and Greg Locke and Roman Catholics like Archbishop Carlo Vigano, Bishop Joseph Strickland, and Fr. Frank Pavone further stoked the fires, predicting dire consequences if Trump left office. Metaxas even said he would give his life for the cause. (He didn't. He did punch someone in the back of the head, however.)

7. For the whole assessment, see "The Consequences of Nuclear War: An Economic and Social Perspective," by Hal Cochrane, PhD, and Dennis Mileti, PhD, from Colorado State University in Fort Collins (1986), available here: https://www.ncbi.nlm.nih.gov/books/NBK219185/.

8. For example, see this account of Secretary of State Mike Pompeo in the Trump administration: Edward Wong, "The Rapture and the Real World: Mike Pompeo Blends Beliefs and Policy," *New York Times*, March 30, 2019, https://www.nytimes.com/2019/03/30/us/politics/pompeo-christian-policy.html.

9. It is not. I come from the denomination/sect that created "rapture theology" in the 1830s. For more on the subject, see Barbara Rossing, *The Rapture Exposed* (Basic Books, 2007), and Zack Hunt, *Unraptured* (Herald, 2019).

10. See, for example, Mustafa Akyol, "The Problem with the Islamic Apocalypse," *New York Times*, October 3, 2016, https://www.nytimes.com/2016/10/04/opinion/the-problem-with-the-islamic-apocalypse.html.

11. A plausible description of the world after climate change is offered by John Michael Greer in *Dark Age America* (New Society Publishers, 2016). Brace yourself for one of the more disturbing reads of your life. It is also available as an audiobook here: https://newsociety.com/books/d/dark-age-america-audiobook.

12. I originally heard this term from Thomas Beaudoin (see https://indexarticles.com/reference/currents-in-theology-and-mission/the-church-defender-of

-theocapitalism/) and have explored it in a number of books, most notably, *Everything Must Change* (Thomas Nelson, 2007). For an alternative vision for capitalism, see Paul Knowlton and Aaron Hedges, *Better Capitalism* (Cascade, 2021).

13. Basic Books, 2015. See also Jeff Sharlet, *The Family: The Secret Fundamentalism at the Heart of American Power* (Harper, 2009). See especially the connection Sharlet points out between the founders of "The Family" (known to me as "The Fellowship" when I was involved with it in the 1970s and early 1980s) and anti-union organizing.

10. Because Christianity Is a Sinking, Shrinking Ship of Wrinkling People (Demographics)

1. That something else may have been a huge infusion of cash from donors eager to send Evangelicals out as defenders of Theo-Capitalism, as discussed in Chapters 5 and 9, and in Kevin Kruse's *One Nation Under God* (Basic Books, 2015).

2. See David Masci, "Five Facts About the Religious Lives of African Americans," Pew Research Center, February 7, 2018, available here: https://www.pewresearch.org /fact-tank/2018/02/07/5-facts-about-the-religious-lives-of-african-americans//.

3. See Diana Butler Bass, "Nothing Is as It Was," October 13, 2020, https:// dianabutlerbass.substack.com/p/nothing-is-as-it-was. She concludes, "We need a new story of American faith—what it means to be a citizen, to love the land we inhabit together, and to treat one another with grace and dignity."

4. See Sarah Pulliam Bailey, "Church Membership in the U.S. Has Fallen Below the Majority for the First Time in Nearly a Century," *Washington Post*, March 29, 2021, https://www.washingtonpost.com/religion/2021/03/29/church-membership -fallen-below-majority/.

5. See Kate E. Temoney's "The 1994 Rwandan Genocide: The Religion/Genocide Nexus, Sexual Violence, and the Future of Genocide Studies," in *Genocide Studies and Prevention* 10, no. 3 (2016), available here: https://scholarcommons.usf.edu /cgi/viewcontent.cgi?article=1351&context=gsp/.

11. Because Leaving Hurts Allies (and Helps Their Opponents)

1. See Lisa Wells, *Believers* (Macmillan, 2021).

2. See the Center for Action and Contemplation's Daily Meditation, "The Edge of the Inside," September 12, 2017, available here: https://cac.org/the-edge-of-the -inside-2017-09-12/.

12. Because Leaving Defiantly and Staying Compliantly Are Not My Only Options

1. In Appendix IV, I'll briefly address the special challenges for pastors of staying and leaving.

2. The poem was actually composed by Bishop Ken Untener. See "A Prayer of Oscar Romero," bread.org, October 26, 2018, https://www.bread.org/blog/prayer-oscar -romero.

3. I have substituted the word *Christians* for her *evangelicals* because her observation applies broadly. See Kristin Du Mez's blog post "#LeaveLoud and the Evangelical Reckoning," March 19, 2021, available here: https://www.patheos.com/blogs /anxiousbench/2021/03/leaveloud-and-the-evangelical-reckoning/.

13. Because . . . Where Else Would I Go?

1. I have rendered the Greek phrase *zoein aonian* as *new way of life* rather than *eternal life*, as it is usually rendered. I believe Jesus' primary message was not a contrast between biological life on earth and spiritual life in heaven but rather between *life in this present age* and *life of the ages*—or between *life in the current regime and economy* and *life that transcends this regime and economy*. If I am right, *zoein aonian* is not a synonym for *life after death*, but rather, it is a synonym for Jesus' key phrase *kingdom of God: a new way of life* that seeks for God's loving desires and dreams for the earth to come true.

2. From the February 4, 2021, podcast, available here: https://podcasts.apple.com /us/podcast/reformation/id903433534?i=1000507689651.

3. These are the stories of hostility described in a children's book (for all ages) I cowrote with Irish peace activist Gareth Higgins, illustrated by Heather Lynn Harris, *Cory and the Seventh Story*. We also wrote a companion volume for adults: *The Seventh Story: Us, Them, and the End of Violence*. Information on both books is available here: https://www.theseventhstory.com/. In addition, I highly recommend Laura Alary and illustrator Sue Todd's beautiful children's book (for all ages) *Mira and the Big Story* (Skinner House, 2013).

14. Because It Would Be a Shame to Leave a Religion in Its Infancy

1. From "A Response to John Haught's *A New Cosmic Story*," Center for Christogenesis, September 25, 2017, available here: https://christogenesis.org/response-to -new-cosmic-story/.

2. White men dominated in the modern period. You'll notice more diversity in the list of postmodern leaders at the end of this paragraph.

3. For more on this overview, see *The Cosmic Timeline*, available here: http://visav .phys.uvic.ca/~babul/AstroCourses/P303/BB-slide.htm.

4. *Making All Things New: Catholicity, Cosmology, Consciousness* (Orbis, 2015), pp. 197–200.

15. Because of Our Legendary Founder

1. *Freeing Jesus* (HarperOne, 2021), p. xxii.

2. I borrow the phrase "mechanism of domination" from the twentieth-century German philosopher Theodor Adorno. While exiled in America in 1944, he watched from a distance as the horrors of Nazism unfolded in his native land. He was appalled to hear Germans minimize the horror with platitudes like "Life's good, in spite of it all." No, Adorno said: "The admonitions to be happy . . . have about them the fury of the father berating his children for not rushing joyously down stairs when he comes home irritable from his office. It is part of the mechanism of domination to forbid recognition of the suffering it produces." From *Minima Moralia*, no. 38 (1944), available here: http:// johnshaplin.blogspot.com/2012/10/invitation-to-dance-by-theodor-adorno.html.

3. I'm using *literalist* as a general term here, including literalism about the Bible in general and miracle stories in particular, along with all Christian teaching as being literally, factually, ontologically true as opposed to being contextually wise, metaphorically meaningful, or profoundly insightful.

4. Differences like these are more common than many people realize. For example, in the stories of Jesus' resurrection, different lists of women came to the tomb; they were greeted by either one man or two angels who were either inside or outside the tomb; either Mary or several women met the risen Christ first; the women touched him—or were told not to touch him, and the risen Jesus later met the disciples either in Jerusalem or Galilee.

5. By the way, journalism is often called the first draft of history. But even journalistic accounts posted in the next day's news reports often contain differences based on which witnesses were interviewed, and when.

6. Thanks to Mike Morrell for this Barfield quote: Mike Morrell, "God Is Not a Math Problem: Feasting on the Holy Trinity," mikemorrell.org, May 30, 2021, https://mikemorrell.org/2021/05/not-a-math-problem-feasting-on-the-holy-trinity/.

7. I've written elsewhere at length about this literary approach to the Bible. See *A New Kind of Christian* (HarperOne, 2010) and *The Great Spiritual Migration* (Convergent, 2017), along with *We Make the Road by Walking* (Jericho, 2014).

16. Because Innocence Is an Addiction, and Solidarity Is the Cure

1. Maham Hasan, "'A Car Crash Between Nicholas Sparks and *Mein Kampf*': In the Tangled World of Far-Right Chat Rooms, White Supremacists Are Getting Organized," *Vanity Fair*, October 13, 2020, https://www.vanityfair.com/news/2020/10/talia-lavin-in-the-tangled-world-of-far-right-chatrooms.

2. See Nadia Bolz-Weber (@Sarcasticluther), "Yes. It's the cult of innocence . . . ," August 21, 2020, 2:02 p.m., https://twitter.com/Sarcasticluther/status/1296915708224315392.

3. See Brian McLaren, "A Letter to My White Christian Pro-Life Friends, Part 1: My Story," brianmclaren.net, September 8, 2020, https://brianmclaren.net/a-letter-to-my-white-christian-pro-life-friends-part-1-my-story/.

4. It may also be exactly the kind of thing Jesus warned about in Matthew 6:1–18 and 7:1.

5. Playwright and actor Ted Swartz has captured the great social and personal utility of enemies in his powerful play *I'd Like to Buy an Enemy*. See https://www.tedandcompany.com/shows/id-like-to-buy-an-enemy-2-0-the-fear-version/.

6. Actually, it's not hard to imagine: the only place left is physical violence, as demonstrated on January 6, 2021, in Washington, D.C. To watch a well-known pro-life leader come to terms with the violent dimensions of the movement, see Abigail Disney's documentary, *The Armor of Light*, 2015, https://www.armoroflightfilm.com/.

7. See, for example, Rebecca Ann Parker and Rita Nakashima Brock's account of Charlemagne in *Saving Paradise* (Beacon, 2008).

8. https://twitter.com/TheRaDR/status/1299448988630949888?s=20. The irony is both subtle and strong: pro-lifers see themselves as valuing the full humanity of the unborn. However, to the degree they objectify the unborn in unconscious pursuit of innocence, to the degree they commodify them for political leverage, they are actually dehumanizing them, just as they accuse their opponents of doing.

9. When the unborn aren't available as innocent victims, demagogues find others to supply the needed innocence: fallen war heroes, religious or political martyrs, jailed or persecuted leaders, veterans, or other victims of violence or exploitation, for example.

10. See, for example, recent estimates of the numbers of abuse victims and abusive priests in France (https://abcnews.go.com/International/wireStory/major-report -expose-sex-abuse-frances-catholic-church-80408030), or new discoveries of mass graves in Canada (https://www.bbc.com/news/world-us-canada-57592243).

11. This acknowledgment, no doubt, is the thrust of Paul's message in Romans, especially chapters 1–3.

17. Because I'm Human

1. If I'm preaching in a context where I think the people can handle it, I present this as a double healing. Jesus heals the woman's daughter, but she heals him of his prejudice.

2. In this light, the story dares to suggest that being labeled unclean is actually a moral advantage. If you don't have purity or innocence to maintain, you can be more humane.

3. *Faith After Doubt* (St. Martin's, 2021), p. 215.

4. John Pavlovitz grapples with this very question in a blog post, "I Don't Like America, But I'm Staying," johnpavlovitz.com, June 15, 2021, https://johnpavlovitz .com/2021/06/15/i-dont-like-america/. He says, "I'm trying to stay to be a builder of the country I dream of living in, the one whose glory I have seen brief flashes of; the one that has always been made better by good people who decided to be loud in the face of a really powerful violence that seemed to be winning. . . . And yes, I fully believe it's all going to get worse before it gets better, but I'm staying so that hopefully the worse isn't quite as bad and so the better arrives a little bit sooner. . . . If things continue to devolve and our systems further fail and fascism gets a greater foothold, I may decide that remaining here is morally impossible. . . . But for now, I'm going to roll up my sleeves, steady myself, double my resolve, and work tirelessly alongside millions of others here." See also John's powerful book, *If God Is Love, Don't Be a Jerk: Finding a Faith That Makes Us Better Humans* (Westminster John Knox, 2021).

5. *No Cure for Being Human* (Random House, 2021). She adds, "but we are all good medicine."

6. Thanks to Cliff Berrien and Tom Eberle for introducing me to this song, available here: https://youtu.be/vdsidTtcvMk.

7. Thanks to Valarie Kaur for this distinction drawn from Guru Nanak, founder of the Sikh religion, explained here: *See No Stranger* (One World, 2020).

8. For a musical exploration of these proposals, see Bruce Cockburn's songs "Orders" and "Us All," available here: https://youtu.be/5ly1fKZa_lQ. Lyrics available here: https://www.brucecockburn.org/lyrics--four-new-songs.html.

18. Because Christianity Is Changing
(for the Worse and the Better)

1. See his book *A Bigger Table* (Westminster John Knox, 2017).

2. Howard Thurman, *Deep River* (Eucalyptus Press, 1945), 36.

3. See Andrew Brown, "The War Against Pope Francis," *The Guardian*, October 27, 2017, available here: https://www.theguardian.com/news/2017/oct/27/the -war-against-pope-francis, and see also Tom Roberts, "The Rise of the Catholic

Right," *Soujourners*, March 2019, available here: https://sojo.net/magazine /march-2019/rise-catholic-right.

4. See Tara Isabella Burton's article "The Religious Hunger of the Radical Right," *New York Times*, August 13, 2019, available here: https://www.nytimes.com/2019 /08/13/opinion/sunday/religion-extremism-white-supremacy.html. See also Pascal-Emmanuel Gobry's "If You Didn't Like the Christian Right, You'll Really Hate the Post-Christian Right," available here: https://theweek.com/articles/687808 /didnt-like-christian-right-youll-really-hate-postchristian-right.

5. Here's how Matthew Fox put it: "Christianity has to back up and begin all over. It's not that hard really. Many are the wonderful mystical teachers who have taught us these things. From Mary Oliver to Hildegard of Bingen; from Emily Dickinson to Julian of Norwich; from Thomas Merton, Thomas Berry and Teilhard de Chardin to Thomas Aquinas, Meister Eckhart and Mechtild of Magdeburg. From Jesus and Paul to poets and musicians everywhere." "We Are Because the Universe Is," daily-meditationswithmatthewfox, June 3, 2021, https://dailymeditationswithmatthewfox .org/2021/06/03/we-are-because-the-universe-is/.

6. See, for example, the work of the Poor People's Campaign: https://www .poorpeoplescampaign.org/.

7. See, for example, the work of Fr. John Dear: https://beatitudescenter.org/, and the work of Pax Christi: https://paxchristi.net/.

8. See, for example, the work of the Convergence Music Project: https://www .convergencemp.com/.

9. *The Church Cracked Open: Disruption, Decline, and New Hope for Beloved Community* (Church Publishing, 2021), pp. 22–23.

10. "Notes for a Novel About the End of the World," in *The Message in the Bottle* (Farrar, Straus and Giroux, 1990), p. 117.

19. To Free God

1. Frank Schaeffer (2014). I tried to convey a similar message in a song I wrote and some friends recorded, available here: https://brianmclaren.bandcamp.com/track /atheist.

2. From *The Grain of Wheat: Aphorisms*, translated by Erasmo Leiva-Merikakis (Ignatius, 1995), p. 46.

3. For a prayer that grapples with the challenge of addressing God in prayer, see C. S. Lewis's *A Footnote to All Prayers*, available here: https://www.journeywithjesus .net/poemsandprayers/632-cs-lewis-footnote-to-all-prayers.

4. I use the word *insistent* in homage to the creative theological work of Catholic philosopher Jack Caputo, especially in his *The Insistence of God: A Theology of Perhaps* (Indiana University Press, 2013).

5. Dr. Michael Ferguson, in his TEDx talk *This Is Your Brain on God* (https://youtu. be/ocuqguH1OIw/), notes that religion, like sex, is something we can forbid, but people will still be curious about it and explore it. So, just as we need to teach and practice safe sex, we need to teach and practice safe religion.

6. One of our best contemporary thinkers who works tirelessly to rid us of false notions of God is Pete Rollins: https://peterrollins.com/.

7. Thanks to Samir Selmanovic for this "bigger than God" insight, from his book *It's*

Really All About God: How Islam, Atheism, and Judaism Made Me a Better Christian (Jossey-Bass, 2011).

8. Thanks to Mike Petrow for this quote.

20. Because of Fermi's Paradox and the Great Filter

1. See Elizabeth Howell, "Fermi Paradox: Where Are the Aliens?," space.org, April 26, 2018, https://www.space.com/25325-fermi-paradox.html/. See also *The End of the World with Josh Clark*, a podcast series available here: https://podcasts.apple.com/us/podcast/the-end-of-the-world-with-josh-clark/id1437682381. See especially the November 7, 2018, episode.

2. See William R. Catton, *Overshoot* (University of Illinois Press, 1982), and see also Jared Diamond, *Collapse* (Penguin, rev. ed., 2011).

3. Thanks to Tripp Fuller and John Haught for this language. In his podcast interview with John Haught, Tripp Fuller said, "People who read the universe in the flattened way fundamentalists read the Bible, as cosmological literalists, . . . are taking the life out of it." See "The New Cosmic Story," *Homebrewed Christianity*, May 13, 2019, available here: https://trippfuller.com/2019/05/13/john-haught-the-new-cosmic-story/. For more on the noosphere, see "What is the Noosphere?", available here: https://humanenergy.io/projects/what-is-the-noosphere/.

4. The transcript of Yunus's talk is not currently available. However, he expresses a similar line of thought in this interview: https://www.osservatoreromano.va/en/news/2020-07/the-project-for-a-new-world.html.

5. Thanks to Rev. Jeffrey Petersen for directing me to this spoken-word masterpiece on living in light of Fermi's paradox, *Vlad the Astrophysicist*, by songwriter Peter Mulvey: https://www.youtube.com/watch?v=sNGUkdovn_8&t=475s.

21. Include and Transcend

1. See *Falling Upward* (Jossey-Bass, 2011).

2. For more on Rob's framework, listen to four episodes of his podcast *The Robcast* (November 12–December 2, 2020), available here: https://podcasts.apple.com/us/podcast/me-we-everybody/id9567426386.

3. *Include and transcend* are helpful terms derived from the important work of Ken Wilber. See, for example, his *A Theory of Everything* (Shambhala, 2001).

4. Thanks to Matthew Fox for this rich image from Hildegard: "Two Visions of Hildegard About Original Goodness, Original Blessing," dailymeditationswithmatthewfox, August 18, 2019, https://dailymeditationswithmatthewfox.org/2019/08/18/two-visions-of-hildegard-about-original-goodness-original-blessing-part-one/.

5. I deal with this concern in depth in Chapter 9 of *Faith After Doubt* (St. Martin's, 2020).

6. See, for example, the work of Kaitlin Curtice, Randy Woodley, Ray Aldred, Terry LeBlanc, Richard Twiss, George (Tink) Tinker, and Steven Charleston.

22. Start with the Heart

1. It's worth noting that the message of both Jesus and Paul in the New Testament stood diametrically opposed to the primacy of self-interest. Jesus did not say,

"Whoever tries to save his life will save it," but rather, "Whoever tries to save his life will lose it" (Luke 17:33). Similarly, Paul wrote, "Do not look only to your own interests, but also to the interests of others," and "Love does not seek its own way" (Philippians 2:4, 1 Corinthians 13:5).

2. Recalling our conversation about freeing God in Chapter 19, I want to add that when we think of God loving creation, that doesn't necessarily mean that God does so from the outside only, with God as subject and creation as object. It could also mean that God loves creation inter-subjectively from the inside, as the love that flows through all creatures. We'll return to this insight later in this chapter.

3. What is often called the New Trinitarianism celebrates this understanding of God as flow. See Richard Rohr and Mike Morrell, *The Divine Dance* (Whitaker House, 2016). And see Cynthia Bourgeault's *The Holy Trinity and the Law of Three* (Shambhala, 2013).

4. Barbara Brown Taylor, *The Luminous Web: Essays on Science and Religion* (Cowley Publications, 2000), 73–74. This selection appeared in the Center for Action and Contemplation's Daily Meditation, "An Infinite Web," https://cac.org/an-infinite-web-2020-06-25/.

5. Mirabai Starr, *The Showings of Julian of Norwich: A New Translation* (Hampton Roads, 2013), 23–24. See also Matthew Fox, *Julian of Norwich* (iUniverse, 2020).

6. It's interesting to note, in this light, that English Bible translators had another option when they translated the Greek word *thelema* into the English word *will*, as in the Lord's Prayer: *your will be done*. The word can also mean *desire* and could have been translated *your desire be fulfilled*. Where *will* sounds like an act of domination, *desire* sounds like a process of love.

7. HarperOne, 2019.

8. For those uncomfortable with the first-person plural pronoun *We* being used to include God and creation, it might be useful to contemplate John 17:21, where Jesus uses *us* to refer to himself, God, and the rest of us. This Trinitarian unity-with-diversity is seen throughout the Fourth Gospel, where Jesus, the Spirit, and the Father invite our participation in their one-anotherness, as seen in John 14:23 and 15:1–5.

9. *Cloud of the Impossible* (Columbia University Press, 2014), 306.

10. See Bruce Cockburn's song "Lord of the Starfields." You can hear a live performance of the song here: https://youtu.be/4GsSkrdY9qM.

11. For one exciting endeavor in this regard, see the Revolutionary Love Project, launched by my friend, colleague, and Sikh activist-author Valarie Kaur: https://valariekaur.com/revolutionary-love-project/.

12. For more on the idea of liturgy as secular as well as religious, see David Dark's interview here: "Ep. 5.7: David Dark on Pop-Culture and Policy as Liturgy," YouTube, December 18, 2018, https://youtu.be/oa91EvoMXDI (beginning at 6:20), and see his book *Life's Too Short to Pretend You're Not Religious* (IVP, 2016).

23. Re-Wild

1. See *Grounded: Finding God in the World* (HarperOne, 2015).

2. See http://www.orth-transfiguration.org/st-augustine-354-430/. I have replaced masculine pronouns with the noun *God*.

3. Meister Eckhart, Sermon on Sirach 50:6–7. Quoted here: https://cac.org/every
   -creature-is-an-epiphany-2021-10-03/.
4. For more on this subject, see Nadia Bolz-Weber's *Shameless* (Convergent, 2019);
   Linda Kay Klein's *Pure* (Astria, 2018); and Tina Schermer Seller's *Sex, God, and the
   Conservative Church* (Routledge, 2017) and *Shameless Parenting* (Topsecret, 2021).
5. For a helpful summary of natality, see Wolfhart Totschnig, "Arendt's Notion of
   Natality," available here: http://www.scielo.org.co/pdf/idval/v66n165/0120-0062
   -idval-66-165-00327.pdf/.
6. My book *The Galápagos Islands: Spiritual Journey* (Fortress, 2019) describes one
   such quest.
7. See *Rewilding the Way* (Herald Press, 2015).
8. See Australia and New Zealand School of Government, *Respect for Indigenous
   Peoples and Cultures: ANZSOG Learning and Action Protocol*, https://www.anzsog
   .edu.au/preview-documents/publications-and-brochures/5223-indigenous
   -protocol-final/. Also, see Choctaw elder and Episcopal priest Steven Charleston's
   beautiful *Ladder to the Light* (Broadleaf, 2021).
9. See https://watersheddiscipleship.org/.
10. https://www.seminaryofthewild.com/.
11. From Wendell Berry's commencement address to the College of the Atlantic (Bar
    Harbor, Maine, 1989), available here: https://www.teachthought.com/education/
    commencement/.
12. See, for example, the Methodist Theological School in Ohio: https://www.mtso
    .edu/academics/academic-programs/masters-degree-programs/master-of-arts-in
    -social-justice/. Or see the work of Bill Plotkin and the Animas Institute, https://
    www.animas.org/about-us/our-founder/.
13. As part of that re-wilding, many congregations are reconnecting with the original
    human inhabitants of the land, to return the land to the peoples from whom it
    was stolen. See Emily McFarlan Miller, "Churches Return Land to Indigenous
    Groups as Part of #LandBack Movement," religionnews, November 26, 2020,
    https://religionnews.com/2020/11/26/churches-return-land-to-indigenous-groups
    -amid-repentance-for-role-in-taking-it-landback-movement/.
14. See https://www.crcc.org/.
15. I've been honored to work alongside Eco-America and their outreach to the faith
    community, Blessed Tomorrow: https://blessedtomorrow.org/.
16. Indigenous wisdom is often contained in proverbs. Here are two that are espe-
    cially relevant to this chapter: "When all the trees have been cut down, when all
    the animals have been hunted, when all the waters are polluted, when all the air
    is unsafe to breathe, only then will you discover you cannot eat money" (Cree),
    and "In our every deliberation, we must consider the impact of our decisions on
    the next seven generations" (Iroquois).
17. *The Galápagos Islands: A Spiritual Journey*.
18. See, for example, this video from Dawn Perez, "The Wild Woman Archetype: 10
    Signs YOU Are a Wild Woman!," YouTube, March 8, 2021, https://www.youtube
    .com/watch?v=SI6RRx-ioKw.
19. In the same oft-quoted passage, Thoreau also said, "Nature is not, of course, al-
    ways benign and beautiful. It can be frightening and terrifying also. Not too

many generations ago, raw nature and wilderness tended to inspire fear and dread in 'civilized' people. They represented Otherness and the Unknown. That which is 'wild' is also 'bewildering.'" But, he said, "We are attracted by wilderness, the Otherness of it, the sense it is something inevitably outside of us. Always beyond us, it is what is ultimately real. We cannot adequately appreciate this aspect of nature if we approach it with any taint of human pretense. It will elude us if we allow artifacts like clothing to intervene between ourselves and this Other. To apprehend it, we cannot be naked enough." This quotation is probably derived from lectures Thoreau gave based on his 1851 essay "Walking," available here: https://www.theatlantic.com/magazine/archive/1862/06/walking/304674/.

24. Find the Flow

1. See, for example, Umair Haque's use of the term in 2011 in a *Harvard Business Review* article, "The Protests and the Metamovement," October 4, 2011, available here: https://hbr.org/2011/10/the-protests-and-the-metamovem.
2. See Vincent Donovan, *Christianity Rediscovered* (Orbis, 25th anniversary ed., 2013) and *The Church in the Midst of Creation* (Orbis, 1989).
3. Ilia Delio, "Love at the Heart of the Universe," in "The Perennial Tradition," *Oneing*, vol. 1, no. 1 (Center for Action and Contemplation, 2013), 22. Out of print.
4. On making violence unthinkable, see the work of the Raven Foundation (https://www.ravenfoundation.org/) and UnRival (https://unrivalnetwork.org/).
5. I explore some of those practices in *Finding Our Way Again* (Thomas Nelson, 2008), as does Tony Jones in *The Sacred Way* (Zondervan, 2010). See especially Barbara Holmes, *Joy Unspeakable: Contemplative Practices of the Black Church* (Fortress, 2017) and *Crisis Contemplation* (Center for Action and Contemplation, 2021). For more on resilience, see Kira Newman's article "Five Science-Backed Strategies to Build Resilience," *Greater Good Magazine*, November 9, 2016, available here: https://greatergood.berkeley.edu/article/item/five_science_backed_strategies_to_build_resilience. And see Gareth Higgins, *How Not to Be Afraid* (Broadleaf, 2021).
6. For a good introduction to reparations in the United States, see Kelly Brown Douglas, "A Christian Call for Reparations," sojo.net, July 2020, https://sojo.net/magazine/july-2020/christian-call-case-slavery-reparations-kelly-brown-douglas. Other nations and regions will have their own approach to reparations.

25. Re-Consecrate Everything

1. From James Baldwin's 1980 speech, "Black English: A Dishonest Argument," as quoted in Raoul Peck's documentary, *I Am Not Your Negro* (2016).
2. From his sermon, "Loving Your Enemies," available here: https://www.penguinrandomhouse.ca/books/572778/a-gift-of-love-by-dr-martin-luther-king-jr/9780807093245/excerpt.
3. See Danielle Shroyer, *Original Blessing* (Fortress, 2016).
4. This is the subject of my book *The Last Word and the Word After That* (Fortress, 2019).
5. For another short summary of doctrines that can be constructively recycled, see my *Faith After Doubt* (St. Martin's, 2021), pp. 156–157.

6. It's almost always wise to find experienced outside consultants to help in processes like these. One good source in the United States is https://convergenceus.org /strategic/.

7. Thanks to Wendell Berry for the connection between desecration and consecration. In "How to Be a Poet," he wrote, "There are no unsacred places; / there are only sacred places / and desecrated places." The poem is available here: https:// onbeing.org/blog/parker-palmer-how-to-be-a-poet/.

8. For a leader in this realm, see Pamela Wilhelms, https://www.wilhelmsconsulting .com/soul.html.

9. See, for example, the Auburn Senior Fellows: https://auburnseminary.org/senior -fellows/.

10. https://bayoakomolafe.net/project/the-times-are-urgent-lets-slow-down/.

11. For more on this subject, see Rob Bell, *Everything Is Spiritual* (St. Martin's, 2020), and listen to Carrie Newcomer's "Holy as the Day Is Spent" from *Kindred Spirits* (New Rounder, 2015) and Peter Mayer's "Holy Now" from *Million Year Mind* (Blue Boat Records, 2007).

26. Renounce and Announce

1. See https://eji.org/projects/community-remembrance-project/ and https://fb .watch/5_h5DpBsvg/. See also Rob's exemplary sermon, "How I Became a Racist," June 27, 2020, available here, beginning at 0:29:00: https://www.facebook .com/connectionsparis/videos/803104350220553/.

2. On common memory, see Mark Charles's TED talk "We, the People," YouTube, January 24, 2019, here: https://youtu.be/HOktqY5wY4A, and see his book, co-written with Soong-Chan Rah, *Unsettling Truths* (IVP, 2019).

27. Stay Loyal to Reality

1. See Ron Suskind's *New York Times* article, "Faith, Certainty, and the Presidency of George W. Bush," October 17, 2004, available here: https://www.nytimes .com/2004/10/17/magazine/faith-certainty-and-the-presidency-of-george-w -bush.html.

2. Diana Press, 1975, 350.

3. From Timothy Snyder, *On Tyranny* (Tim Duggan Books, 2017), quoted in this article: Sean Illing, "'Post-Truth Is Pre-Fascism': A Holocaust Historian on the Trump Era," *Vox*, March 9, 2017, https://www.vox.com/conversations/2017/3/9 /14838088/donald-trump-fascism-europe-history-totalitarianism-post-truth.

4. See David Dark (@DavidDark), "Thank you . . . ," 6:06 a.m., January 29, 2021, https://twitter.com/daviddark/status/1355155332176228359?s=27.

5. See *Why Don't They Get It? Overcoming Bias in Others (and Yourself)* and *The Second Pandemic: Authoritarianism and Your Future*, available here: https://brianmclaren .net/store/.

6. Crown, 2016.

7. You'll notice that instead of using the term *God* in this prayer, I use other names. I have nothing against using the word *God*, but in recent years, I find myself employing other terms, for reasons that I hope became clear in Chapters 19 and 22.

8. *Nonsense* (Crown, 2016), from the epilogue.

9. "This Is an Apocalypse," in *The Call to Unite: Voices of Hope and Awakening*, ed. Tim Shriver and Tom Rosshirt (Viking: 2021), 54–55.

28. Stay Human

1. For example, Jesus spoke of people who epitomize peace as *sons of peace*, and he called James and John, who apparently epitomized boldness, *sons of thunder*. See Luke 10:6 and Mark 3:17. Similarly, we find phrases like *sons of the devil* (John 8:44) or *sons of God* (Matthew 5:9). In each case, there is a "like father, like son" similarity. The term bespeaks family likeness.
2. This new model of humanity is at the heart of what Paul means by his pregnant and frequently used phrase, *In Christ*, which could be rendered, *in the new model of humanity*. See Romans 6:6; Ephesians 2:15 and 4:22–24; and Colossians 3:9–11. In some modern translations of Paul's *new humanity* passages, the Greek word *anthropon*, meaning *man* or *human*, is translated *nature, self*, or *way of life*. Something is gained in these translations, but something is lost too. If I were writing a translation, I would probably render the contrasting terms *old humanity* and *new humanity*. Paul's old and new humanity, in this light, would parallel the contrast Jesus makes between the old kingdom of Rome and the new kingdom of God.
3. *Christian humanism* is the term proposed by David Gushee in *After Evangelicalism: The Path to a New Christianity* (Westminster John Knox, 2020). The term has roots in the Renaissance, in figures like Erasmus and Thomas More.

Afterword

1. In his commentary on Matthew, the American theologian Stanley Hauerwas said, "Prior to Constantine it took exceptional courage to be a Christian. After Constantine it takes exceptional courage not to be counted as a Christian." From *Matthew* (Brazos, 2006), p. 62.

Appendix II: Images You Can't Unsee (Addendum to Chapter 2)

1. See George Rosenthal, "Auschwitz-Birkenau: The Evolution of Tattooing in the Auschwitz Concentration Camp Complex," jewishvirtuallibrary.org, https://www.jewishvirtuallibrary.org/the-evolution-of-tattooing-in-the-auschwitz-concentration-camp-complex/.

Appendix IV: A Letter to Pastors (Addendum to Chapter 26)

1. I recommend the work of Convergence: https://convergenceus.org/consultants/.

About the Author

Ken O'Renick (kenorenickphotography.com)

A former college English teacher, **Brian D. McLaren** was a pastor for twenty-four years. Now he's an author, activist, public theologian, and frequent guest lecturer for gatherings in the United States and around the world. His work has been covered in *TIME, Newsweek, USA Today, The New York Times, The Washington Post,* CNN, and many other media outlets. The author of more than fifteen books, including *Faith After Doubt, Life After Doom,* and *A New Kind of Christian,* he is a faculty member of the Center for Action and Contemplation. McLaren lives in Florida.